the Dream
the Dreamer
the Therapist

A guide to understanding dreams

DEBBIE PAULIK FORD

First published 2024 by Debbie Paulik Ford

Produced by Independent Ink
independentink.com.au

Copyright © Debbie Paulik Ford 2024

The moral right of the author to be identified as the author of this work has been asserted.

All rights reserved. Except as permitted under the *Australian Copyright Act 1968*, no part of this publication may be reproduced, stored in a retrieval system, or transmitted in any form or by any means, electronic, mechanical, photocopying, recording or otherwise, without prior written permission from the publisher. All enquiries should be made to the author.

Cover design by Neil Turner at Turner Design
Back cover author photo: Sauvage Photography
Edited by Daina Lindeman
Internal design by Independent Ink
Typeset in 13/18 pt Bembo MT Pro by Julian Mole at Post Pre-press Group, Brisbane, Qld

ISBN 978-1-7636739-0-8 (paperback)
ISBN 978-1-7636739-1-5 (epub)
ISBN 978-1-7636739-2-2 (kindle)

Disclaimer:
Any information in the book is purely the opinion of the author based on personal experience and should not be taken as business or legal advice. All material is provided for educational purposes only. We recommend to always seek the advice of a qualified professional before making any decision regarding personal and business needs.

To Ruby and Hector.
Sweet dreams my beauties.

'The dream is a little hidden door in the innermost secret recess of the soul …'
— CG Jung

Contents

FOREWORD 1

PROLOGUE 3

1: THE EFFECT OF DREAMS ON MY LIFE 5

2: THE PRACTICE OF PSYCHOTHERAPY AND DREAMWORK 19

3: DREAMS FROM THE STAGES OF LIFE 41

4: DREAMS THAT FACILITATE CHANGE 87

5: DREAMS AND CANCER 121

6: DREAMS AND HEALING: THE MAP OF MY JOURNEY THROUGH DREAMING WITH BREAST CANCER 151

7: DREAM MOTIFS 191

APPENDIX: STARTING A DREAM JOURNAL 231

GLOSSARY 239

ACKNOWLEDGEMENTS 247

Foreword

I first met Debbie Paulik Ford when she was accepted to a training institute for psychoanalytic psychotherapy at which I was teaching. Her outstanding characteristic was curiosity: the desire to know what was just over the horizon. During training, she was interested in the nature of dreams and how to go about interpreting their complex and coded language of images.

Debbie has a natural insight into the world of dreams, which is comparatively rare even among psychotherapists. It is a gift, and she rapidly gained an understanding of how to probe the nature of dream images, each of which has not a single but multiple possible meanings, and how these together create a context or narrative that is relevant to the dreamer. After more than thirty years as a qualified practitioner, Debbie has a mastery of dreamwork that the multiple examples and their interpretations in her book demonstrate.

She has called her study *The Dream, the Dreamer, the Therapist: A guide to understanding dreams*. The dreams she has selected from her clients have been chosen according to set themes, each dream being pivotal in the process of the therapy and frequently showing the potential for healing. Debbie and the dreamer discuss the dream to arrive at meaning. In so doing, they bring to consciousness hidden aspects of the dreamer's life. By making the dream narrative conscious, the potential for change and healing is opened, though this does not always occur. In her book, each dream and its interpretation is placed in the context of the dreamer's life and problems, so not only is the specific dream discussed but many a glimpse is afforded into the dynamics of the consulting room.

Debbie has also had the courage to share her own dreams with commentaries on them, including a cycle of dreams experienced while she was suffering from cancer. And for the reader who has something of her curiosity to engage further with their own dreams, she has provided a detailed guide on how to go about making a dream journal.

Curiosity is the key word. If you have it towards dreams, you will learn much from Debbie's expertise.

Dr Sally Kester

Prologue

This book isn't a memoir; rather, it's a narrative woven with threads of my personal experiences, both as a dreamer and as a psychotherapist. Its essence lies in the exploration of dreams, tailored for those outside the professional sphere, delving into the understanding of dreams within the context of the therapeutic relationship. My aim in writing the book is simply to share my passion and love for dreaming and to spark curiosity within you, the reader, about the profound journey of self-awareness that can come from examining your dream life. I also wish to share some of my thoughts, insights and experiences around dream understanding.

Dreams have profoundly shaped my life, prompting introspection and unveiling insights into both my inner world and the world around me.

I aim to offer you a hint of the mystery of the working relationship in the therapeutic alliance, which is the relationship between the therapist and the client. Drawing from my personal experience and case studies from my nearly 30 years of practice, I have selected dreams to show how meaning can be unearthed and brought to consciousness, and the consequent changes that can occur within the client. Each dream I share is more than 15 years old. Included within are case studies spanning various stages of life, instances where dreams have effected change, encounters with clients navigating cancer, and my journey through breast cancer, guided by the wisdom of my dreams.

My clients gave me permission to use their dream material, and I have altered their identities to maintain their anonymity. All dreams are written in italics.

1

The Effect of Dreams on My Life

I stumble then tumble. Down a hole, like Alice. I am falling, falling. I am a child, lost, afraid. There is damp dirt underneath my skin and up my nose. My feet touch down on cold concrete. I am somewhere yet nowhere. I peer into the dark. An eerie wind blows the naked globe hanging from the rafters. Light swings across the room in shafts. I am transfixed.

Tiny hospital beds stretch out in rows. Stiff sheets tightly tucked. White, neat as a pin. Children's beds.

Then, silence.

The calm before the storm.

Bombs explode. It's a war zone. The roof splits open. Windows shatter. Ice-blue sky falls in. Thin glass splinters fly like heat-seeking missiles searching for their target. They are searching for bodies. I smell gunpowder. Bitter. The canvas walls flap in and out. Everything shakes. I feel the building shake, my body shake.

Then the little white beds smash into a pile of rubble. There's blood everywhere. Children flying everywhere. Dead. Murdered. Not normal children. Broken children. Broken into pieces, their deformities exposed. A head, the size of a huge pumpkin, rolls along the floor past me like a beach ball.

I panic. Run as fast as I can. I am so scared, and I know I am somehow responsible.

I woke from this nightmare gasping for air, tore my sweaty T-shirt from my breasts, and fumbled for the light switch. I was sure this nightmare was brought about by having to face these deformed children and the horror it caused me. I knew I must see Matron. I needed to tell her I was not cut out to be a nurse. Quickly, I showered, put on my blue and white check uniform, and tied my starched white pinafore tight, so it held me together. I slipped out of the nurse's quarters and headed for the Administration office. Nursing was a baptism by fire. As first-year student nurses, we gave it everything we had, care, skill, gentleness. Most of the time, it was joyful, with the satisfaction of making a difference in the children's lives, but there was no support for our anxieties and emotions. Together we faced trauma, suffering and death. We were teenagers. Not old enough to vote, but old enough to care for tiny babies in humidicribs.

The hospital had a policy of keeping grossly deformed children with diseases like hydrocephalus in single rooms at the far end of each ward. As young girls, inexperienced in life, these patients terrified us. These children rarely had visitors as the sight of them was so confronting, often horrific. It seemed even their parents had abandoned them. I recalled shamefully thinking they looked and sounded like wild animals.

I was still new, the most junior nurse on the ward, on the day I saw my first severely mentally and physically retarded patient. I was petrified. It was as if I had looked on to mythical Medusa with vipers for her hair and turned to stone! Tommy was a boy of about twelve with microcephalus. He had an incredibly tiny head, gross mental retardation and gross physical abnormalities. His dimly lit room was at the end of the ward, room 34. I was told to bathe, change, and feed him. I can still recall his strength, his smell, and his animal scream as his twisted, tangled body thrashed about on the bed. I ran away, straight back to my senior. Tears were streaming down my face. 'I can't. Honestly, I can't.' But I was no exception; I had to do my job. I returned to Tommy in room 34, bathed him, changed him, fed him. It was a nightmare in full light.

That night, as I sat on my friend Sandy's bed in my pyjamas, I was weeping. I shared my feelings of guilt for having those harsh thoughts and feelings. About children. We were so grateful we could share this with each other. We felt ashamed of our reaction, and our reaction shocked us. We were unprepared. Were we going to be strong enough to do this work? Of course. We both adjusted. Sandy was already accustomed to suffering, having recently lost her brother in the Vietnam War. I was venturing on wider seas than I was accustomed to, but Sandy had already faced the darkness of life.

A few nights later, I had this shocking dream. I was having an *Alice in Wonderland* experience of falling deep into the unconscious. Into a war encounter with darkness, the gruesome, the macabre.

I insisted on seeing Matron. The secretary's eyebrow met her tightly rolled hair. I sat outside until Matron was ready. Eventually, she appeared and ushered me into her office—polished brown desk, heavy brown drapes over thin sashed windows that looked on to a lone sapling. There was a sepia photograph of Princess Margaret trapped behind glass. The princess peered at me. Matron seemed unimpressed. She stood erect, tall in starched white, her arms folded across her flat chest as she listened to my dream. My skin prickled as I told it.

I kept talking, trying not to cry. 'I fear these retarded children. I'm really scared of them, but I would never harm them. I'm scared of how they look, and smell, the noises they make, and how at night, when they have epileptic fits, their sheets violently shake. I am terrified to walk into their room. I am scared to be alone with them.' Matron stood as still as a statue and listened, lips pursed, eyes narrowed. She was unperturbed. I continued on. 'Clearly, I am unsuitable to be a nurse. Should I resign?' I was crying now. I whispered, 'I am not the good person I thought I was.'

There was silence. She thought before she spoke.

'Nurse, you are exactly the sort of person I want as a nurse. It is good that you are being so honest. Thank you for your honesty.' Her thin lips split into a hard half-smile as she walked over and opened the door. 'We shall not mention this again. I suggest you get back to work.' I was dismissed.

I felt confused. I certainly was in a place that was foreign to me. What was this dramatic and shocking drama that I had fallen into? Surprisingly, a few months after my discussion with Matron, the world transformed. All the deformed children were placed in a dedicated ward of their own, staffed by nurse assistants who wanted to work with them. Sandy and I were overjoyed. As student nurses, we were relieved as we no longer had to face our fear.

I realised my frightening nightmare had shocked me into speaking my truth and sharing my inner turmoil. Sharing the dream facilitated change. Matron heard me and took me seriously. I also became briefly aware of the dark, hidden part of myself that was capable of murderous thoughts. There was an awakening awareness of how important my dreams were and that I didn't understand them. However, I had a knowing that without that nightmare, nothing would have shifted. Change quietly occurred within my self, and within the structure of the hospital. This was amazing!

My nightmare helped me to adapt to the changes in my life as a young nurse. At work, I was frequently confronted by issues involving life and death, pain, and suffering that, as a naïve schoolgirl, I had no knowledge or experience of and limited ways of processing. I was afraid of that which I didn't understand. Rather than acknowledging these overwhelming feelings, I had repressed them. Which is what we do.

This was the beginning of my looking inwards. It was also an introduction to my career, my vocation as a psychotherapist.

Many years later, I was able to link this dream to a deeper level of my inner world. I became aware that there was a parallel story of my own childhood experience and to what we now know as inter-generational trauma. Inter-generational trauma occurs when devastating experiences are unacknowledged and flow on from the person who experienced them to members of the next generation and affect them in the depths of their being. If trauma caused by such things as war, genocide, sexual and physical abuse, criminal situations, addictions, and suicide is not resolved, it is passed down a family's lineage, changing lives and possibly accumulating more trauma each time. Until the issues are consciously confronted—often these days in therapy or deep meditation, or ideally through open loving communication between generations—then the effects are unresolved. Negative patterns are repeated and transmitted through attachment and impact in destructive ways.

My grandfather was badly wounded as a young soldier in WW1. Bombs were thrown into the bunker where he and other soldiers lay wounded. They were attacked by soldiers on the ground, in tanks, and from the air. He returned from Villers-Bretonneux in France disabled, his body and soul wounded, unable to walk unaided. My grandfather was such a quiet, kind, philosophical man who escaped feeling by thinking. Living his life with objectivity separated him from the world around him and also from the trauma within him. He had men friends, returned soldiers who would quietly gather on a Friday afternoon. They would sit in a rough circle on my grandparents' sunny veranda discussing religion, philosophy, the meaning of life, but never the war. I only learnt of my grandfather's war in whispers.

I remember being intrigued as a child. Maybe their gentle study helped delicately wrap their trauma and suffering in a sense of purpose and meaning that released them from the horror. Later in life, I read Viktor Frankl's *The Search for Meaning*. He reported that survival itself may depend on seeking and finding meaning. Prisoners in concentration camps survived by maintaining a sense of purpose in their suffering. My grandfather and his friends were perhaps still searching for this meaning through thoughtful inquiry. Now we know that in searching outside of ourselves, we miss what is going on within.

My father was a young RAAF bomber pilot during WW2 who returned to Australia with what I now recognise as undiagnosed post-traumatic stress disorder (PTSD). PTSD symptoms include grief, fear, shame, guilt, depression, anxiety, numbness or heightened sensitivity, anger, insomnia, flashbacks, nightmares, frightening thoughts and intrusive memories, feeling 'on edge', difficulty regulating moods, and self-destructive beliefs and behaviours. American psychiatrist Jon Shay calls this a 'deep soul wounding'. Like his father before him, his youth and innocence were taken away by war trauma. These brave men never spoke of their wartime experiences and therefore did not resolve them. This is the inter-generational trauma that was passed down to my generation from my father and my grandfather standing behind him, the trauma that was expressed in my nightmare of the explosions and falling bombs.

I wonder if their silence about their war experience was because of the shame of what they did rather than what they saw. Perhaps they naively believed that by not sharing, discussing in depth, and resolving their experiences, the memories and horror would disappear. Both men left the shores of Australia as boys and returned as men. Damaged, wounded men. Their experiences were uncelebrated with awareness. There was no imagining the unimaginable, no contemplation of their sacrifice as they gave their innocence and their lives so we could thrive in a free nation and world. The shadow of war remained repressed, pushed deep into the unconscious. Trauma had found its way down the line. Invisible until it erupted. My nightmare was triggered by my fear, which had become activated in my unconscious and had pushed its way into consciousness.

I also discovered this link of inter-generational trauma through an embodied physical and emotional experience. It was 1977, and my husband and I were camping around Europe before heading to London. This was a common exploit for those in their early twenties, a rite of passage. It was the Brezhnev era, and we discovered the Soviet Union was a poor and harsh country that seemed happy to despise us denim-clad, hippy-like youth who knew only democracy and affluence. One evening while we were in Moscow, the whole campsite was robbed. All the tents were silently slit open, and all our possessions were stolen. When we reported this crime to the authorities, we were told we were lying capitalists. There was no crime in the Soviet Union.

We drove through Checkpoint Charlie, past the Berlin Wall, and were naturally unable to stop in East Berlin. It was eerie, as if WW2 was still in the air. Now we were entering Germany with mixed feelings. Hamburg was our next destination. The city had been completely rebuilt after the war, and we were looking forward to visiting the infamous red-light area. We arrived late in the day to the main campsite, which was circled by unwelcoming barbed wire. The sky was heavy, gunmetal grey. It was pouring with rain, and the campground had turned into a quagmire. We found a small suitable area on high ground and pitched our tent. The rain stung our faces like tiny needles. I was starting to feel unwell. Perhaps I was coming down with a virus? Friends went joyfully to the red-light area, and I stayed behind as I was taken over with a feeling of impending gloom and darkness. I was unable to sleep or settle myself. All I wanted was to leave Hamburg as soon as possible. I felt the anchor holding me steady and keeping me connected to Mother Earth was losing its hold.

As the morning sun struggled to break through the heavy sky, I pushed my way through the grey mud to the tired and graffitied phone box at the camp entrance. Intuitively, I knew I needed to call my father. We hadn't spoken for the five months I had been overseas. It was expensive to call home and a luxury reserved for emergencies. This felt like an emergency. 'Everything okay? Broke already?' He was often the joker. I shared with him how I was feeling physically unwell and felt overwhelming sadness and how bizarre this experience was. I didn't understand what was going on within me. It was something I had never experienced previously. Why did I imagine he could understand and find some sort of meaning for me? Was it to do with my being in Hamburg? I tried to make sense of what was happening. How was I picking up and connecting to a story that was my father's? I was then a nurse, not yet a psychotherapist, so I knew nothing of the effects of trauma on the unconscious.

On hearing my experience, my father hesitantly informed me that his most challenging mission during WW2 was when the RAAF (Australian Air Force), with the RAF (Royal Air Force), was to bomb Hamburg. He sounded sad when he told me they were commissioned to 'flatten Hamburg'. With night after night of deadly strikes, they accomplished this mission. He shared that they lost many men, including his good mate from London who was his gunner, and many aircraft in the battle. The words I recall he finally spoke to me were: 'I'm so sorry.'

He felt shame, and we never spoke of this again. I, too, felt his shame. Through the miracle of the telephone that graffitied box became the confessional in a long-gone cathedral. There, in Hamburg's mud and rain, I heard my father's shame, like Matron heard mine. Shame visited on me and my brother, almost innocently, certainly without my father understanding. Importantly, in this moment, I felt his vulnerability. This facilitated an unspoken shift in our relationship. Something within him changed; it was as if a light had been shone onto a hidden and dark part of his inner world. Healing had taken place, a rapprochement of sorts.

We left Hamburg that day, and I immediately felt fine. We all talked of how Hamburg was once a busy trading city, a city of music and culture, of the arts. It was still rebuilding to its former days. I had no further unsettling experiences.

Now I understood that my father drank to forget the war and the shame and remorse he carried, and why occasionally when he was overwhelmed, he unintentionally dropped metaphorical bombs, an explosion of unexpressed feelings that erupted on us, his own innocent children. War trauma had left an imprint on him and on us. Alcohol helped distance himself from his feelings and actions. This adaptive behaviour helped him survive. When my brother and I were very young, he was still in fighting mode. His everyday life was often a battle. A war. He could be attacking, a persecutor. This was traumatic for little children. But we were not the enemy. We were allies. We were all on the same team. Had he forgotten? He did it for us.

ANOTHER IMPORTANT DREAM

After Hamburg, we travelled by bus to Poland, a country invaded first by Germany during WW2, then by the Soviets. Six million Polish citizens including three million of the country's Jews perished during this time. We were in another poor and confronting country. While in Warsaw, I had this beautiful dream, the first half of which I re-dreamed over forty years later in October 2020.

> *I'm in a foreign country I am sure is Poland, probably Warsaw, in a very old home with thick limestone walls. It is primitive and foreign. I wonder if it is an art gallery, as the walls are lined with unframed, naïve paintings and drawings on canvas. I am walking around as if in a gallery, inspecting the paintings.*

the Dream the Dreamer the Therapist

A little old woman stands up from a grey wooden kitchen table. She tells me she is Polish. Her clothes are old and worn. She has a dirty cloth as an apron, tied around her thick waist. Her legs are badly bowed, like she has rickets. She looks at me directly. She has the old, wizened face of a crone. I hold her gentle gaze. In broken English, she says, 'For you, for you, thank you.' She hands me a large, rolled-up, calico canvas. I take it and unroll this old, worn canvas.

It comes alive. It is filled with a huge glass fishbowl full of clear water and brimming with little green frogs and fish. There are three large, beautifully lustrous goldfish. They are all swimming and jumping. The fish scales are shiny, metallic, iridescent, colourful. I can see their gills moving as they breathe. I am looking at this canvas in disbelief. This is magical! The fishbowl is in three panels of colour, blue, gold, and pink. What a gift it is! I can hardly believe what I am seeing. It is like a Matisse painting, but even more beautiful. I feel so alive, light, joyful, swimming, floating. I feel the opposite to how I felt in Hamburg.

Then I am back inside the gallery. I tell her I will buy it—100 pounds. I don't care that this equates to 200 Australian dollars. She is pleased I want to buy it. But she says again, 'No, a gift.' I pay her anyway. I'm happy to.

As I leave, it is raining. I am in a very neglected garden. Someone gives me a small cat to take care of, and I doubt it will survive if I don't take it. Carefully, I make a sheep-skinned pouch, attach it to my belt, and carry it with me. I leave with my now rolled-up canvas and kitten, which is snug in the soft pouch, safe and warm.

What did this dream mean? I woke up feeling content, like my reservoir was filled. The dream lit up the dark night of my soul. It seemed potentially lifesaving, with light that replaced all the darkness. It gifted me a lovely world, alive and colourful. A shimmering life. From my dream, I also have the little kitten and a special interaction with the wise old crone.

When I first had the dream in Warsaw, it felt like it was a gift of kindness, a story to balance out and compensate for my unsettling experience in Hamburg. I didn't understand dreaming then, whereas the second time I had the dream, in 2020, I gained a different meaning. I had the dream following a sharing, an unwrapping of client stories in our long-standing peer supervision group. One of the therapists was from Germany, not far from Hamburg. We were the same age, daughters of our fathers both fighting in the same war. They were unknowingly enemies, and here we were, the next generation, colleagues and girlfriends. This time, meaning-making was ensconced in the talking cure, psychology.

Deep in that night following the supervision session, my Warsaw dream returned. I hear the 'For you, thank you' from the same wise old crone, the elderly Polish woman. Her words echo through my high, blue sky. Again, I step in and out of this wondrous image. An incandescent watery place of bright beings alive with enigmatic messengers from the deep. The huge glass fishbowl full of clear water brimming with little green frogs and three large, lustrous goldfish. Everything is moving, swimming and jumping, shimmering, iridescent. It is magical. I am in disbelief. It is such a gift!

That night, the spindle spun shadows into the light, one generation at a time. I had been unconsciously shouldering my father's shame for the destruction he caused as a young pilot carrying out his duty to his country. He was carrying this shame without the gift of a thank you, as was my grandfather. In my dream, the woman had given me the 'thank you'. We had paid the price. I heard it this time. My relationship with dreams and imagination, my ability to walk in and out of two worlds, inner and outer, facilitated receiving this gift.

The war against the German Nazis and Soviets saved the lives of millions. I needed to shift this guilt to gratitude, so this debilitating emotion was not passed on any further. The archetype of the wise old crone, the wise woman within who knows my destiny, was gifting me a thank you and a new life. An emancipation. Gifting me spiritual new beginnings, feminine intuition, and transformation, a gift from the inter-generational feminine. The symbolic message was powerful and valuable.

I now felt differently about my father's actions in the war. He facilitated and contributed to freedom for much of Europe. Like his father before him, he had contributed to world peace. Two generations of the masculine had to leave their comfortable life and face fear, danger, darkness, and death in a dimension of life that was unknown and unexperienced. This was a massive sacrifice, made to create a world in which my German girlfriend and I, and everyone in our generation, were able to flourish. My father and grandfather were not gifted and touched by the feminine wisdom from the depths, so they had to carry their traumatising shame and guilt in silence. Unfortunately, the wisdom found from the deep was unexpressed and seldom communicated to anybody; thus, it was kept as a secret, a shameful secret.

Following the dream, I was able to be responsive to my father's unexpressed negative emotions. This dream had answered many questions. I was able to see how my father's suffering led to an influential dream in my life. As the story of my life unravelled, my guilt transformed to gratitude, and I was emancipated from my father's shame. It was an ending, and it was a beginning.

MY DREAM INITIATING MY PRACTICE

In the early 1990s, I finished my training as a psychoanalytic psychotherapist. I had completed my own thorough training analysis and supervision with psychoanalytic psychotherapists and Jungian analysts. My studies and my inner work were done, but I was unsure about setting up my own private practice. Was I ready? Before going to sleep, I gently asked for a dream.

> *My daughters are in junior school. They are working together in the art room. The room is rich with warmth and laughter. Their lovely creative art teacher is taking the class. They are about eight and ten years old. The girls are moulding a clay pot. It is nearly complete, looking wonderful. I smell the clay, see the rough texture, the patterns. I can see the outline of ancient humans, animals, pyramids, chubby cherubs carved amongst a garland of leaves and flowers, chiselled deep in the clay. The girls are playing around and being silly. I am there in the room and notice I, too, have clay on my hands.*
>
> *While watching them play, I begin feeling upset they aren't taking more care of my special pot. It is valuable, and they might break it. They are laughing and reassure me they can make another if they break it. They are covered in a clay that is a deep mustard colour. I can smell its earthy scent. It is wet and glossy and rich. I think it's sticky like amniotic fluid. I think aloud, 'It is important to me, and not to them. It is for my room, not just for fun. I am an adult; they are children. It is precious.'*

The dream reassured me and gave me the confidence I was ready. I was an adult, and I could do it on my own, the symbolism of the pot being it was the vessel to hold the past, present, and future. A place where I could imaginatively play and create. Where all could be contained, added to, and stirred, facilitating change, growth, and hopes, an alchemical container, a cauldron, a deep holding reservoir in which we could explore and discover meaning. It was an encouraging gift for me from the psyche. Swiss psychologist Carl Jung said, 'Your vision will become clear only when you look into your own heart.'

A month later, I started seeing clients in my office. I was ready.

2

The Practice of Psychotherapy and Dreamwork

As we travel through life, we have an increasing curiosity about our interior world. Generally, we have a drive to understand our behaviour, our feelings, and our relationships, with others and ourselves. Our unconscious finds a way to show us and illuminate the unknown, so we can find a way forward and discover this meaning imaginatively that we long to understand. Our unconscious mind conceals content we are totally unaware of, which comes into consciousness through intuition and dreams.

We can gain understanding by looking at our dreams as they can hold many of the answers. The dream comments, corrects, teaches, offers help and guidance, and contributes to balancing the dreamer's waking life and thus supports psychological growth and development. It can be thought of as aiming to broaden self-awareness by presenting a bigger picture beyond our limited conscious everyday world. The dream lives a parallel existence within us. In therapy, our goal is to help bridge this space that lies between our conscious and unconscious worlds so they can co-exist with awareness.

Recalling a dream is rather like receiving an email from an unknown person. Sometimes we can't decipher the message or even the language. Often this message is ambiguous. Occasionally the message is clear, and we understand it straight away. The dream may show us where we need to focus our attention. The dream also offers the possibility of healing in this space.

Carl Jung believed it is through paying attention to our dreams that we are able to find balance internally and externally. The balance of masculine and feminine, good and evil, light and dark, fluid and rigid, order and chaos, objectivity and subjectivity; these opposites are always trying to rebalance and heal.

As a psychotherapist, I love working with dreams, those of my clients and my own. My own inner world is awakened through dreaming. The dream is such a powerful and purposeful tool. It gives me a glimpse of my client's inner world and offers an understanding of their external world. It is through the power of the therapeutic alliance that the client and the therapist can mutually work with imagination towards understanding the dream presented. I am a witness to the dream. It is the client's ability to feel the reverberation of the dream deep within, to accept and make use of their own associations to their dream symbols as it unfolds, that brings healing. This inner work builds consciousness and self-awareness.

The client gradually experiences connection with me and parts of their own self as we work with the dream material. This is a shared dynamic interaction. As therapist, I try to think symbolically, cognitively, and imaginatively. There is a framework of theory that is the foundation of these thoughts. I listen with compassion, attention, and curiosity while processing and investigating the deeper, unconscious layers of their story.

When working with a dream, it is through the client's associated feelings and thoughts that their dream story begins to unfold and come alive. We stay as close to the dream as possible. Over time, recurring images and patterns appear that we don't have access to in life. It is exciting when the dreamer can use the insights gained as they grasp an image in a dream, leading to an 'aha' experience: *'I get it.'* This is a powerful step towards self-realisation that can inspire and motivate the dreamer as the awareness has the capacity to free them from entanglements and lead to clarity. It is as if we translate the dream together; we attempt to de-code and bring into the present that which has been hidden from view. The dream can offer a new point of view, a fresh perspective. Each dream has its own rhythm, emotional tones and colours, feelings or lack of them. There is no set formula.

Yet sometimes, the dreamer is quite disconnected from their dream, as if the story doesn't belong to them. It takes curiosity on both our parts to work with their associations and feelings that travel with the dream images. It also is an opportunity to look at their defenses that can get in the way of the dreamwork and, naturally, get in the way in life. These defenses are presented within the dream as obstacles, for example, walls, soldiers or armies, prisons, veils, or roadblocks. Their function is to protect the ego. The defense mechanism may also be an unconscious attempt to sever the connection within the therapeutic relationship between myself and the client, to avoid the distress associated with vulnerability and emotional exposure, or to prevent an attachment forming. This self-protective action helps maintain psychological stability, even if it disrupts beneficial processes like therapy.

One client dreamt of vomiting up a little toy soldier who was guarding what she had repressed. Her defensiveness was making her physically sick. By becoming aware of these defenses, barriers, and inner constraints and letting go of them, the hidden part has more space and can gradually become a more tangible and knowable part of themselves. There is tension here as the defenses that have guarded our conscious world against this knowledge are strained. The therapeutic space holds this tension. The dream needs to speak. Our unconscious needs to be heard. The dream speaks to the dreamer in a new coded language. Interpretation assists the dreamer to gain an experience of the dynamic that has kept them imprisoned emotionally and possibly physically stuck. Then they can see and accept 'this is me; this is who I am' and are able to comprehend a basic truth about themself, a relationship, or a problem they may have been trying to solve.

Dreams will nearly always lead one towards an answer. I encourage you to hear your own inner voice and explore the story and images that emerge. Our inner world waits patiently for us to pay attention and gradually become a little more conscious as the dream is revealed. Deep within us lies an infinite wisdom that can guide and support us through our daily lives. Our goal is to connect to this source.

We will never fully understand our dreams, even if at the time of elucidation or interpretation, we feel we have understood the meaning. Dreams when revisited often take on a new meaning, sometimes months, or even years later, as with my dream in Poland about the 'thank you'. It went from being a kind gift of a thank you to me, then my father, and then my grandfather to holding a broader meaning about the making of a peaceful world.

If you are not seeing a psychotherapist, your dreams will still talk to you in an emotional way. Be assured the psyche is working its magic deeply within your alchemical kitchen. Journal your dreams. Share your dreams with a friend. Keep the dream alive and dynamic. Often, I hear people say they don't dream, when the truth is they do not remember their dreams. We mostly all have five or six dreams a night. We dream about every hour and a quarter when we are in rapid eye movement (REM) sleep. It is about setting the intention, paying attention, practice, and taking the process of recall seriously. Then the dreams will start to come to you on waking. I have found in my practice that deeply depressed clients seldom recall a dream, but as their depression lifts, they gradually begin to dream, often just an image or dream fragments to start with.

During REM sleep, there is no engagement with the pre-frontal cortex of the brain, so there is no rational or logical thought. There are vivid visual, hallucinogenic, irrational images with movement, memory, and emotion. The dreamer has a heightened sense of awareness, remaining vulnerable while the body is experiencing sleep paralysis. During this state, dreaming helps consolidate memories by sorting through and processing the events of the day.

Dreamwork is a small yet important part of the therapeutic work. It occurs within a quiet, reliable, consistent, and non-judgmental framework. Both the space and relationship are containing and enabling. It is here we safely explore the client's suffering and deep pain as a shared encounter. We sit with the many emotions that arise. We sit with ambiguity and uncertainty, which may provoke anxiety. It is my role to tolerate and process this anxiety. Sometimes we laugh together out of relief, joy, or love as we sit on the edge of awareness. This shared therapeutic space goes beyond a physicality, as it also occupies a space within the therapist's mind. Psychotherapist Irvin Yalom succinctly calls the work 'the therapeutic act, not the therapeutic word'. This shared therapeutic space is still present when working remotely by video call, like most therapists did during COVID and now continue to do so.

Clients come to therapy to understand themselves and be understood. They feel a need to talk as their feelings are causing them suffering and may be tripping them up in their daily lives. These feelings have meaning and are a symptom of something else. Dreamwork is one way to uncover and reveal the hidden meaning.

Together, we build our therapeutic alliance, and we explore the conscious and the unconscious, the tangible and the intangible, what is real and what is imagined. I listen. There may be talk of love and hate, trust and betrayal, and the many issues involved in the problems of living. We each live a unique story, and we all have our own drama. The story gradually comes alive from within as the client's narrative unfolds. Dreams are a special part of this process. The dream conveys information about the client's relationship within, with others, with the past and present. Developmental patterns and capacities are revealed.

I am aware that the healing work happens because of our relationship; it is the key to understanding, insight, and potential change. Clients come to their own understandings as the work progresses. These realisations, meanings of behaviours, events, images, or symptoms are processed and become integrated into the personality. It is as if there is an instinctual drive towards wholeness within each of us, towards becoming what one potentially is, our total self, enabling us to become complete. Jung called this 'the process of individuation'.

OUR INNER WORLD: SOME TERMS

The unconscious

Central to psychotherapy is the concept of the unconscious. The picture of our mind is that of a space divided into two. Consciousness is actually a very small part of this picture, the tiny tip of the iceberg. The remaining area is vast and complex, powerful, timeless, and obscure, and is known as the unconscious. It is totally invisible and not accessible to rational thought or deep feelings. It is an immeasurable reservoir of feelings, thoughts, memories, desires, and instincts. This is the dream-making space. The only way these two spaces, the conscious and the unconscious, can communicate with each other and work together is to speak the language of the unconscious through dreams, imagination, visions, and intuition. The language is that of symbolism.

Engaging in inner work in psychotherapy using clients' dreams is a way of communicating with and understanding the symbolic language of the unconscious. A symbol can be thought of as an outwardly projected image of inward feelings and thoughts. It has a very deep meaning and refers to the mysterious and unknown. It is usually at times of psychological stress or conflict that we become aware of the unconscious as we experience urges that are foreign to us—destructive, primitive, irrational. The relationship and equilibrium between the conscious and the unconscious has ruptured, and we feel discomfort as anxiety is provoked.

The ego

Within our inner world sits the ego as the centre of consciousness with its feet in the unconscious. It is the 'I'. The ego expresses personality, manages identity—that is, our sense of self—and provides a unity for this personality. It navigates the demands of the reality of our external world, organises our thoughts, feelings, sensations, and intuitions, and can make use of memories that have not been repressed.

The ego evolves through our lifetime from childhood. Gradually, it develops 'ego strength', having the ability to cope with the reality of life. We all develop ego defenses to protect from anxiety arising from inner conflicting impulses. Throughout life, the old defenses die in most people, as is appropriate, in response to what is happening in life, and new defenses develop. The ego deals with ongoing matters of consciousness as it maintains psychological stability and integrity. When there is not good enough parenting, healthy ego development is undermined and therapy may be needed to restart the process and develop more adaptive ways of relating to yourself and others.

The ego is like the orchestra's conductor. This is a powerful position. The conductor chooses the music, interprets, decides the tempo, maintains the beat, and communicates with all the different parts of the orchestra. With an eye constantly on all the players, the conductor relays a vision of how the music should feel, sound, and even look. So too, the ego seeks harmony by bringing all the parts of the personality together. When an unanticipated dissonance occurs in our lives, we are thrown back into the more primitive stage, perhaps with unexpected emotions, like rage, sorrow, or deep anxiety. It is as if the sound is not synchronised. The ego is there to run the conscious score and conduct life.

The persona

The persona is the mask of personality one shows to the public, the world. Each of us wears several masks as we travel through life. These are external masks, the interface that helps protect, hide, and enhance our identity. The origins of 'persona' can be found in the masks worn by actors in ancient Greece. Unfortunately, we can lose touch with our true self that lies deep within. Having a persona is a necessity in living our everyday lives, but it is only a small part of who we are.

Jung applied the persona to those aspects of the personality one adapts to the outer world, the face we show others that is acceptable and presentable. This is the face we choose to show. That which we don't choose to show becomes shadow. Sometimes we even hide things not only from others but from our selves. This is often shown in dreams. This difference causes inner conflict. English psychoanalyst Donald Winnicott wrote about the 'false self' that develops and hides the inner 'true self'. In dreams, the persona shows us how it is fulfilling its task and illustrates to us what is not visible, for example, how clothing veils our body and facades of buildings cover their deeper layered interiors. Dreams may reveal tensions or conflicts between the true self and the external persona.

The shadow

Jung defines shadow as 'the thing a person has no wish to be'. The shadow resides in the unconscious and holds the personality traits one hides from oneself and the world. These are qualities we do not want to be identified by as they don't fit with who we think we are. They may be shameful, negative, or unacceptable. Therefore, they are denied, disowned, and repressed, or projected onto others. We are resistant to allowing the dark sides of our nature to come to consciousness, to our awareness, because they stop us from feeling good about how we see ourselves. These are the negatives beneath our ego's positives.

Jungian analyst Robert Bly simply and beautifully described the shadow as a 'long bag we drag behind us.' He said, 'We spend our life until we're twenty deciding what parts of ourselves to put in the bag, and we spend the rest of our lives trying to get them out again.'

From the time we are one or two years old, our parents start to not like things about us. We are too boisterous, too loud, too messy, and on it goes. In this invisible backpack, we store feelings like rage or hate that are associated with these undesirable traits. Throughout life, we continue to repress qualities that we or others reject, placing them into our metaphorical bag. This process occurs as part of normal ego development. When we dream and these qualities emerge into our awareness, some aspects of our life story are revealed, leading to a sense of emancipation.

It is the hidden darker aspects of our self that we carry as shadow within us, embodying the aspects of our personality that our ego considers inappropriate or undesirable. It is so easy to unknowingly project our shadow onto others, onto other races, other societies. If we recognise that we are experiencing heavy negative emotions, then we can be sure that we are encountering our shadow. The shadow is Robert Louis Stevenson's Mr Hyde. Dr Jekyll is the positive ego. The shadow is an always present and essential component of our personality. Our work is to become aware and familiar with it and accept its existence. Only then can we take responsibility for bringing it to consciousness and allowing our self to assimilate this once-repressed part. Owning our shadow parts that we have been unaware of is part of our journey and enables us to integrate them in our pursuit of wholeness and living an authentic life.

Meeting a Part of My Shadow

I recall many years ago, on commencing my training analysis, a meeting with an unknown woman in my dream. She represented a part of my shadow, as she was so unlike my regular ego self.

I am at a night-time party that is noisy and fun. There is even a Ferris wheel in the background playing music. It is going around and around. I notice a woman, and I am instantly curious about her. She is a sexy brunette. She looks sassy and full of herself. I'm thinking she looks very much like a tart, a hussy. She looks across at me as if she knows me, but she is smiling with a slightly crooked smile. She knowingly looks me straight in the eye. I feel somewhat awkward. As I get closer to her, I see that she is very similar to a woman I met in outer reality at a party a few months earlier.

Suddenly, she vanishes, and then, just as suddenly, approaches me from behind. Someone gives her a microphone, and she steps up onto a table as if to either sing or give a talk. Everyone is looking at her and is certainly paying attention. How strange it is that she has no voice! She is unable to speak or be heard. This woman is unaware that she is without a voice. Someone asks me, 'Why don't you tell her?' I don't know why.

I woke up from the dream with a start and felt very emotional. My throat was dry. I then found I couldn't stop thinking about this woman. She was going around and around in my mind, like the Ferris wheel. I recalled seeing the young woman at a real party, and I was judgmental of her and didn't like her. She was very sexy, loud, and opinionated. Everyone seemed to be swarming around her like bees to a honey pot. I asked a friend if she knew who she was. She told me she was an internationally famous author. Oh, my goodness. No wonder I didn't like her—I was envious of her! It is so easy to not accept in others what we are unable to accept in our selves. It was so much easier to project upon her than to face her and own her as a part of my self that had been rejected.

I had quickly forgotten about her until she appeared in my dream. In my upbringing, I was encouraged to be beige. Be beige, act beige, and you won't draw attention to yourself. That was being a good and safe girl. This young woman was every colour but beige. The more I explored my feelings around this woman, the more I became acquainted with this shadow part of myself that was living hidden in the dark recesses of my psyche. In the dream, she turned and faced me, even looked me in the eye. It was time to face a part of myself. I recall protesting that I wasn't that bad. I also recalled feeling shame at my judgement of her and guilt that I didn't help her to be heard in the dream. I could have happily labelled her as shadow, intellectualised this, and lazily moved on.

The Ferris wheel going around and around was another aspect of the dream that held a message. I needed to piece together all the images, as they were all of equal value and connected. Until I really found meaning within the dream, my life would continue unconsciously to go around in circles.

Primarily, I was facing the erotic self in the dream, the self that I saw as a 'tart'. While I was experiencing emotions that were connected to my shadow, I wrote down all the imagined qualities this woman had. The list was substantial. Then I read it aloud. 'This is me,' I spoke to the list. How unpleasant. Gradually, I was able to let myself be free of this judgement as I was able to take responsibility for the shift within me. I was beginning to 'know myself', all of myself. That surely is our mission. This shift deepens and widens our conscious self, gives a sense of solidity, and seems to also energise the inner self. This process takes time and patience.

The shadow in the collective shows us the dark unknown side of mankind. History is littered with examples of this dark side being expressed in wars, art, literature, and culture. Individuals and communities have also been scapegoats and have had the sins of their society projected onto them. Virtual spaces online can exhibit collective shadow communities and behaviours. Certain online communities may foster a voice for repressed or taboo thoughts, beliefs, and behaviours that stay hidden or unacknowledged in broader society. Social media platforms, algorithms, filter bubbles, and the spread of misinformation can lead to an amplification of the shadow, a lowering of inhibitions due to distance and anonymity, and lead to expressions of aggression, violence, prejudices, and unconscious bias. Trolling and cyberbullying are manifestations of this shadow. The concept of the collective unconscious shadow underscores the importance of confronting and acknowledging these societal aspects of the psyche to promote healing, reconciliation, inclusivity, and ethical social progress both offline and online.

There can also be a shadow carried by a family or family member. Domestic violence, homophobia, and child abuse are examples of what can be hidden in the shadow of a family and hidden in society. Secrets kept in families may arise from a factual foundation or they may arise from fantasies. If these secrets do not get expressed, for example, feelings of love or hate, and are hidden, individually and collectively, they can become shadow. This shadow can be passed on as inter-generational repetition or trauma, as I spoke of earlier. Unspoken, unknown, unacknowledged, and unimaginable—especially the unimaginable. It may reside in our physical body as a cellular memory.

In my practice, I have encountered the dream shadow being presented as a dark intruder, trying to break into a house or a car, attempting to break into consciousness. My client Philip had a recurring dream of Tony Soprano (of the TV series *The Sopranos*), who he described as dangerous, bad, cunning, and without morals. Philip was a quiet, very good law-abiding man who lived his everyday life trying so very hard to be perfect. This is his dream:

> *I am in a small shop. It's like a newsagency; it has Lotto and magazines. It is a family business. There's a man at the counter, cowering. He's quietly crying, and when my brother and I come in, he sends his young daughter into the back room. He tells me he doesn't have the money, so he can't make the payment. My brother*

> *is pushing magazines off the shelves and causing some chaos. The man is still quietly sobbing. He knows what this means. My brother stands next to me. I am Tony Soprano, and I pull the baton out of my belt. He puts his hands on the counter, and I am about to start smashing them with the baton, which is like a hammer. I look around and can't see my brother.*

Together, Philip and I dialogued with this Tony part of him; we engaged creatively with this aspect. He was drawn to and intrigued by Tony's complex and multi-dimensional character and the drama of his life. Over time, he became familiar with this dream figure and integrating him into his personality, transforming masculine weakness into strength, thus turning a negative shadow into a positive force. Like Tony, Philip was a family man with psychological struggles who sought therapy so he could be vulnerable, express anger, and acknowledge repressed violent thoughts. Our imaginative play made Tony more real to Philip. Dreams facilitate individual growth by offering the opportunity to face and resolve our shadow aspects, including the family shadow. This makes understanding the meaning of dreams worthwhile.

The following case is an example of family shadow.

SIMON

Simon was a quiet man in his mid-forties who was having difficulty relating to his fifteen-year-old daughter. He was feeling a disturbing disconnect between them, which was troubling him. He didn't understand why he was concerned. 'She is just a teenager, so of course I'm going to struggle.' Simon said he was happily married. His wife thought he was overreacting about his daughter, and maybe he was. He shared this dream during his first session.

> *It's night, and I am driving in an old car, and I'm really lost. An unknown man is anxiously clutching the steering wheel. It's raining*

and the windscreen wipers are going rhythmically back and forth, back and forth. As I look, searching, out of the windscreen into the night, I can see a huge dark shadow in the sky that has morphed from a threatening black rain cloud into a huge black wild dog. I see it has sharp teeth. It is hovering above the family home of my childhood and is putting the home in permanent darkness. There are people inside, but they are thin stick figures, it's as if they're not real. Tiny little children are scurrying around inside who look like little grey mice. I am really scared.

We began our work together discussing how Simon felt during the dream. He said he felt lost and afraid throughout, and especially terrified of the huge wild animal hanging over their house. He described himself as a timid and anxious child who was afraid of adults and dogs. Simon said he was continually trying to be unnoticed by being as quiet as a mouse. He wondered if he and his sister, Maria, were the little grey mice in the dream. His association was that their house was not a home; it was a soulless dark building inhabited by soulless people. His father controlled everything and everyone. On the outside, the house was immaculate, as was their family persona, yet inside, it felt unstable and dangerous.

Simon told me he was brought up in a strict, conservative, church-going family that seemed unable to express love and kindness to each other. Occasionally, there was violence. There were no signs or discussions of intimacy or affection, yet within the community, the family was admired and held up as exemplary until Simon's older sister, Maria, became pregnant at fifteen, which brought shame to their family. This secret was hidden from the school and church community. When her pregnancy started to become obvious, she was sent away to a home, where she stayed until she delivered the baby. Maria was forbidden to touch or see the baby, which was adopted. She returned home as if nothing had happened, and the experience was never discussed. It became a secret held within the family to keep up appearances. Perfection was maintained on the outside, but inside, Maria was the scapegoat.

Simon remembered sadly that Maria had wet patches on her shirt when she came home. She was obviously still lactating. Simon said he had to turn away. He was twelve years old, and he didn't understand. Maria was now withdrawn and depressed and was always blamed for tensions within the family. At seventeen, she ran away from home and was never seen or mentioned again. The family shadow was pushed onto Maria. She was known as the one who did evil. Simon said it was as if she never existed, just like the baby. She was just a trace, a stick figure left in his imagination, a stick figure flickering in his dream. Simon was flooded by previously repressed fear, sadness, and grief. How cleansing the downpour of tears felt.

In coming to therapy, Simon had opened a door, providing the opportunity to find language and feelings for his emotionally deprived life as a young boy, and the longing he felt for his lost sister, Maria. For twenty-five years, he had no knowledge of her whereabouts. All he had was a distant fading memory and longing. During therapy, he began to open himself up to his vulnerability so we could process and safely bring these feelings to his awareness in a way that he was unable to in his childhood. He began to realise and see that this dynamic of a lack of intimacy and connection was being played out in his own family, even though at a much less toxic level. By Simon being able to flesh out his family figures and their dynamic, he became available in his own family to share their love and connection.

We could talk about his daughter being the same age as his sister, Maria, when she fell pregnant. This had silently terrified him. Simon told his children about his upbringing and shared his feelings of sadness. Now it was safe, and there was no need for the shame and the secret to be passed on. His new lexicon of feelings was a pocket of connection. He passed on his secret bundle with consciousness, with words that could be understood. Simon had mourned his loss and now approached his relationship with his daughter with insight, hope, and anticipation. This was healing for his daughter and the family unit too as it fostered open communication and empathy. He had a clear vision as he faced their future and felt he was in control. He also began his search for Maria. Simon's brief dream offered us the foundation for our work together on his path of self-discovery and personal growth.

INNER MASCULINE AND INNER FEMININE

Other figures we carry in the unconscious are the images of both male and female. It is as if every man has a representation of a woman within and every woman has a representation of a man within her unconscious, so all human beings incorporate both masculine and feminine. It is as if we each carry within the whole human potential. These figures appear in our dreams as the opposite sex. Jung named a man's inner feminine as the 'anima' and a woman's inner masculine as the 'animus'.

Twice in my life, I have dreamt of my internal masculine being inadequate. The first time was when I was confronted by a major problem in my love relationship and had not yet commenced studying psychotherapy. This is the first dream of my inner masculine.

> *I am searching everywhere for a man; I think it is my husband I'm looking for. I am at home where everything is peaceful and familiar, yet I am feeling anxious. I cannot see him anywhere. I call to him, 'Where are you?' I open the door, and a young male who is familiar is standing behind the door in another room in my house. He is passive, saying and doing nothing. I assume he is sitting down. 'Stand up!' I cry. I badly want him to stand up. Then I realise he is standing up, but he is a dwarf.*

I rolled over and went back to sleep, feeling disappointed. My masculine was without language; he was passive, and he was chromosomally challenged. I wanted more from him. I wanted to connect and communicate with him, but he was unable to meet any of the needs I desired of him. This was a time in my life when I needed him to act, to be a strong champion for me, within me. I needed him for my internal growth. Unfortunately, he stayed hidden behind the door. He remained passive and hindered my growth and development as a young woman. At this time, I assumed this dream was about the man in my life, as he was not standing up for me. I was unaware this was about my own internal masculine self. This inner masculine drive was hiding from me.

Approximately ten years later, I again experienced a similar relationship issue in a second dream.

> *I am at the airport and feeling so excited as I know I am going on a journey. I am going to a psychotherapy conference in America. Before I depart, I am to meet an unknown male colleague and teacher who is going to travel with me. Searching, I look around, and there he is. He is handsome and is smiling at me. I am filled with joy and anticipation. 'Stand up!' I call to him. But once again, he is standing up. He is a dwarf.*

I awoke from the dream heartbroken. As a young psychotherapist, I was conscious the dwarf figure was of psychological importance as a masculine symbol, a part of myself, my inner world. I also knew this important dream image was a repetition of the first dream. I needed to understand this and process the dwarfed masculine, facilitate his growth, and bring him to consciousness. This time, I knew the dream was not about another. It was about me.

I was on a journey to meet a part of myself yet unknown, deformed or an unformed and repressed masculine part. The feelings I had associated with him were disappointment, sadness, and anger, and yet there was also affection. He was the teacher, the holder of wisdom and knowledge. He was a part of me. Yet there was no connection between the inner masculine and feminine. He was hiding his strength and power and was thus estranged from my feminine identity. He was the teacher I needed to travel with internally. I needed to learn from him. It is through our very abnormalities and imperfections that we come to know and develop our self. It is undertaking a journey of immense suffering that enables healing. One emotionally suffers, as one needs to give up an old way of being, an old way of being identified. I suffered.

My dwarfed masculine was gradually able to transform. This enabled him to live and speak his wisdom. The issue stemmed from within me. The inner imbalance was mine, and during our journey together, he became expanded, stronger, more courageous and spirited. I undertook therapy, and I consciously attempted to become more potent. Once developed, my masculine helped me become independent and more accomplished. It was as if I now had internal resources I earlier had not possessed.

Previously, my masculine was negative and was unable to protect me or encourage me. I experienced him as projected onto my male partner at times of disappointment. Instead of hindering, my masculine now assists me. I am still able to talk and communicate with him. This is creative, and it is healing. My inner figures became more balanced, my masculine no longer dwarfed by my strong feminine. The dwarf image has not reappeared in my dreams.

A later stage of inner masculine development is seen in my dream of the Wise Old Man.

> *I meet a very old, wise, spiritual man. His robes are white and flowing; his hair and beard are long and white. 'I have a gift for you,' he says. He hands me a very old, heavy, ancient text. I look down at the open page, but I am unable to read it as it appears to be written in Sanskrit. Sadly, I give it back to him. We are both disappointed.*

I awoke feeling I was very close to something unknown within me. But it was not close enough for me to understand or grasp. I was feeling sad, as I wanted it so much. However, a second dream on the same motif came a year later.

> *I am living in a harem. There are so many women here, and we are all the King's women. There is only one very important man living in the harem. We women are wearing beautifully coloured silk fabrics draped around our bodies like saris, and sheer veils across our heads, leaving only our eyes exposed. I am happy here, but there is a deep knowing we are his women, and we belong to him. He is powerful, and I know he loves me. My mother is here living in another compound. We are emotionally close and protective towards each other. I help her with her life and make her life comfortable as best I can.*
>
> *I am the city healer, and I am being called to go out. I arrive at my destination, and there is the Wise Old Man wearing long, white robes. His hair is long and white, as is his beard. I wonder to myself, 'Is he Buddha?' I know he is a spiritual man as I have met him before.*
>
> *He greets me. 'I have been waiting for you to come.' He is holding a large, old, and ancient text. He offers it to me, pointing to the page. I am surprised I can now read the Sanskrit text. I read out loud: 'Let go and heaven will be yours.' It is a beautiful knowing moment.*
>
> *I return to the harem. One of the women tells me I am to marry the King this afternoon. 'No,' I tell the women. 'I must escape this destiny.' My mother begins dressing to impersonate me. We all help cloak her in veils and beautiful bridal fabric. The ceremony has*

begun, and as he hears her begin to speak her vows, he knows it isn't me.

He is furious. He yells, 'Where is she?' I am running from the back of the ornate temple. Magically, I have an incredible power that transports me over the walls of the harem, into a forest of tall, strong, autumnal trees, leaves of yellow, brown, and green, and some of the trees have blossoms. I can hear music. It is Handel's 'Messiah'. I am awake, and I am peaceful in heaven.

When I woke from the dream, I felt that, somehow, I had experienced a form of transformation and was aware of all my senses. I recorded the dream immediately in my journal.

These were the notes I wrote to ponder in the morning: 'Is heaven the end or the beginning? Is this part of the Eastern or Western philosophy of letting go? My dream was Eastern in its setting. I need to think about attachment in Buddhism.'

I was aware I was desiring too much the first time this masculine wisdom appeared. In the second dream, I could hear his wisdom. I let go, and, yes, heaven was mine. At last, I was ready to hear and process this inner wisdom. I was able to let go. The image and accompanying spoken words unlocked unconscious psychic energy and allowed it to flow and create a transforming effect. When the inner masculine figure is developed, the internal and external worlds both become dynamic.

To happily live in relationships, in work, love, and play, we need equality. Similarly, we also need our internal figures to be equal and living in harmony.

THE ARCHETYPE OF THE SELF AS SPIRITUAL EXPERIENCE

In the depths of the unconscious lie the primordial energies of the archetypes, which express themselves as symbols when they come to consciousness, and this can sometimes be accompanied by powerful emotion. These universal symbols are very often familiar, as we have met them in our childhood in fairy tales and myths. They embody our everyday human instincts, experiences, and qualities. A dream will occasionally point to a centre as a wise woman or wise man, a spiritual guide, an inner city, or a shape of a circle or perhaps a square. This centre may be a mandala, which means 'circle' in Sanskrit and is a geometric configuration of symbols. This is a symbol for wholeness. The dream can lead the dreamer into a deep appreciation of an inner spiritual reality. This is often a glorious, humbling, and grounded inner sensation, though I find it is difficult to find language to describe this sensation. Interpretation is not required. It very clearly speaks to our spiritual side. It is as if it offers a direct transmission of the spiritual. For Jung, these images were manifestations of the archetype of the self that unifies both body and psyche in wholeness. They may be expressed through powerful emotion.

I recall about twenty years ago entering the Fraumünster, a renowned landmark in Zurich, on my way to the CG Jung Institute. I entered the church, and there in front of me was the amazingly impressive and beautifully mesmerising stained-glass window created by Marc Chagall that depicts the Virgin Mother and Child. I was moved beyond language. Then my eyes fell onto the Christ Window: Christ crucified and resurrected. Tears flooded down my face, and my body was covered in goose bumps. This was an archetypal experience. I was emotionally, spiritually, and physically overwhelmed by the energy generated by these incredibly powerful and meaningful images. Later, I read this was a common reaction. The emotional force was so very powerful.

These collective figures, symbols, and patterns exist deep within us all but only rarely generate such feeling.

On reflection, this was a time of change for me, and the experiencing of this energy and the deep meaning of the image of crucifixion and resurrection facilitated the need for change and transformation that I was unknowingly undergoing. Such an unexpected and divine gift I received that day in Zurich, a gift that left me with a feeling of awe.

3

Dreams from the Stages of Life

Dreams often reflect where we are at in our lives. The following dreams represent different stages of the life cycle, like the stages and ages of man in Jaque's famous speech 'All the world's a stage' in Shakespeare's play *As You Like It*. Shakespeare was aware of these stages long before a scientific psychological classification was formed.

These clients had a significant problem at a time that corresponded with a chronological and developmental stage. Each stage needs to be negotiated for a satisfactory progression to occur, and at each stage, there are challenges to be faced, emotional, intellectual, spiritual, and physical. These challenges trigger dreams which help ease our transition into the following phase of life, offering important tools of self-discovery. The dreams I have selected cover some of the issues faced as we grow older in life.

STAGE 1: Childhood

Childhood is a journey from complete dependence towards independence. It is a physical, emotional, cognitive, and social journey.

In infancy, the child's world is magical, as if they are the magician. There is an innocence that allows them to believe that their thoughts and actions can magically make events happen. Then gradually reality creeps in; they become aware of the objective world, and their magical world sadly has to be let go. Play and exploration serve as a conduit for learning, creativity, and developing social skills.

It is common and normal for children to recall and be fascinated about their dreams, and their nightmares. These dreams reflect this magical and often frightening world of the imagination. They may contain allegory, symbolism, and metaphor. These engage the child as a creative story. As parents, we need to listen to our children's nightmares with care and the kindness they deserve. Talking with them about their dreams can provide an insight into their inner worlds and provide an opportunity for connection, understanding, and reassurance. Children's dreams are less complicated than adolescents' or adults' dreams, are shorter and less inhibited, and gradually become more rational. Their dreams provide expression of emotions and ideas they have no language for. They are diverse and creative and reflect their inner worlds, emotions, and experiences.

Children's dreams offer deep psychological wisdom as Jung believed they have greater insight into the unconscious. Cultural and social factors, beliefs, and traditions may influence children's dreams. Parents' responses to their children's dreams can offer support and reassurance, soothe their fears, especially around nightmares, and help promote healthy sleep patterns.

My grandson shared a short dream with me when he was three years old.

> *I'm holding hands with my little playmate Nic. We are happy because we're getting married!*

When sharing his dream, he was smiling, but then he looked a little confused and said, 'I love Nic, but I thought I was going to marry Mummy!' A new aspect of my grandson's personality was coming into being as he was discovering otherness. He was also finding a way to process his longing for his mother. This occurred when there was an unconscious knowing that his mother and father were a couple with a relationship from which he was excluded.

Until that time, his capacity for love and relationships only included his mother, father, and sister. The boundaries that had contained these relationships were now stretching to allow others in and enable his internal world to expand. At this age, he was beginning to explore the idea of separateness. The dream of marriage symbolised the emerging of the internal masculine and feminine qualities that would one day create a harmonious whole.

LOTTIE

Working with children is a privilege and is to be taken seriously. It takes calmness, clear boundaries, compassion, and a gentle, mindful approach. I would only see children who were working directly with a specialist, so it was a parallel and supported process. Six-year-old Lottie was referred to me by a paediatrician to try to make sense of her recurring nightmare. She arrived with her mother and was a pale, pretty girl tall for her age. When she finally looked up at me, I noticed her eyes were the colour of forget-me-nots. Her presenting problem was a nightmare of a huge red dragon who spat orange fire.

Lottie quietly told me she was in Grade One at school; I was impressed by her sharing this with me. Her referral told me that she struggled socially and didn't walk till she was nineteen months old. The parents had separated, and she spent every second weekend with her father. Lottie's angry mother believed he was the cause of Lottie's nightmares, and she was working with a lawyer towards gaining full custody of their daughter. Lottie began blinking rapidly when her mother said this, a sign she was experiencing anxiety. I quicky directed her mother to my waiting room, where she sat during each session, but I always insisted a parent was close by.

I discussed with Lottie that she might draw for me what she could see in her dream. In my office, I had a small child's table and chairs, coloured pencils, crayons, and large sheets of white paper. The language of drawings is like dream language; it is the language of the unconscious. Lottie drew a huge red dragon living inside a house, and from his mouth, he spat orange fire. My first thought was perhaps the dragon was her mother, who seemed as angry as a fire-fuelled dragon. Was this an internal fear or did it represent an external intimidating force?

Lottie then drew a picture of her home. In the drawing, Lottie was tiny and outside her house. Her dog was close to her. Lottie's mother was huge by comparison, and she was drawn inside the house, with the dragon. The mother and child were not closely connected in the drawing, and Lottie's father was missing. She had drawn herself with legs but no arms. I wondered if this was showing me how helpless she was feeling. This was Lottie's recurring nightmare, which she had dreamed again the night before our first session.

> *The big red dragon is fighting with another scary dragon. They are spitting fire at each other. I'm really scared. I have lost my sunhat, and I go into another room to try to find it. I'm sure the dragon is going to find me and eat me.*
>
> *I wake up crying because I'm scared.*

Lottie said her mother didn't come into her bedroom to settle her when she woke from her nightmare. I wondered if her mother was meeting Lottie's needs. It was important I let Lottie know that I understood that the dream was a very real experience for her. I understood her fear was that she would be destroyed and she would disappear. She had faced once more the archetypal image of the dragon, and she had lost her sunhat, her protection.

From my bookshelf, I retrieved Carl Jung's *Man and His Symbols*. I opened the book to the coloured image of St George slaying the scary dragon to free a maiden. This was the hero's journey. Lottie's eyes were glued to the picture. I assured her lots of people dreamed of colourful, fire-spitting, scary dragons, just like St George did. Lottie loved this idea, and I could see she was feeling reassured.

I asked for Lottie's father, Martin, to come for a session. He appeared to be a gentle man who cared deeply for Lottie. Her nightmares upset him, and he wanted to be helpful. He shared he had a brother who had recently been diagnosed with drug-induced psychosis. His brother had now ceased taking recreational drugs and was maintained on a mood stabiliser. As his brother was homeless, Martin let him stay with him in a bedroom at the rear of the house on the condition he stayed well out of sight on the weekends Lottie was there. Martin didn't tell Lottie or his ex-wife that his brother was living with him. This was a secret. The parents' relationship appeared to be unloving and unforgiving, and they were always fighting each other, just like the dragons.

After our session, Martin discussed with his ex-wife that he was providing accommodation for his brother. Now that the brother's presence was out in the open, both parents concluded it was for the best if he moved out. This he did. As the brother wasn't dangerous and was keen to again be a part of the family, I suggested he gradually become integrated into the family and come to visit when Lottie was there.

Our talking enabled Lottie to find her own language for her fears and to process her drawings, and this helped her resolve her feelings of fear during a time of upheaval. Her nightmares stopped, and Lottie's drawings began to feature normal childlike images: herself, her house, both her parents, and her dog. The fiery dragons were missing. They had been slain.

JAMIE

Jamie was a nine-year-old boy referred to me by his paediatrician. He suffered anxiety and had once again started to wet the bed. On his first visit, his mother, Mikayla, explained Jamie had been a bed-wetter until about four, but this habit had returned. She said she felt helpless and didn't know what to do. His doctor prescribed Tofranil, which had made some difference. Jamie was a pale, thin boy with sandy hair and soft brown eyes. I noticed he had very long, dark eyelashes, which he batted like a doll. There was something loveable about him when he came into my office with his mother. She was in her fashionable leisure wear, looking as if she was off to the gym. She was pretty and tossed her dark mass of hair about in a coquettish way. Jamie didn't take his eyes off her.

Jamie sat in the waiting room as she explained the situation. Her husband, Robert, was an engineer who worked away for two weeks, then was back home for two weeks, so he wasn't a constant part of the family. She assured me everyone was happy with the situation. Thankfully, he earned good money because, as Mikayla explained, she loved to spend money. 'I just can't help myself,' she said happily. Their daughter was doing well and an easy child. But Jamie! 'Such a little darling. He has a bad dream, wets the bed, and I can't be bothered changing the sheets, so he comes in with me. It's so sweet. Bob can't stand it. But it's fine with me, especially when he's away.'

Jamie was happy to chat with me. Mikayla sat in the waiting room reading the magazines. I suggested he draw me a picture of his family. He drew his mother big, dad little, his sister smaller than him, even though she was older, and he drew himself standing close to his mum, wearing armour and carrying a sword. 'He must see himself as a fighter or a protector,' I thought.

'Why are you wearing armour?'

'Well, I'm the little man of the family, so I must be ready, just in case.'

'What do you think might happen?'

'Oh, you never know, an invasion from out of space, maybe an invasion of an alien.'

'Does that make you a bit worried?'

'No, I'll be ready.'

Such bravado.

I was curious about his sister.

'Oh, she's a bragger. She has lots of friends, she talks too much, and she's smart.'

'What about you? Aren't you just as smart?'

'No, I'm not that smart. I'm like mum,' he said quietly.

I wanted to know more about his mother. It seemed Jamie felt his mother needed him. I explained she had Jamie's father; they were both adults and a couple. He shared she wasn't very strong, and it was obvious to him that she couldn't cope if he was just an ordinary kid. I was thinking how in normal development the mother was protective of her child, offering nourishment and support. Jamie was confused about his role as a child. He was seeing himself as the protector.

As time went on, Jamie started to share his imaginary life with me through his drawings. He was just an ordinary kid who went off into a forest in a land where he was magically transformed into an adult warrior called Link. Jamie drew him for me many times. Link had four different coloured tunics for different occasions and different moods. Red was for fighting, blue was for when he was feeling sad, purple was for when he wanted to find peace, and yellow was for the times he visited the sun, moon, and stars. Yellow was his happy tunic. Sometimes, Link was a child and made high-pitched noises; then he transformed into an adult who made low-pitched noises. Link was a good person; he only fought the bad guys, the monsters. Link always carried a sword and a shield.

At the end of a session, Jamie asked me if I could give one of these pictures to his father. There was no time to ask why. I had my thoughts, my own imagination. When I went to fold one of the drawings to give to Mikayla, he said no; he'd changed his mind. At this stage, I was being held in high regard by Jamie. He did a drawing of me. I was valuable, protected, and protective, and he believed I would go into battle for him. A link was forming in my mind.

At the beginning of the next session, I asked him about his dreams, and he shared one.

> *I'm in a spaceship. It's like a huge silver bubble, and I can drive it to visit other galaxies. It's my actual home. It's powered by the sun. So fast. I have all sorts of guns, tanks, and bombs on board. I'm lethal! Everyone is scared of me. I'm getting a bit lonely, so I'm going to land on Earth soon. I zoom down to Earth and decide to rescue Mum. I can see her; she's waiting for me. Then there's a big fight. Luckily, I have guns that fire rounds of bullets. Dad doesn't recognise me, so he's trying to kill me first. I kill Dad with my guns. There's blood, and finally, I stab him with my magic sword. I'm trying to get Mum to come with me, but it turns out it's not Mum but a witch with a big nose. I'm running back to the spaceship, but my legs won't go fast enough. I'm running and running but not moving. The police get me. I'm crying out, 'I'm just a kid.'*

Jamie said he often would wake up scared and crying. Then he would notice he had wet the bed. We talked quietly about how everyone feared him, yet at the end of the dream, he's calling to the police and telling them he's just a kid. I said in a family, the dad and mum are the police because they make the laws for their family. Jamie wasn't sure about this idea. He said he wanted to be both the kid and the grown-up. I explained we all have different parts of ourselves—some are young, some are older and wiser, some just want to play and live in a make-believe world. This was normal and nothing for him to worry about.

Just like Link, we have different colours and outfits to wear to show how we're feeling. It's not till we're older that we know the words to express exactly how we're feeling. Even then, it's not always so clear. We were smiling together. Jamie said he was feeling more purple, more at peace.

At our next session, Jamie used little stamps for his drawing of himself. Again, he was dressed in full armour and carrying a sword. I did not interpret. I just asked Jamie to tell me how he felt. 'I'm happy now doing the pictures, but I'm not happy at home, except when it's just me and Mum. Then I'm happy.' He looked at me as if he was going to test me. 'I love being in bed with Mum. It's so warm and lovey-dovey.' I was now really getting the picture of a little boy who could see a gap between his mother and father, a gap he felt able to fill. His Oedipal stage had not been resolved, and Jamie was developmentally regressing rather than separating and developing and identifying with his father.

We started to talk about his father. 'Mum says he's a bit of a hippy. He says things like, "Out of my heart pours music." I say, "Out of my heart pours blood!" Who is the man here, eh?' He had stepped into the bravado self. I asked what colour tunic he was wearing now. 'Red, blood red.' At the very end of the session, Jamie looked across at me and said, 'Gosh, you have got such bedroom eyes!'

On arrival at his next session, Mikayla said Jamie had a headache and wanted to stay in the car. She asked if I had a Panadol, and I said I didn't. I suggested perhaps Jamie could sit in the waiting room and she and I could talk until his headache was better. Perhaps Jamie was feeling awkward about his flirtatious behaviour with me at the end of our last session? It seemed to me Jamie was possibly resistant to doing the work together as we were getting close to the issue at hand. I was mindful that his flirtation was a defense, his unconscious attempt to sexualise the relationship as a way to control his anxiety and our therapeutic interaction in the room.

There was time for me to suggest she and Robert could work together on their relationship. It needed to be made clear to Jamie that they were the parental couple and a boundary around their relationship put in place. Jamie was growing up and too old to be in bed with her, especially as a reward for wetting his bed. I suggested she just change his linen without saying anything about his bed-wetting and then go back to her own bed. She was okay with this but shared she really wanted to keep him as her baby for a bit longer. 'He's not a baby. He's a little boy needing both a mother and father who can protect and nurture and love him. That is your role.' I was aware I was being directional with Mikayla. Jamie was struggling to develop an independent sense of self. My understanding this pattern was the first step towards it not being repeated and for him to be able to separate from her.

There was no time for Jamie to come in, but he said he would be fine for our session next week. I was wondering if I was to be the wicked witch in his dream, having gotten between him and his mother and putting an end to his fantastical imaginary wish. For two weeks, Mikayla cancelled our sessions. Finally, Jamie came for his session. He seemed somehow different. He was doing a few drawings in his diary, which he showed me, and his feelings of anxiety were less. No more flirting, no more talk of bedroom eyes. He was just an ordinary kid, and I was just an ordinary therapist. The bed-wetting was stopping. Mikayla said the boundaries were working, but it took her some time to adjust. She didn't seem that happy about the changes. Jamie and his dad were getting along. Therapy had provided a place where Jamie and his mother could experience new possibilities and learn how to move away from regressive behaviour. Here was the opportunity for new growth and development individually and as a family.

STAGE 2: Adolescence

I have always enjoyed working with teenagers. It is frustrating yet rewarding. As the child becomes an adolescent, he/she has commenced the journey of crossing the metaphorical bridge from the safety of childhood towards becoming an adult. This can be a time of ambivalence towards themselves and their parents. They can feel shame and pride, frustration, bewilderment, fear, or excitement. So many emotions are experienced that appear to have no rhyme or reason. Often the developing ego is overwhelmed by these emotions. One minute, the ego is bulging with self-grandiosity, then it is fragile and self-conscious. One minute, they long for connection, then become distrustful, turn inwards, and choose to be solitary. There is anxiety centred around developing a strong ego. This is also a time of role and gender confusion.

Teenagers need their parents to maintain their values and rules, but not take too active a role in asserting them. They need an unconditional and the secure relationship to push up against. Just as children thrive on exploration from a healthy loving base, so does the adolescent. Here, the parent is to accept the behaviour, which is often unpleasant and antagonistic, without approving of it. It is best for the parent to build a bridge rather than a wall to connect with their teenager.

To separate, one needs to let go. This means both the teenager and the parent are required to trust and gradually let go. We cannot separate without experiencing loss. This is the loss of innocence and the loss of one's childhood. Understandably, dreams at this stage reflect their changing emotional, physical, and social world. Dreams of loss and fragmentation are common during this time. With loss comes depression and mourning, which need to be felt and endured. This is developmentally necessary for adolescents to become whole and more separate. This suffering is the gap between where they are and where they want to be. Dreams are often dark and sad. At this time, adolescents are becoming greatly influenced by their peers rather than by their parents, who can no longer provide the same level of safety and protection they have in the past. Adolescents are also being greatly influenced by social media, technology, and academic pressure.

Much of their time is spent in the virtual world, and this has influenced adolescent mental health. Rising rates of depression, anxiety, self-harm, especially among girls, online bullying, and suicide have been reported. Sleep patterns can change due to screen and content exposure. Dreams may be centred around online interactions—for example, video games and movies—and include superheroes and fantasy situations. Due to early exposure to pornography, adolescent dreams are becoming more sexualised and violent.

I encourage parents to normalise teenagers' dreams by offering open discussion and support to help them navigate their journey with greater resilience and self-awareness.

PAUL

Fourteen-year-old Paul was a pale, fair-haired lad who seemed child-like. He didn't seem to have any definition. He came for psychotherapy because he was struggling to form peer-group relationships. He was suffering from anxiety and lacking motivation in school. The night before our first session, Paul had a nightmare, which he shared. It gave us a snapshot of the lack of balance and the actual dynamic of the mother and son relationship.

> *My mother is trying to swallow me! She doesn't have any teeth, just big, red, wet gums. I am terrified. I am a young child, not fully formed, pink and naked. The boy here doesn't look familiar; I just know it is me. Am I Peter Pan? Am I living in a fairy tale? I wake up.*

This was a short but shocking and disturbing nightmare for Paul. He felt terrified in the dream as he felt powerless and at his mother's mercy. His mother was a strong, powerful, and charismatic woman. He was her only child. Paul's father had suddenly died when Paul was two. The boy had no available father figure to identify with or to support and travel with him on his journey. In this dream, Paul was terrified he was going to be swallowed up. She was a 'devouring mother'. While Paul was telling me this dream, I thought of the big bad wolf who lured Red Riding Hood to come closer and how quickly and unexpectedly it devoured her. This was a castrating mouth. He was sensing death. The hero refuses to be swallowed in the unconscious. Now I was thinking of the witch figure, while Paul said he was thinking of Peter Pan.

Peter Pan, the eternal boy, needs to move away from a mother complex towards maturity, responsibility, and hard work. He needs to avoid a psychological death. It seems if the adolescent male does not physically and emotionally separate from his mother, he will psychologically remain stuck in an infantile, dependent relationship without the capacity for independent thoughts and actions and adult relationships. We see and hear of men who remain 'mummy's boy'.

Paul wanted to have friends, but fear was stopping him take the step away from his mother and on to the metaphorical bridge towards his potential peers. I was aware I needed to help Paul get in touch with his feelings. Gradually, Paul started to share his emotions. He expressed his growing feelings of dislike, even hate, towards his mother. He felt afraid and ashamed of these thoughts. Quietly, he shared his fantasy that his mother killed his father. He knew this was not true, but he couldn't get rid of this thought. In his nightmare, his mother was trying to swallow him, and if she succeeded, he, too, would be devoured and no longer exist. Just like his father. Paul shared quietly he was afraid he may have to destroy his mother before she destroyed him. He was truly suffering. He was suffering as he had a strong survival life force.

Gently, we explored the dream images. Paul was undeveloped and infantile. He said how tasty he looked as the infant in the dream. All pink and soft—such an intimate image and feeling at such a horrendous time! I imagine Freud would say this was a sexual dream of the child's desire to be eaten and consumed by his first love object. I was resistant to go there at this time, as I might be perceived to be the big bad wolf.

Instead, we explored the fantasy image of wholeness. Paul felt this was his mother's desire. 'But this idea has come from you?' He shared he did love the idea, when he was young and there was no father, that he and his mother were one. 'In a bubble?' I asked. Paul agreed, but now he wanted out. He wanted freedom. The symbiotic union was coming to an end. All these thoughts and feelings were now being given a voice. He had repressed these feelings, and now the dream had created some inner change. With this tension, he was feeling emotions that were unsafe to express. Paul admitted to feeling sucked dry and without hope. What was the point of trying? He longed to feel strong and to experience some mastery over his life. To achieve this, we explored ideas around examples of strong men in his life. His PE teacher at school was a man he admired. He was strong, available, and encouraging to all the boys. Paul decided to engage in after-school swimming training run by his PE teacher. There was at last some energy in the room, and energy within Paul gradually replaced his apathy.

Psychotherapy provided a safe space for Paul to explore his feelings, fears, fantasies, and hopes. He gained an understanding that his mother had just been lovingly trying to be both mother and father to him, and in this undertaking had over-parented and over-protected him. Paul made his life-giving choices.

EMMA

Emma's mother called to make an appointment for her fourteen-year-old daughter, who was becoming withdrawn and quiet. She said she wanted to accompany Emma to her sessions. I suggested Emma come alone and said I would call her if I needed her to join us. This, I explained, was my policy when seeing adolescents. Reluctantly, she agreed.

Emma presented as a quiet, softly spoken, young teenage girl with long, straight, brown hair and pale, watery, blue eyes. Her shoulders were slightly rounded, and she appeared to be lacking in self-confidence. But Emma was keen to talk.

She said she'd had to grow up way too quickly, as the fun of childhood had ceased at six years old when her father left the small family and moved interstate. There was no struggle, just an emptiness where her father had been. Emma was afraid her mother wouldn't be able to survive in life without her help. She felt trapped and believed she had a duty to support her mother. I could see Emma was stuck. There was consequently a very young part of Emma who was fearful she also might not survive without her mother. This part was the six-year-old Emma who silently suffered when her father left. Emma said she always tried not to burden her mother with her own physical and emotional needs.

Emma shared a dream she had a couple of nights before our first psychotherapy session.

> *My mother is driving an old red car. I am in the passenger's seat. There isn't much room in the car, and it is cramped and uncomfortable.*
>
> *I feel angry and trapped sitting next to my mother. I want to either wrestle the steering wheel away from her or just jump out of the car. She is really annoying me, and I am feeling incredibly frustrated.*
>
> *I know my girlfriends are also in a car that is an awesome convertible. They are in their bikinis and are heading to the beach. I see my face as large as a dinner plate and as red as a beetroot. I feel very unattractive.*
>
> *My mother and I are heading in a different direction. I could scream! 'I want to be with my friends, not with you! I want to go to the beach,' I yell at my mother.*

Emma said when she awoke, she was feeling sad and stuck. It was very clear to Emma what the dream meant. She said in an animated voice that the dream spoke to her about her fear of taking control of the vehicle, but how she wanted to be in the driver's seat, with her hands firmly on the steering wheel. 'The dull red car is just like me. It is sad. It hates being small and dull. I want to be in the driver's seat. I want to be behind the wheel of a convertible, shiny and cool.'

I could see that Emma's interpretation represented where she was in her life. I could also see her grief of losing her father had been passed over and not dealt with. Emma was grieving and angry. We began by working together on issues around unexpressed grief and the feelings she had never felt it was safe to have. Then we spent time dealing with her anger. 'I wanted to cry, to sob, to be held like a baby, but my mother was doing all that. So selfish! What about me? Who was going to care about me?'

Emma at last was able to cry, to sob like a baby, like a six-year-old child, like a fourteen-year-old teenager. It was safe here; she was being held within the framework of our session. Emma's anger was the energy required to developmentally separate from her mother. Emma associated the colour red with anger. The car, her face. Both were red. Both needed to be understood, felt, and used to provide her with a sense of agency, some drive to move forward. Once we had processed these issues, we could deal with how she was going to separate and take control.

Emma again shared she wanted to be in a convertible. I suggested this was symbolic of converting from childhood to adolescence and eventually to adulthood. 'Yes, then I can feel free, with the wind in my hair.' We did a visualisation around this image and the accompanying feelings. Emma loved that imagining. She longed to be with her friends, her peers, where she belonged. Imagining them being with her in her car was meaningful. Emma wanted to be going to the ocean, a common dream image of the unconscious and of one's feelings. Her associations around the ocean were having fun, being with her school friends, and wearing a bikini. She also felt she had an ocean full of tears inside her. These tears were now able to flow.

Dreams from the Stages of Life

STAGE 3: Young Adulthood

This is a time of expanding consciousness as there now is an awakening of the inner world. There is a developing sense of self-knowledge and self-hood. There comes an appreciation of the lessons learned from the games played when younger, of the presence of virtue and a higher cause than winning. The young adult is no longer an awkward adolescent but is not fully a mature adult. They are now beginning to define and embrace their function and role in life, and tools and skills are being acquired. It is a time of career exploration, educational pursuits, and getting established in the workplace. Commitment and responsibility are now achievable and not so frightening. Intimacy in romantic relationships and friendships is experienced. Young adults are starting to align themselves with their parents' values and way of living or may be still reacting against them.

Dreams at this time are becoming more memorable and thought-provoking. They may reflect themes of self-discovery, identity, and the challenges of this dynamic and transformative stage of life. Mythical figures appear commonly, as in the cases below of both Jodie and Mark.

JODIE

Here is a dream example of a myth introducing Eros, the god of love, to the dreamer. Jodie and I had been working together weekly for about nine months, interestingly a gestation period. She came to psychotherapy as a well-groomed young woman in her mid-thirties. Her hair was cut in a sharp bob, and her clothes were stylish yet severe in their cut. Jodie was clinically depressed and had little motivation. She said she had nearly given up on life as she felt life had given up on her. Together, we identified she was not at risk of self-harm. Jodie struggled to find love within herself and in relationships with others. She worked as an accountant in a large firm. She was disconnected from her interior emotional world as she was most comfortable in her head, intellectualising, thinking, and working with numbers and spreadsheets. During her time in therapy, her presenting depression had lifted. This was her dream.

> *I am living in a two-storey house. There is something familiar about this house. The upstairs level is divided in two. In one half of the upstairs lives Elizabeth Jolley, the famous West Australian author. Elizabeth is thin, elderly, grey, and looks quite severe. She is sitting silently, quietly writing at her desk. In the other half lives a young, beautiful yet frail female musician who is playing the cello. The cello is big and round and curvaceous. The girl playing has long, orange, curly hair and looks angelic. I like looking at her. These two women are completely unaware of each other's existence. I am aware of each of the women, and I seem to know them somehow.*
>
> *I hear a flapping and knocking noise at the French doors of the upstairs balcony. I ignore the sound of the insistency and the obvious presence of a mythical figure at the doors. All I can focus on is the gentle playing of the cello. It sounds soothing.*
>
> *Neither of these women pay any attention to the disruption on the balcony. I'm looking at them amazed they aren't noticing. What is wrong with them! I peer through the doors outside. There is a young, tall, strapping male whose body is covered in white feathers! He is bird-like, has wide, white-feathered wings, which are flapping. He is amazing! Yet, I feel afraid. Is he trying to fly or trying to get inside? He seems determined to come inside. The two women remain unaware of his presence and continue with their work. How can they be so blind? I successfully pull myself out of the dream. It is like getting out of a pool of thick honey.*
>
> *Now I am awake, tearful, and somewhat physically fearful.*

Jodie had quickly written down her dream before she lost it, as she knew at a very deep level this dream was significant.

We talked about her dream. Jodie felt the birdman was some sort of god. I suggested that Eros, the Greek god, was at her door. He was outside of herself, on the balcony. She felt sad and afraid that she could not enjoy the imaginative drama being played within. Eros was representative of her life force. Eros, charged with desire and passion for another, was attempting to enter her conscious self.

Jodie was fearful. We talked about the two women. It was as if Jodie was stuck, unaware and unable to dwell in her creative self, which inhabited both parts of herself that were split in two. One part naïve and one part mature. She liked the idea of having creative parts of herself. When we dream a myth, it has such power that it can shake us and may even have a physicality, which usually leads to an insight or a revelation. Jodie was concerned about the sensation of flapping wings in her chest, which felt like anxiety. A loud metronomic beating. Jodie suffered anxiety in her everyday life. Occasionally, she could feel her heart beating noisily in her chest.

Here was beautiful and powerful Eros, the god of love and sexual desire, but Jodie had been closed off from the possibility of a relationship with Eros. I showed Jodie an image in a book on Eros. She couldn't believe he was a part of her internal world. Jodie knew nothing of Greek mythology, yet she knew she was feeling anxious, a little excited, and a sort of pleasure. She shared she felt this pleasure as an excitation and curiosity within her body, which she described as unformed and adolescent.

Together, we worked on how Jodie could open the French doors and welcome Eros into her life. She needed to not be fearful. There was much in her life she was afraid of. She had been busy creating and writing stories in her mind of all that could go wrong in the future. These stories kept her emotionally stuck and unable to feel or live in the moment peacefully.

We also worked on bridging the split parts of herself. Jodie began to become acquainted with the internal storyteller represented by Elizabeth Jolley who had been keeping her stuck in busyness and the frail romantic cello player who was fearful and not robust enough to embrace life. She just kept playing the same old tune. Jodie felt drawn to the cello player with her curly orange hair. She felt she looked soft, spiritual, and angelic, and that she played the strings of her cello like heartstrings. Jodie was getting in touch with a spiritual, heartfelt part of herself.

She commenced a journal and gradually started to write about life within her family, where there had been an absent father figure, unavailable to lead the way forward. Also, she recalled her mother suffered from chronic depression and described her as anything but jolly.

Jodie was able to engage a new masculine energy that enabled her to feel more powerful.

> *I am a young boy setting out on an adventure. The land is rather barren, rocky, and unfamiliar to me. I wonder where I am.*
> *I stumble over a rock, and I am concerned that I am disabled.*
> *I look down, and I seem to be okay. My little young feet are on the ground.*

I asked Jodie the approximate age of this boy. She felt about three or four years old. This question is often relevant as there is likely a significant experience that has been triggered. Jodie said her family moved to the east coast around this time. It was also the time of the birth of her younger brother.

We talked about this young boy child in her dream. Jodie said she was sure it was her rather than her brother. Perhaps this signified the innocent part of Jodie that was full of wonder and wanting to explore the new, unfamiliar, and somewhat barren world. This nascent masculine energy didn't seem to know what to do or where to go. He hadn't yet come into his own. It's not that he was disabled, just young and not surefooted.

Our work together involved consciously sitting with Jodie's fear and sadness as felt in her depression. She no longer suffered anxiety. Gradually, this weight lifted and she had a desire to allow Eros into her conscious world.

ERICA

Erica booked her appointment in a distressed state. Her voice was high-pitched and thin, and her message was verging on hysterical. I had an appointment available later that day, and Erica arrived twenty minutes early. While I was eating my afternoon tea, I could hear her sitting in my waiting room. *Do I see her early?* I had never done that previously, but I noticed I was feeling some anxiety about what may be coming, so I decided to just sit with this discomfort.

White-faced and red-eyed, Erica sat across from me on the edge of her chair. She had a shock of long and untidy brown hair, and she looked washed out. Immediately, she was crying gut-wrenching belly cries. The desperate cries of a baby. I wondered if she would be able to speak.

At that time, I was revisiting the work of British paediatrician and psychoanalyst Donald Winnicott as I was teaching his ideas to trainee therapists. I remembered him saying an analyst has to display all the patience, tolerance, and reliability of a mother devoted to her infant. This was my way of working with attachment. As I sat there with some foreboding, Erica began, 'You have to help me. Last night, I dreamt I drowned my baby, Veronica!' Oh, relief! I expected her to say she actually drowned her baby. Really drowned her. But it was real to her.

Erica was in her late thirties. She emphasised she was extremely close to being forty. It had taken years for her to conceive. Excitement and anticipation followed by disappointment. Month after month. Cycle after cycle. Her husband, Jay, was getting performance anxiety.

She explained she was a Virgo, a perfectionist, and this situation was far from her expectations. That was another disappointment. 'I could have killed him! But he did it. Eventually!' Erica was having murderous thoughts without awareness. Would she have those thoughts about me if I didn't perform?

She told me Veronica was now nine months old. Erica had not suffered post-natal depression and was not taking any medication. 'She's been a very irritable baby and has irregular sleep patterns. I'm up all night. I hate it. I'm so tired. Jay hates it too. He mostly sleeps in the spare bedroom. Well, there certainly won't be another baby!'

I was wondering if Jay still wasn't sexually performing. Was he feeling humiliated? Was this adding to her rage? I ask about her dream.

> *I can see myself pregnant. My skin and the shape of my body look like an elephant's. I am big, heavy, slow, wrinkly, and as loose as a used paper bag. I am watching myself from a distance. I don't want to get close as I look gross. Then I squat down by a riverbank and push out a baby. It is like going to the toilet, you know, like having a shit, not a baby. Next, I am bathing the baby in the river. The baby is covered in shit. It is screaming, kicking, red-faced like a monkey. I have had enough! I hold the screaming baby underwater. It kicks and struggles until it is finally still. Floppy, dead. Quiet. Peace has come.*

Erica said she woke up gasping for air. It was like she had drowned, as if she was the screaming baby. Erica was more settled now. The telling of the unspeakable had allowed her to calm down and be present. She was surprised by how much better she felt. 'Gosh, perhaps that was all I needed to do. Confess.'

There was so much of Erica in the dream and so much going on within. She was scared. Afraid of her unexpressed rage and hate that had been weighing her down. Now it was coming out, shit and all.

Was she going to kill off this new beginning? I needed to check in to see if the baby was at risk of harm. No, she loved Veronica. She could never harm her. Then I needed to check in to see if Erica was at risk of harming herself. Gosh, no, she could never do that. She had visited her local GP to be sure she wasn't suffering post-natal depression. We had a 'no harm' contract in place, just in case.

The session was coming to an end. For some reason, I felt I needed to give Erica something to take home, to think about. Psychotherapy would be helpful to both mother and child. This unknown, unexpressed hate would otherwise be unhealthy to Erica and all her relationships. I asked her if she ever sang nursery rhymes to Veronica. No, she hadn't thought of doing that. I said it helped to settle and soothe both the mother and baby. It is a way of releasing pent-up feelings, such as anger or even hate, without harming or hurting the baby. 'Just sing without an attachment to the meaning of the words, or the feelings. It will be enjoyable for both of you.' I suggested she sing this traditional lullaby:

> *Rockabye baby, on the treetop,*
> *When the wind blows, the cradle will rock.*
> *When the bough breaks, the cradle will fall.*
> *Down will come baby, cradle and all.*

Now Erica was curious, and a little teary. She was keen to engage in some inner work.

In the following months, our work began as educative and emotional as we discussed (using the framework and ideas of Winnicott) the unthinkable concept and feeling of hate towards your child. Winnicott came up with the phrase 'good enough' to move parents away from idealisation, as the expectations of parenting were unrealistic. Erica like most new mothers had a fantasy of perfect maternal and infantile bliss. These expectations were placed across a range of areas in our lives. They were demanding, and actually impossible. You could learn to be good enough rather than perfect, I assured Erica. Perfection was unattainable, so by attempting to achieve this, all one felt was lots of little failures every day. This could be demoralising. Perfection was neither necessary nor possible in parenting.

Gradually, I was able to let go of the role of teacher. Taking on this educative role was unusual. Perhaps Erica was unconsciously forcing me into this role so she didn't need to hate me? At times, I found her presence quite pressuring. She was a big woman and took up a lot of space in the room. Was she elephant-like, just like in her dream, thick-skinned, measured, and powerful? Perhaps feeling hate towards me could have really overwhelmed her. I also became aware that I had some of my own resistance to the idea of hate. How could I have ever felt hate towards my own babies? I had frequently sung that rhyme to them, completely unaware of what I was singing. I had found it soothing and joyful. Being a therapist was always opening an unexplored window into my own psyche through the working relationship.

Hate gradually seeped out of Erica. Her resentment, frustration, and blame were placed upon her baby. She voiced that all these associations with her feelings of hate that were surfacing were shitty. She felt like shit. Jay was a shit. Her life was shit. It stank.

Erica shared freely the strong and passionate emotion of hate she felt towards:

- her ineffectual husband,
- her lazy husband,
- her ineffectual father,
- her body for letting her down,
- her body for staying fat,
- her baby for distorting and destroying her body,
- her baby for not being the idealised baby she wished for, upsetting her reality,
- her baby for spoiling her breasts,

- her baby for hurting her nipples as she chewed and sucked her dry,
- her baby for having a mind of her own,
- her baby for expecting her to be a slave to her every whim,
- her baby for allowing her no peace and taking up all the space,
- her baby for demanding she love her unconditionally,
- her baby for spitting out the food she had spent hours preparing,
- her baby who ate everything for Jay … who did nothing to help,
- and hate for her baby as she no longer thought about sex, and she no longer enjoyed sex as her vagina was still sore.

So much anger, sadness, and grief, and so much hate. All her fantasies of a perfect baby and family had become strongly challenged. This was not at all what she had bargained for. Wished for. So many contradictions were overwhelming her. These feelings were affecting Erica's self-esteem and her relationship with her child and husband.

The dream opened up the therapy. I asked how this drowning related to her life. Did she feel she was drowning as a new mother? As a wife? Did she wish the baby was dead? Erica found it freeing just being able to talk about these unthinkable thoughts in a safe space. It unburdened her of her self-criticism for these failings. We discussed how her expectations had not been fulfilled. Erica felt she was drowning in her unexpressed and unacceptable emotions. But the reality of having this much-wanted baby was not as she'd hoped.

She and Jay shared so many fantasies of life with this longed-for child, dreams and plans of the perfect, happy family. She had read all the books, gone to all the classes, bought all the clothes and toys, painted the nursery. Pink was everywhere. But all she could see was red. Unfulfilled expectations were always a major source of unhappiness. She had not just felt unhappy; she was full of rage and hate. Her internal and external worlds were out of balance. Here was the possibility of a new beginning. A symbolic birth, a new baby.

We worked for a year on Erica being a good-enough parent, not the mother in an 'ideal' family. We were working with reality, not some fantasy. We revisited her thoughts, feelings, and memories of her own birth stories, her memories of her childhood, and experiences of being a part of a family. Her family laughed that they thought she had undiagnosed Down syndrome. So very funny! They thought she looked ugly. Erica believed from these stories she was unlovable. It was healing for her to share as she dived into the deep well of these forgotten memories, to have her feelings of rejection seen and acknowledged.

We also had to think about her relationship with her husband. She had been feeling let down and unsupported. Her husband, Jay, was able to share with Erica his feelings of being emasculated and lonely. At times, he felt jealous of the baby. They all had needs, and they each were needing connection.

At the end of our therapy, Erica shared a final fragment of a dream.

> *We are on a seesaw in a school playground. I am on one side, and a small boy is on the other. We both are playful and happy. We are suspended in perfect balance. It feels powerful, childlike, and fun.*

Erica had given up sitting on the edge of the spectrum on which we all sat. Extreme positions tended to be unhelpful. Being over-perfect, over-conscientious, and over-obsessional kept Erica out of balance. It also kept her emotionally out of tune and unavailable to Veronica. Her dream of balancing on the seesaw gave her a reassuring image and feeling of stillness, balance, and fun. I discussed with Erica how she was balancing her life, again in reference to Winnicott's good-enough parent. The 'good enough' applied to many areas and could be used in all interactions to provide a happy life, free from performance expectations.

Speaking her truth, her hopes and disappointments was healing. She had gained insight and skills to enhance her pleasure in parenting and relationships. Now Erica was confident in being a good-enough mother and leading a good-enough life.

MARK

Mark was in his early thirties and appeared confident and self-assured. He was of average height and walked with a bit of a swagger. His hair was dark and always well-groomed, and he looked fit and strong. Mostly he wore tight denim jeans and a very white open-necked shirt. Mark was a successful stockbroker in a large firm. I noticed when he sat, he had a slight tremor in his right hand. Ever so slight. Perhaps he was ill at ease, after all. He told me he had been using cocaine recreationally at the weekends, which he said kept him high, excited, and pumped up. He made a big fuss as he assured me he wasn't addicted to the drug, but I wondered if he protested too loudly.

Mark was referred to me as he was having difficulty sleeping and sustaining meaningful relationships. He said he found it difficult to turn off at night. He didn't appear tired, but I occasionally felt tired when he left our sessions. It felt like it took a lot of energy to keep up his persona, the mask he presented to the world. Mark grew up in a working-class family. He said he couldn't get away from them quick enough. As the oldest child, he was the first in their humble family to go to university. His parents were so proud of him.

The night before his second appointment, he had this dream.

> *I am a young boy playing with my father. I am a long way off the ground, and I am climbing on a very high wall made of stone. My father is calling to me to be careful. I'm not listening to him. I am having so much fun. He is now yelling at me to be careful. His voice is loud and shrill. I leap off this high wall, and then I'm flying around in circles, going higher and higher. I am so excited! I think I'm a bird, an eagle maybe. The view is amazing. I am in the clouds; they're fluffy and white, like in a picture book. Everything below looks so small and insignificant.*

I'm feeling so strong and powerful. Suddenly, I seem to lose power and I'm falling. My arms, my wings, won't work. Down I come. I'm falling still. I'm screaming to my father, 'Help me, help me!' I crash into land. I am broken. I feel like I am dying.

Mark said he woke up crying. He was fearful this dream may be a warning or, at worst, may come true. I felt sure there was a fall coming.

We talked about his father, who was a bricklayer. Mark said his father was proud of his son, but I sensed Mark felt he was above his father, just as he was physically in the dream. I asked if he saw himself as equal to him, but he looked away as if embarrassed. Now his hand was tremoring. Mark admitted he never shared anything about his loving but simple family with his friends or work colleagues. In fact, he never thought or spoke about them at all.

'I wonder if you are ashamed of them?' I enquired.

'Yes, if I'm honest.'

'In the dream, your father was trying to warn you, but you didn't listen.'

'I never listened to him. He's barely educated. He knows nothing.'

He was dismissive of his proud father.

I said to Mark that his dream sounded like the myth of Icarus. Mark had not heard of this myth. I explained how Icarus was a Greek mythological figure whose father made some glorious, expansive wings out of feathers and wax so Icarus could fly. His father warned his son he must follow his instructions carefully. He was not to fly too close to the sea as his wings would get wet and he would drown. Also, he warned him not to fly too close to the sun; he would fall to his death as the wax would melt from its heat. In the myth, Icarus flies too high, and, thus, he travels too close to the sun. Icarus didn't heed the wise words of his father, and the heat of the sun melted the wax holding his wings together, and he fell into the sea below and drowned. This dream felt like a warning from the psyche as Mark was living a fearless life and soaring like a bird.

Mark had not been listening to the wisdom of his father. He also had not acknowledged him in his role as his father, and the importance of this role. His father gave him the tools to fly—the love, support, and education. Just like in the myth, he made him expansive wings to give him the freedom to fly the nest and go out into the world. Mark had also lost touch with his own internal father and wasn't listening to the inner voice of caution and self-preservation. The dream showed Mark was not grounded; his father was. Mark's ego was inflated and was taking him towards dangerous heights. He was quite shocked at hearing about the myth, and how there were such parallels to the risk-taking life he was now living. He looked fearful. 'I don't want to drown. I want to live my best life.'

Mark was beginning to have some awareness that he had made some imprudent lifestyle choices that were against his better judgement. His work and the emphasis he placed on money had taken him away from values he had once held dearly. He had virtually disowned his family because they were poor and uneducated. Mark felt he was like a child, wanting more and more excitement and ego-driven pursuits. These, he could now see, were taking him away from himself.

We talked of the wall of stone in the dream representing Mark's defenses, the high wall being made of stone, solid and impossible to move. He felt this wall was significant. Interestingly, Mark's father was a bricklayer and a stone mason. Mark felt the wall was preventing him from connecting with others and keeping him lonely. He told me this was one of the reasons he had come to see me. Relationships with others seemed impossible. Not just with women, with anyone he considered inferior. He became aware he was looking down on everyone, not just his family. They appeared small and insignificant. Relationships need to be respectful, trusting, supportive, and conducted on an equal footing to be successful, which was an impossibility with Mark's head in the clouds.

Our work involved gently getting in touch with the values he had become estranged from. There was grief and sadness as he became aware of the hurt and pain he had caused others, especially his father, and it became very clear to him how his life choices were also causing him much suffering. Mark also understood he was harming himself by drug taking. The drugs were keeping him inflated, high, and artificially feeling above others. It made it more difficult to relate. We talked of Oscar Wilde's children's book *The Selfish Giant*, which I had on my bookshelf.

The giant built a wall around his beautiful garden to keep the children away, but the garden was now permanently in shade and no longer blossomed. The giant missed the children, and he was lonely behind the big wall. Mark was lonely. He was no longer blossoming. His wall was keeping him from forming meaningful relationships and playing in a free and healthy way. The giant took down his wall, and, likewise, Mark began to pull apart his wall of defenses. Just as the poignant allegory spoke of the importance of empathy, kindness, and generosity to others, Mark was gradually able to welcome and integrate these transformative qualities. Through our working relationship, Mark became more in touch with his authentic self.

STAGE 4: Mid-Life

Mid-life shifts the focus from becoming established in the outer world to a coming to terms with the inner world. This shift provides a new sense of power and identity, and there is the coming of wisdom in the gaining of ever-increasing consciousness. Aspects of the self are integrated as the individual is striving for wholeness and authenticity. At this time, there is a transition of identity and self-confidence, which can lead to the 'mid-life crisis', feelings of anxiety and depression as inevitable mortality becomes real and life to date is evaluated. Changes are sometimes actioned; careers or sexual partners are changed in an attempt to regain the energy of a sense of purpose, of youth and vitality, accessing parts of themselves that have been unexpressed to date.

This can be enriching and create a sense of completion, but not always. Roles in mid-life shift as children are growing up and leaving home, while parents are ageing and needing care and attention. This awareness may come with feelings of sadness and sometimes despair. There is a need for internal balancing of these changes. Dreams at mid-life reflect these inner and outer challenges and changes that are being navigated. Reflecting and exploring these themes offers insight, clarity, and integration. This is a transformative stage of life.

ROSE

When Rose entered my office, she looked fragile and anxious, so much so that her anxiety was infectious and instantly attached itself to me. She was in her early forties, worked part-time as a teacher, and said she was happily married with two children. She said she never worried about her son as he was no trouble. It was Zoe, her fourteen-year-old, who was the problem. 'She avoids me, is rude to me. I don't seem to know how to talk to her, and I'm concerned about her.' Rose said she had had a nightmare. It had frightened her as she was afraid it might come true.

> *I am in our family home. I look out of the front window. Across the road, I see my fourteen-year-old daughter, Zoe, on the roof of the neighbour's house. She is drinking alcohol with her three girlfriends. The girls are dressed up in wild and crazy outfits, as if they are going out to a fancy-dress party. It is daytime. They are animated, excited, and happy, as if they're at a party.*
>
> *On another rooftop, I can see a group of young boys the girls know well. They are calling out to the girls. The boys, too, are laughing. They are youthful, handsome, and full of bravado. Zoe is frenetically dancing and keeps getting very close to the edge of*

the roof. I am watching this and am consumed with fear and panic. Zoe is waving to the boys in a carefree manner. She is not looking where she is going. I try to call to her to take care, but she doesn't hear me. 'Stop!' I yell.

One of Zoe's friends dares her to jump. Without thinking about it, Zoe jumps. She hits the concrete below. I hear the thump. She falls apart like a China doll, broken into pieces.

I am overwhelmed, shocked, and full of sadness.

The nightmare woke Rose up, and she was flooded with tears. She knew she needed to talk about this dream, so Rose and I discussed it and were able to see this was a parallel to something happening in her life. We began to engage in work on her own internal, adolescent Zoe. Her experience of adolescence was frightening, and Rose was rather apprehensive to talk about it. She described herself as having been an out-of-control teenager in an environment of drama and chaos. She didn't get on with her parents, who drank too much and were often abusive towards each other. They also appeared disinterested in her, and she was an only child.

Rose used to sneak out of the house at night-time and meet up with boys from school. They drank cheap alcohol but, luckily, didn't get into serious trouble. She said she probably was depressed so she self-medicated with alcohol, which made her even more depressed.

We invited her teenage self into the room. This part of Rose needed to be seen, heard, and understood. Rose shared that during this time she'd had suicidal thoughts, which she never acted on, and certainly never spoke of. It was a very moving experience for Rose to revisit and process this troubled time in her life. I find if these experiences aren't healed, they can be re-enacted by the next generation, as was perhaps starting to happen with Zoe. Rose began to understand that

Zoe needed the same, to be seen, heard, and understood.

Up until now, Rose had been an anxious parent and seemed to take a firm and inflexible position. She wanted Zoe to develop her own personality in her own way, yet Rose was concerned her parental values and ways would crumble and smash into pieces if she took risks in her role. She desperately wanted a relationship with Zoe. She wanted the relationship she had longed for with her own mother. Rose didn't have a model of parenting in place and felt the way she was parented wasn't effectual. We spoke about allowing Zoe to gradually get close to the flame she was naturally drawn to, but for her to be protected so she didn't get burned. Zoe was testing her abilities and wanting the space to do this while affirming her identity.

The evening after working together on her dream, Rose spoke with Zoe about risk-taking behaviour and how to cope with pressure from friends and peers. She said she spoke without imposing her strict adult values, which had worked when Zoe was a child; now she spoke with love and concern. Previously, Zoe wouldn't listen to her as she couldn't stand her mother being so dominating and controlling. But now, Zoe started to listen and also started to share with Rose some of her concerns in her rapidly changing world. A connection was forming.

A couple of weeks later, Zoe was at a party with school friends. During the evening, a group of eight girls were taken to hospital by ambulance because they had overdosed on alcohol and a party drug. Zoe shared with Rose that she had refused the shooters and drugs because of their discussion. The dream had been a catalyst for a change in her behaviour and relationships. It also showed Rose how her mother–daughter relationship was dead in its original form but now had the potential to change. It was like a jigsaw puzzle that needed to be broken apart so the pieces could be put back together to create a new picture.

ANTONIO

Antonio came to therapy and told me he was having 'an existential crisis'. He was suffering from anxiety and wondering about the meaning of his life. He said it felt futile. For forty years, he had spent all his time looking after the women in his life, first his mother, then his wife. 'I've had enough.'

He came to Australia as a little boy in a migrant family from Europe. His mother missed her home country and never fully grieved for her parents and siblings left behind. His father worked two jobs to try to make his wife happy, which didn't work. He had a massive heart attack and died at work at the age of forty, just the age Antonio was now. Antonio then took on the role of looking after his mother, sisters, and brothers. This was exhausting. He married a lovely woman from the same European village his parents came from. It turned out she was just like his mother. Antonio wanted to make changes but didn't know where to start.

After a year of us working together, Antonio felt he had established his own identity and had found his own voice. We worked on his resentment that his father died so young, leaving him to inherit the patriarchal role. Antonio had to leave school and become the provider for the family. He was never able to find his own path and form his own individual identity. As a child, he was always in trouble with his father, so his memories of being loved were overshadowed by threats of violence.

Antonio understood now that his father was financially and emotionally stressed. He, too, must have missed his country and his family left behind, but there was no space for his grief. Then he died. Antonio suggested he died of a broken heart, and he didn't want to experience the same fate. He became clear on his responsibilities within his own family and that it was not his role to make everyone happy.

Towards the end of his therapy, he had this dream.

I am busy making and baking loaves of bread all night long. First, I measure the flour; it is white and looks like snow. I add salty water from a vessel I have filled from the ocean. Then I add pink and frothy yeast. There is lots to stir with the wooden spoon my father used to threaten us little ones with, and I am getting hot. I roll the dough, back and forwards, back and forwards. It is hard work. I pummel the dough and make small loaves ready for baking.

I look around. I'm in a dusty old basement. There are no windows. My apron is old canvas and covered in flour. My arms seem very long, heavy, and thick. They are white with flour. Dough is stuck to my huge hands that look like paddles. My brow is glowing, sweaty. The oven is an enormous open firepit, and very hot.

Eventually, the loaves are cooked. I labour as I pull the heavy trays out of the oven. There are trays and trays of golden-brown loaves! I can't believe my eyes! The loaves are glittering like gold bars.

The next morning, he felt exhausted yet rewarded. Antonio was thrilled to have this dream and to be able to process and share his inner wealth with me. His dream took place in the kitchen that was in the basement of his family home. He said he felt like he was living in earlier times, maybe a generation or two ago. Antonio was working so hard in the dream, just as he was in therapy. His dream kitchen was now full of golden loaves. His association around the golden loaves was that gold was strong, valuable, and precious. He recalled both his parents used to wear gold chains around their necks. He didn't want to continue this tradition. He wanted his own identity.

We talked of how bread was a wonderful example of being the ultimate alchemy. It took very little to make, and it transformed into a lot. The precious gold was the symbol of transformation. Antonio recalled the biblical story of the loaves and the fishes easily providing sufficient goodness to feed and sustain many thousands. He felt sustained by the dream. Now he felt he had the resources to provide emotionally for himself and his wife and family. The dream showed us he was undergoing the process of transformation deep within himself. Antonio had found a way to bring his underground stream of gold to the surface.

JULIE

Julie was a forty-year-old woman who had come to therapy as she felt unfulfilled in her life. Her hair was fair, and her beautiful pale skin was luminous. Her eyes were green and calm; she was quiet in her manner and softly spoken. She described how she was feeling 'spiritually empty, even soulless'. This was troubling her. We talked about her being forty years old. She was midway through her life. Julie never expected to feel like this. She was surprised her life was now full of dread and unhappiness that had snuck up on her. Julie could find no fulfilment in her daily life, and she did not know where to start with the sadness she was feeling. She decided to try talking about it with me and search for the answer. She said she worried this state was her destiny. Julie was adamant about not seeing her GP as she did not want to take antidepressants. She had watched her mother go down that pathway, and as she explained, 'There's no sunshine down there. Nothing grows. There's just darkness.'

'You are worried your destiny is to be like your mother?' I asked.

'I hadn't thought about that connection, but yes,' she said quietly.

Julie grew up on a wheat and sheep farm miles from anywhere. It was hot, dry, and barren. She was the eldest of six children, five of them girls. She felt she was raised to be a boy. She had a basin haircut and wore old jeans and boy's clothing. Her skin always burned as she was fair. The other children were allowed to be themselves; only Julie was treated like a boy. Eventually, a son was born, and she was sent to boarding school at twelve. Julie believed this saved her. After school, she went straight to university and became an accountant. She never returned to live on the farm and distanced herself from farm living. Her life she described as uneventful. She had dated boys at university but never fell in love.

At the age of thirty-six, she saw a specialist about freezing her eggs in case she wanted a baby. He suggested she not wait for Mr Right, that Mr All Right would do. 'Just go out and get pregnant.' She was shocked at this attitude and decided against taking his advice. Julie then said she'd hoped I may have a down-to-earth philosophy that she could embrace. My response was, 'Let's look inside and see what the psyche comes up with.' The night before her next session, Julie had this dream.

> *I am lost. I look around me, and I'm in a green jungle of tall trees and fronds and ferns. It smells moist and dank. Up ahead, there are signposts. I'm so relieved! Quickly, I run towards them and look up. I can't read them. They are in a language that is foreign to me. I am about to cry. I look down and I see my feet are bound in clean calico ribbons as if I'm a doll or a geisha. I try to feel my toes, wriggle them, but they're numb, dead. Then I am suddenly aware I have this swollen tummy. It is huge. It's not swollen ... I am heavily pregnant. I feel big and heavy, in fact bursting. I am thinking I am stuck here in the jungle, alone, that I'm forty, and I don't want a baby. I feel afraid.*

Julie woke fearful and worried the dream may be prophetic. We went straight into discussing it at her next session. I asked her about the jungle and the feeling she had being there. She felt afraid as she was immediately aware she was lost. This jungle was the opposite environment to the dry and barren farmland she grew up in. She felt relief when the signposts appeared but let down as she could not read them. Julie knew they held the answer, the way out, just like she was searching for an answer in therapy, to find the way ahead. She was intrigued her feet were tiny and bound.

'That was torture; that was what men did to women who were geishas. Why can't they just be women?'

I asked how she felt seeing her feet so neatly bound, and she quickly responded with anger.

'My father tried to stop me from being a girl, so in his way, he bound and prevented my growth.'

I was thinking her bound feet were also out of contact with Mother Earth and were preventing her from being grounded. As Julie in the dream was clearly full-term, it seemed unlikely this was a prophetic dream about literally falling pregnant, as she was not in a relationship and lived a solitary life.

We talked about how she felt in the dream, heavy and bursting. This was a symbolic pregnancy, a pregnancy of ideas, or a metaphorical baby representing new life in her future, and this was lying deep within her. Perhaps it was a story to be written, a project, or a business venture. Whatever it was, it had been conceived and was growing. Soon it would be time for this baby to be delivered or birthed into the world. Julie felt she was bursting. Her association with that was her fear of exploding, and then she felt she would once again be empty and left with a void. When Julie said a 'void', I heard 'avoid', and I wondered what she was afraid to face. Even the feeling of talking about being pregnant in the dream was far from enjoyable.

Yet I was feeling excited at the prospect of a new beginning for Julie. I then realised this was my desire and not hers. Julie related to the dream as she did to life—with dread. Perhaps the psyche was showing us where Julie had been going wrong in her life. The weight of her dread prevented her imagination from being playful. She wanted also to pursue the idea of spirituality.

I shared that an internal spiritual mother may give birth to a spiritual part of the self who could help guide her through the second half of life. This may be an instinctual desire for wholeness. We all have a need for spiritual connection, and as we age, a yearning for a sense of a higher power in our world. Julie did not stay working with me for very long. Over the next few sessions, we explored Julie's ideas around the spirit and soul. Her soul was searching for some form of nourishment. Gradually, she came to accept that everyday spirituality was ever so ordinary and available to her. All she needed to do was pay attention to her everyday life. Like a baby, the soul needed time, nurturing, and attention. Julie's dream was a generator of change and meaning, the pregnancy being linked to her spiritual self and not to the body's desire for a physical child.

WILLIAM

William presented as a serious, neat, and quiet man in his forties. He seemed to wear a lot of grey—suit, tie, shoes and socks—and his shirts were all either washed-out blue or grey. His hair was greying at the temples. His energy was flat, and I wondered if he was rundown. William said running his own business was stressful, so he thought I could help him cope with this stress. William had married his childhood sweetheart, and after a year of marriage, they decided not to have children. He spoke of his love relationship in a matter-of-fact way. It was data, just information. I wondered where was Eros, where was the passion?

He was surprised when I asked him about his dreams. Interestingly, he had a dream about his car breaking down.

> *My car keeps breaking down. I am frustrated as I am unaware*
> *the car has a problem. I hop out of the car on the side of the road,*
> *walk around it, and inspect the tyres. It looks fine. I can't see that*
> *anything is wrong. I get back inside the car, but it still won't go.*

When William woke, he felt lethargic. Because of the dream, and the fact that he was feeling flat, I was concerned William may be unaware he had a physical problem. Perhaps he needed some self-care and maintenance. Just as a car needs regular maintenance to run smoothly, so do our minds and bodies. I suggested he have a check-up with his doctor. His GP reassured William he was in fine physical health.

The next week, he was rather withdrawn. Again, he had a dream about his car breaking down.

> *My car is broken. It won't go forward or back. There is black smoke coming out of the exhaust. I tow the car to a mechanic. He says he can't fix it. I know I must abandon it.*

There was some sadness around this, and William admitted to feeling like a failure. He wanted to see the car as literal. He said his car in real life was a reliable German four-door automatic that was only a couple of years old. He said it wasn't very exciting, but it was sturdy and adequate. I wondered what it was that he wanted me to fix. Did he see me as the mechanic, or was he?

We talked about the inability of the car to move forward in the dream. William had come to therapy to deal with his stressful yet successful workplace. This was all he thought he wanted to work on. He was a serious and intelligent man, a little like his car, reliable and automatic. He enjoyed his workplace and managing his staff. Goals were set and met at work. He described himself as a thinking man. This kept him operating fully in his head and disconnected from his heart, disconnected from Eros.

Suddenly, it dawned on me. Gently, I suggested we again discuss his marriage. He had always glossed over this relationship, saying he was too busy to give his wife too much attention, in therapy and in life. She also didn't seem interested in giving William much attention. It wasn't William who was broken down; it was the vehicle of love. William was a typical man who wasn't overly comfortable talking about romantic feelings, especially his own. But it seemed his wife wasn't responding to the lack of love between them. Her tank was probably also running on empty. When we lifted the bonnet of the vehicle, the inside was empty. William admitted he no longer felt love or affection for his wife. He believed his wife showed no love towards him or curiosity about him. He said the marriage was broken. Continuing to use the car as a metaphor, it was time to move from automatic to manual. I recommended they see a couple's therapist. After three sessions, they decided a lawyer would be a better option.

William came back to share his progress and to do some inner work. This meant lifting the bonnet. He was very sad yet relieved he was able to deal with the breakdown rather than feel the shame of being a failure. He saw himself as the mechanic. He felt he needed to be the one responsible, to know everything, and be able to make any repairs required. This he did very successfully in his workplace. But when it came to his heart, the engine, he felt he knew nothing. It unfolded that William was angry. Black smoke erupted from within. He finally started to have some colour; it was an angry red. William started to let go—he began to look and feel untidy.

We spent time working through his anger until he reached a new sense of wholeness and his own sense of self as his car was functioning and running smoothly once again.

STAGE 5: Old Age

There appears to be a freedom and a curiosity to explore our inner world as we age. Children have become independent and are starting to form their own families. The attempted climb of the ladder in the work environment, the mastery of skills, the striving for achievements—all this is mostly behind us. The drive for external validation has lessened. There now is a drive away from *doing* towards *being*. Ruminating on the past may evoke anxiety and can lead to cynicism or even bitterness in old age. Fear of death is naturally a source of anxiety. This may be influenced by religious or spiritual beliefs. Existential questions concerning the meaning of life, the purpose of life, transcendence, and spirituality often appear in dreams. Encounters with loved ones or friends can offer comfort, closure, and healing. There may be a processing and resolution of past conflicts or grief.

There is a different inner search or exploration happening. Dreams of loss—for example, loss of one's car and loss of teeth—are common at this stage. Finding secret rooms in a house or keys to doors may also be dreamt about. Finding treasure in a secret room or deep in the garden or in an unexpected place is one of the delights of ageing. As we age, our treasure or inner gold is not overt but rather the opposite. It is now our lived wisdom.

Harold's dream reflects this.

HAROLD

Harold was a tall, frail, quietly spoken gentleman in his mid-eighties. He said he wanted to come to see me as he had a feeling he described as an inner melancholy. His GP thought he was clinically depressed, but Harold disagreed and refused medication. He said he just wanted to sit quietly with someone. This we did. Harold was always conservative and neat in his dress, wearing comfy corduroy pants and a tweed jacket. He had been well-respected in his chosen profession, but he shared he now felt somewhat alone, even lost. He said his children and even his grandchildren did not seem to need him. Harold said he rattled around in his old house, but he planned to stay there if physically possible. He was adamant he didn't want to go into an aged care facility. He did not want to lose his dignity.

I asked Harold if he could recall any of his dreams, and he shared a dream he'd had twice before.

> *I am endlessly searching for something in this old, dilapidated, large, and somewhat familiar house. Every room is misshapen.*

The floor is unstable. There are so many rooms. I don't seem to know exactly what I'm searching for. I walk through doors into rooms that are unfamiliar. Down I climb. Down old stairs into a dusty and empty basement, all the time searching. There is very little light. It is gloomy. There are some blue soft fluffy toys lying around. I feel sad and alone. A bit like a lost boy. I never find what I'm looking for. I just know it is missing.

Harold thought this dream had some importance and was interested to talk about it. He said on waking, a deep sadness had invaded him, a sadness that was not there previously, or he had not noticed. This was the feeling he had called melancholy.

When I asked about his family, he became very quiet. I enquired if he had a wife or partner. He sat in silence. Harold then began to quietly cry. Eventually, he said he lost his wife, Olive, just over two years ago. He said he no longer even dreamed of her. She would appear in his dreams while alive, but not now. He wished he would dream of her, but she never appeared. Harold shared how she had suddenly died when they were on a three-month overseas trip on a cargo ship. They had chosen this unique and slow-paced form of travel for its cost-effectiveness and the opportunity to experience life at sea. Sadly, Olive suffered a heart attack in her sleep. As they were in the middle of the Atlantic Ocean and far from home, she was buried at sea. Harold was with the ship's captain and two officers in uniform for the quiet sea burial held at dawn. There was a prayer, the hymn *Abide With Me*, and she softly splashed overboard wrapped in a flag. That was it. Over in a flash. The loss of Olive was not mentioned on board as Harold said it was apparently thought of as a sign of bad luck. It was as if she never existed.

Harold returned home without Olive. There was no symbolic funeral ritual or service or acknowledgement of her death to be shared with his family as there was no body, no grave, no ashes. This lack of ritual had left Harold unsettled. He said Olive became like the elephant in the room on his return home as no one wanted to mention her death. All his family said was 'sorry'. He said he understood they probably didn't want to upset him. Harold was such a quiet, humble, and reserved man, and he was apprehensive to discuss his experience of losing his beloved wife of sixty-plus years. He didn't want to burden his children with his feelings, so he ignored these feelings. He said he felt separate to them.

As a consequence, Harold was unable to successfully grieve or mourn, unable to deal with this emotional and physical loss, and so he just carried deep within him an unacknowledged empty house that held profound loss. He was far from the position of acceptance. He said while he was on the ship after her secret burial, he felt anger towards Olive for leaving him, and he felt physically and emotionally alone and at sea. Then he felt guilty, as intellectually, he knew she had no say in the matter.

The process of grieving became our shared work. Harold slowly and gently found language amidst a myriad of feelings to tell their life story. I felt so privileged to be immersed in this beautiful narrative. We experienced a form of ritual involving the mind and the heart. Harold shared it felt like his heart was painfully full of sadness. He talked about how he realised his house was empty without Olive, yet her clothes still hung in the wardrobe. Her suitcase remained unpacked in a spare bedroom. Apart from his memories, all he returned home with was her suitcase. We began to unpack it metaphorically.

I only saw Harold for a couple of months of weekly sessions, but he felt the process was very valuable. Olive was no longer invisible. She became alive within Harold, and certainly she had a presence in our sessions. He was aware it was grief he was searching for. In the process of searching, he had discovered parts of himself he had not been aware of. In his dream, these were the doors into rooms that were unfamiliar. Once he located his reservoir of grief within, he smiled and acknowledged how obvious it seemed that this was what he was missing. It was there all the time. It was buried deep within the psyche. Experiencing the range of emotions Harold felt in grief was tiring, but the searching was tiring in a healing way.

We also talked of what Harold felt really mattered in his life. Unexpressed feelings of grief had kept Harold distanced from life. He missed his connection to his family and talking about their family, including Olive. This lost treasure was certainly worth finding for everyone. I gently explained that how we deal with loss shapes our capacity to be present to others and to life. It is the ties of love and affection that bind and hold us together and contribute to a sense of wholeness.

Harold also missed his spiritual practice. He always believed he only went to Church on Sunday to make Olive happy. He admitted he missed the ritual of going to the Sunday service and sitting in the beautiful church because he especially missed listening to the choir. He shared it brought him peace. During our time together, he returned to attending the Sunday service. He was reunited with the church community, and he gained a sense of belonging. Harold was gradually stepping back into life.

In our last session, Harold told me he asked his daughter to help him sort out Olive's clothes, jewellery, and books. This they respectfully and happily did together as a shared task. There was no longer an elephant in the room between them.

Harold also changed his will and discussed with his sons and daughter that he would like his ashes to be scattered at sea, off the side of the Rottnest Island ferry. He was delighted with this choice. He planned a small party to celebrate Olive's life with his family and his few remaining friends. He invited me to join them, but I had to refuse. This is one of the losses a therapist must bear. You engage in a deep and meaningful relationship, but it is a paradoxical relationship. It is the therapeutic relationship that heals. It is not a friendship.

A year or so later, I read in the local paper with sadness yet a sense of completeness that Harold had peacefully died. He was eighty-eight.

He was respectfully celebrated by his family and professional peers. Through Harold's dream of searching, he came to look within himself for what was missing in his life. Not only had he not grieved for Olive, but he had also lost touch with a sense of belonging. He was lonely, not depressed.

As we approach the completion of our life, there is the final step in the hero's journey. Once we have discovered our inner treasure and have implemented changes for our self and our relationships with others, we process and review our learned lessons and knowledge and endeavour to live our truth.

4

Dreams that Facilitate Change

In this section, I present a number of client dreams that illustrate how dreams can facilitate change. As a reader, you may choose to move between these cases, as some of the material discussed may be confronting.

When a client is in therapy, their dreams can provide an insight that the therapist can work with, and sometimes this can change the course of the therapy in helping to provide a successful outcome. The dreams can be a catalyst for self-discovery and personal growth through our working relationship. The psyche may send recurring dreams of symbols, imagery, and metaphors when the dreamer is ready to face these presented insights and bring them to consciousness. When wise to this inner force, we can choose to work to integrate them. The first case of Rebecca's dreams demonstrates both points. She placed limited value on the symbol of the red fox that appeared in the initial dream. However, when the red fox revealed himself a second time, it ensured this exiled trickster part of herself was brought fully to her awareness and could no longer remain hidden deep in her unconscious. This was very enlightening in the process of Rebecca's therapy, which facilitated and empowered her to make tangible life changes.

REBECCA

Rebecca was a lawyer in her early thirties who told me she lived in her head, in her intellect. She proudly admitted that rarely did she allow herself to feel. I vividly recall our first session. She scanned my room with busy, hypervigilant eyes, as if looking for something. I followed her gaze searching for imperfections. What was she searching for, I wondered? Rebecca was smartly dressed, attractive, and frequently smoothed her tight skirt or looked at her watch. I have seen many young women lawyers over the years, often suffering from anxiety and stress. It is a competitive, tough profession that is constantly being measured, as every minute is recorded, billable, accountable, and valuable. Long working hours were expected, and there was a gender bias towards male lawyers, who earned more than women. There can be a large power imbalance, and the profession was thought to be a bit of a boy's club.

Rebecca had been working for a prestigious law firm for more than six years. Some of her peers had already left to have babies. Her girlfriend from university had suffered burnout. 'If you can't stand the heat, get out of the kitchen,' was a mantra one of her bosses chanted if anyone complained about the workload. Rebecca assured me she was there for the long haul. She was married to an academic, and they had decided not to have children. 'I'm happy about that,' she said. I noticed her face didn't look happy when she said this.

One of Rebecca's friends had seen me a few years previously for psychotherapy as she was depressed. She had shared my details with Rebecca at a time when she, too, was struggling. Rebecca told me she got through this time by becoming stronger, working harder, and not dwelling on her weaknesses. When I asked what it was that prompted her to see me now, she said she wasn't sleeping very well and she wanted to work on how to reconnect with her family. Rebecca shared she was longing for family connection now she was an adult. She said the split with her family occurred at seventeen when she secretly applied for and won a scholarship to study law in another state and abruptly left her family behind. Her accommodation was provided, so she was on her way. This path took her away from her family.

'Did you miss them?' I questioned.

'No, I had outgrown them.'

I wondered about all that family provided. It is within our family that we first feel love and compassion, sharing and support, nourishment and strong positive feelings about ourselves as individuals and also in our relationships with others.

'I had all that, but I was smart, and I was pretty much done. They were good people. I was never treated badly. It was me who wanted more.' But now, Rebecca wanted to somehow build a bridge and reconnect with them. She had believed she could be self-sufficient and exist without them.

We worked with her feelings of longing, which she had language for in an objective way, as if this feeling lay outside of herself. Slowly, she moved away from her head and into the domain of her heart. This had an emotionality as well as a physicality, both realms she had been unaccustomed to connecting with.

Rebecca had put out a message to her family on social media suggesting a meeting. This had only limited success. 'They came to our place, but everyone was very cold. I didn't even bother putting the kettle on. Too awkward. I think they're scared of me.' Now she wanted to get to know her parents and her siblings as adults, but she didn't know how to bridge the gap that had widened over the years. She was only just learning how to feel vulnerable; she wasn't ready to share that feeling with others.

'Perhaps next time, you could suggest a picnic rather than a meeting. Then you can step into the child place together, and play will be possible. Staying in an adult place will be formal and possibly intimidating to the others.' As she became more familiar with her vulnerability, she slowly extended an olive branch, which they accepted. A picnic at the river was successful, as everyone's defenses softened. They were all pleased to be reunited.

At our fourth session, Rebecca arrived agitated and restless. She shared a dream she had the previous night.

> *I am up in the attic searching for a school assignment. Where is it? I keep searching throughout the house. The descent down the many stairs seems an incredibly long journey. Eventually, I find my way into the basement. It takes me into a cave. I didn't know this cave existed. Now I am undertaking a deep excavation of my home. It seems to take hours of exhausting digging. Dirt is flying everywhere.*
>
> *Eventually, I find a small, winding stream that I am curious about. I follow the stream, which is quite reflective, even magical, through the dark and dank-smelling earth. There, I find another cave. Carefully, I enter the cave. I can't believe what I am seeing!*
>
> *Even though it is dark, I can see a little fox playing tennis against the cave wall! He has a red racquet and a tennis ball that he hits back and forth, again and again. I am feeling really annoyed.*
>
> *His fur is red, and he has glassy and cheeky eyes. He has a bushy red tail and a pointy face. His eyes are now shifty, beady, like little black glass marbles. He says, 'Ah, you've found me at last,' and he's laughing loudly. His teeth are yellow, sharp, and pointed. Suddenly, I'm terrified, and I wake up with a start.*

Rebecca was anxious about sharing this dream with me, but she wasn't sure why. We worked with her thoughts and feelings about the dream. She was amused she was searching in her upstairs, in her intellect, for answers. This had been her place of comfort, her happy place, but now she was realising the answers were buried far deeper inside her. She commented on how we were engaged in excavating by digging up her memories of her home and her life, and at times, the work was arduous. It had revealed feelings and dark places she didn't know had existed.

This stream had been reflective and what she saw and felt was even magical. She was aware of the stream's connection to a river. She had dreamt of rivers before and loved the idea that the river divided but also joined and united. She described the river as a mysterious flow of life. This, we agreed, was the flow of life she had so wanted to connect with, reuniting and joining her with her family.

But now, the magic was overtaken by the confronting image of the fox, which was at the forefront of her consciousness. Rebecca said she wished the fox would disappear from her mind as she found it disturbing. We talked about her associations and thoughts about the red fox. She saw the fox as a very cunning and clever animal. This fox had dug his den very far away from everything, as if he was hiding, yet there he was, happily hitting the tennis ball back and forth against the cave wall.

I suggested perhaps this was what she did when she left home so abruptly, setting up a home well hidden from family, friends, even from herself. Rebecca said she just knew this cunning fox had the ability to cause havoc. And he was so annoying! Rebecca believed this fox was a lying fox who rarely told the truth. All he did was outsmart everyone and then hide. She felt this little red fox was far too quick and cunning to catch. This was making her feel anxious.

I was now in my intellect, busy thinking about trying to catch the fox, the trickster. Jung said the trickster was a mythological character, a collective shadow figure, a summation of all inferior traits of character in individuals. I recalled shadow figures like this little red fox appeared when we were at emotional crossroads. They were quick, always on the move, duplicitous, and frequently sexually rampant. The trickster archetype was cunning, crude, and primitive. But I felt reassured he could transform what was meaningless into something meaningful and awaken Rebecca to this possibility. Importantly, he was not to be ignored.

I asked Rebecca what the fox's words 'you found me at last' meant to her. She became upset. When she was a young girl, she shared she could be very cunning. Never missing anything, often hypervigilant, telling lies, ready to be clever so she could outsmart her three siblings and even her father. She spoke for the first time of holding her family in contempt. We explored the idea of this clever little red fox representing a part of Rebecca's character that was exiled and had to live in isolation deep within her unconscious in a cave. Rebecca said as a young lawyer she had despised those in her profession who had these fox-like characteristics. One of her legal barristers described how he loved to dig a hole in court for the guilty client to blindly fall into. 'Then we had him!' He was trapped. He had nowhere to hide.

Rebecca was coming to terms with this discovery of the cunning fox. She felt we had made progress as she was becoming aware of this tricky side of her character. I was hopeful she would be in touch with her natural, animal, instinctual reactions as the little fox was now out of the shadow. But he was mercurial. Our therapy came to an end not long after this dream. Rebecca seemed content. She was sleeping better, and her relationship with her family was slowly progressing. I was a little apprehensive, but she was adamant our work was done. She was under a tight schedule and pressure at work to increase her billable hours and bring more revenue into the practice; then there would be the possibility in the future of a partnership in the firm for her. A carrot was being dangled.

Three months later, Rebecca was on my answering machine. Her voice was dark and deep. We had a session, and she was soon sobbing. The image of the trickster red fox had reappeared in her dream, and she was worried.

I'm walking along a path. It seems long and unclear. I am searching for something, but I don't know what. I can't grab onto anything; everything is out of focus. I'm trying so hard to see where I'm going. I think I'm in a grove of pale green olive trees. Suddenly, the red fox comes out from behind a tree. He is there in front of me. His coat is mangy and tufted, matted; he looks neglected. I look straight into his beady eyes. They look tired, less vigilant. I feel sorry for him. I try to touch him, but he has disappeared.

Rebecca woke up beside herself. That morning, she left her message to me. This cunning shadow figure had a small cameo role visible enough to disturb Rebecca. Was he disrupting the chance for unity Rebecca was striving for? Rebecca seemed distraught. I had not seen her vulnerable like this before. She spoke in soft tones as if it was a confession. 'I've been having an affair for a couple of years. Absolutely no one has any idea. I'm cunning, wily as a coyote, quick, clever, and outsmarted everyone, and especially my clever husband. I love my husband. What am I doing?'

She said she also loved the excitement of lying, and of playing a game and winning. She loved the risk-taking sex and living out a part of herself never expressed before. She explained she felt like a stranger to herself. To break the tension, she laughed and said she was foxy. Now she was fully aware she had still been playing games with her family, especially her husband. She shared this was 'quite a racquet'. Just like in her childhood. Rather than show her vulnerability, she was guarded with them, and dishonest. Back we went to the image of the fox.

In this dream, he appeared less powerful than in her first dream and was not in a good way. He was showing signs of being neglected. There was more to be revealed in our work. After acknowledging and allowing feelings of shame, of sadness and grief, the work deepened. Rebecca was gradually able to befriend the clever yet tired fox and bring this tricky aspect of her character into full awareness and acceptance.

Up until this dream, Rebecca had not fully embraced and accepted his presence. This became the body of our work together. He was now the positive, not the negative image. He was now the agent of change and transformation. The fruit of this was Rebecca's decision to have a child.

Rebecca has given me permission to share that we still occasionally work together. She remains married and has an eighteen-year-old daughter. This decision to have a baby had been joyful for both her and her husband. We have maintained a working relationship on an 'as needs' basis since her dream of the fox nearly twenty years ago. He has never reappeared in her dreams. This, she says, is because she fully embraced this part of her personality, took responsibility by being an adult in her world and being fully open as opposed to being secretive and sly. The fox was now integrated into her conscious self, adding strength to her sense of self.

KIMBERLEY

In 2000, I travelled to Montreal and presented a poster at the World Congress for Infant Mental Health. The topic was the unconscious healing in therapy of the mother–infant dyad. My presentation was a case study of a client, Kimberley, who I had been seeing weekly for three years. She was an attractive, heavily pierced, tattooed woman in her late thirties, recently divorced. Kimberley was clinically depressed, on a serotonin reuptake inhibitor (SSRI) antidepressant medication and was acting out her compulsion to wash up to thirty times a day and constantly pick her skin. Her medication did help to ameliorate the intensity of her emotions. Her diagnosis was bipolar disorder and obsessive-compulsive disorder (OCD).

Towards the end of our first session, she revealed her bandaged legs; they were covered in painful sores that she proudly informed me she showed her psychiatrist fortnightly. Her metaphor of the skin as a conceptual framework emerged from this initial session. It was the canvas upon which she painted her despair, and the receptacle of her mother's unpredictable and irrational rage. Kimberley's skin and her mind were both inflamed and subjected to compulsive repetition. It was the site of her shame of being unloved, damaged, and believing herself to being unworthy. She had no one to 'hold her', keep her together, prevent her from spilling out, or contain her anxieties. Kimberley's skin was mirroring this internal process.

Kimberley had intrusive thoughts and compulsive behaviours that interfered with her daily life, thus restricting her relationships with others and her ability to work. Her belief that her mind and her body were contaminated was distressing and provoked anxiety. Excessive activities such as washing, picking, checking, and rechecking were performed without relief.

At her second session, Kimberley pulled up her black T-shirt as she sat down. Before I could take a breath, she revealed heavy breasts pierced with thick silver bars crossed through each nipple. She revealed to me how her mind and body were inextricably linked. The cross. The good in the bad, the bad in the good. With time, I attempted to get the strands straight with Kimberley as they were crossed.

She shared a recurring brief dream she had been having over the last couple of years. It did not reappear after showing me her breasts.

> *I have this image of a cross, which is cold and heavy. I am turned on, as I find it erotic.*

I introduced the idea of a baby who couldn't get to the breast. Kimberley was showing me, 'I couldn't get to the source, the breast.' The breast was an object of need, not desire. These breasts guarded by these piercings reflected the inaccessible breasts of her mother, the failure of her mother to provide the nurturing she needed for normal attachment. Kimberley's mother had a mental health diagnosis of bipolar disorder. Her mother was unable to process and regulate her own fragmented inner world, and as a vulnerable child, Kimberley experienced her explosive rage and thus was not offered containment. Kimberley felt she was used as a receptacle for her mother's rage and all the feelings she was unable to deal with. Her unavailable father was also unable to offer containment.

Kimberley's described her first dream.

> *I have two dirty splinters under the skin in my foot, one large, one small. I am hobbling as they cause pain when I walk.*

Her association was that the sores on her legs also caused her pain when she walked. When I asked who was 'getting under her skin', she felt it was both her parents. Perhaps they needed to be 'worked out', brought to the surface and healed. Something was hindering her path, preventing her from being happy in her skin and moving forward in her life. The dream was showing me the intrusion was both physical and emotional, external and internal.

I felt the splinters may represent Kimberley's internal objects, the mother and the small baby symbolising the relationship that needed to be worked through. This interpretation helped me think about the significance of the mother–infant relationship.

After a year of therapy, Kimberley's OCD had dramatically lessened, her sores had nearly all healed, and her medication was reduced. Her psychiatrist wanted to see me. Kimberley was happy for me to meet him, and I didn't stop to think this through. The boundary that was in place was ignored.

That night, I had a dream.

> *I am having sex with her psychiatrist in his office. We have our clothes on, and it is mechanical and without pleasure.*

In having sex with her doctor, I was living out Kimberley's unconscious desire for me to be the mother in her imaginary family in which her psychiatrist was her father, although he and I both had separate roles in her treatment. Kimberley regressed as our relationship was no longer contained.

Kimberley recounted her next dream.

I am in a changeroom trying on new clothes. I really like them, and I hope they will fit me.

The saleswoman comes in to see how I'm going. She is familiar. I shock her by bending over and showing her my bare behind. We both say sorry, but I'm not sorry. I'm not sorry at all! I'm pissed off with her. They don't fit, and I must wear my old clothes home. I'm furious.

I could see in this dream I was the saleswoman providing the new clothes. Clearly, I had failed in providing what was needed. Kimberley was incredibly angry. This dream represented how I had failed her. As had her mother. I was unconsciously re-enacting repetition in our transference relationship. I was unable to provide the clothes she desperately wanted and needed. Clothes that would contain her. Kimberley regressed and began self-harming.

Working with her dream, Kimberley gradually became aware of her negative feelings of rage and hate she was turning inwards against herself. It was now safe for her to metabolise and feel these emotions. She was able to speak her rage at me for not seeing and providing what she needed. I was able to apologise and put a therapeutic boundary safely back in place.

Slowly, healing returned as I interpreted what was re-enacted. Kimberley wanted to be a baby, dependent on her fantasy family. But it was time for her to take responsibility and be an adult. She could heal again. With secure boundaries in place, Kimberley felt safe enough to attempt an attachment. She became conscious of her behaviour and could begin to lead a normal life. Her symptoms had been ameliorated. Her OCD thoughts occasionally returned when stressed, but she handled these in a healthy manner. A healthy part of Kimberley was wanting change. She was ready for new clothes, a new way of being with herself and within her world.

Kimberley's dreams revealed some of the layers within the psyche, giving us material to work with, patterns and behaviours to notice, and for Kimberley to start to feel in safety.

AMY

Amy came to therapy as an intelligent and curious seventeen-year-old. She had an ongoing eating disorder and had recently been diagnosed as failing to thrive. Her weight was now stable, and she was threatened by her doctor with the consequence of rehospitalisation if she regressed and had any significant weight loss. Like a mangy cat, Amy was thin, and her brown hair was thin and falling out in little clumps. She dressed in oversized grey sweatshirts and very loose tracksuit pants and looked androgenous and childlike. Her head appeared too large for her body. She always wore large headphones and a baseball cap into the waiting room. The headphones were an effective signal to all that she was unavailable to listen or chat.

The night before she started therapy, Amy had this dream.

> *I am dreaming of a grey, skinny, and hungry cat. I'm calling to it to come to me, but it doesn't seem to want to. Its fur is all patchy; it looks uncared for. I try to feed the cat, but it hisses at me and arches its back. It has a huge mouth with sharp teeth. I can see right into its gaping mouth. I'm scared it might hurt me. It looks wild and angry. It is frightening me as I am unable to get close and help it. I try to reach out to pick it up. The cat then tries to bite and attack me. It is so hostile! The cat then turns into a litter of scrawny, hungry kittens in an old, brown case or box. They can't get out;*

> *they are trapped. Then I look deep into the box, and I can see one of the kittens has its head ripped off! There is blood everywhere. It is shocking. There is chaos inside. The kittens are crying; they are terrified. I think they are crying for my help.*

Amy was afraid, trapped, and crying out for help. There was blood, danger, and distress. I always held this knowledge in my mind in our sessions. The dream was a signal, a message to us both.

Amy was the second youngest of six children. She felt she was overlooked and not taken seriously in her family. She wished she was her younger sister so she could always be the indulged baby of the family. Amy and I had an instant connection. I was taking her seriously. I knew she was overwhelmed, angry, self-attacking, and that her ego was overwhelmed. She was still at risk.

I had previously nursed patients with eating disorders, especially anorexia nervosa, and it was frightening for the family and even the staff as the patients flirted with death. It was a fine line they danced between life and death. It was an angry line. Such a powerful yet dangerous position for the patient. The pull towards Thanatos, the death drive, is stronger than the pull towards Eros, the life drive.

Amy said she liked that I was not afraid of her eating issue. She looked at me with a mix of detachment and attention. Not dissimilar to a cat. I certainly was concerned for her psychological and physical health, but I was not afraid. This I shared with her. I felt confidence in myself and in her overseeing referring doctor who offered medical and nutritional support, and I had access to sound supervision if needed.

I had already decided not to discuss her weight or the medical side of her treatment, as her doctor oversaw that role. I needed to put firm boundaries in place. Amy liked this idea and gave permission for me to discuss this with her and contact her doctor at any time I felt she was at risk.

I had spoken Jung's poetic and philosophical idea that 'dreams are the guiding words of the soul'. Amy liked the idea of us working together on her soul as this held some meaning for her. She was eager to understand her dreams. Gradually, she became interested in understanding her disorder. Amy had a desire to study psychology the next year at university, but she was becoming more aware that she needed to understand and heal herself before she could look towards understanding and healing others. There was a part of her that wanted a healthy control. There certainly was no order inside the box of out-of-control kittens. This was a part of her that was self-attacking. This was the part of her that was acting out a form of unconscious suicide. I kept this in my mind.

We came to an awareness from the dream that Amy had not been nurturing and caring for herself. She was starving herself of food as well as of love and self-care. She said she was becoming sick of being tired, cold, and starving. Amy was gifting me the cat in her dream. She was placing it in my lap for me to hold and to think about. I was to find meaning in this symbol, and to take responsibility for it. She had given me her fear. I have relieved her of it.

Understanding the cat as a metaphor of herself in the dream resonated. Now that she was attempting to feed herself, there was a part of her that was hostile and rejecting. Amy had neglected her developing feminine in her attempt to gain some form of control in her life. She was distressed to see the hungry and neglected cat. Before this dream, she had not been able to form a connection to this part of herself, but this was an emotional revelation. The dream was a bridge for us to cross to meet this part. There was a deep sadness that Amy was carrying within. This was the hidden, inner part I wanted to connect with.

We worked with the metaphor of the cat representing the feminine Amy. Gently, we started to imagine that Amy was the cat in the beginning of the dream. She started to feel into the mind of the cat. Then into the body. Amy said she felt alone, angry, and scared. The word 'hostile' was used again. She felt she had a yearning for someone to stroke her, to feed her, to love her. She looked at me with distant, longing eyes. I asked who she craved this attention from, and she sadly said her mother.

Amy had started over-exercising and starving herself after a group of popular girls at school began to bully her. They called her a 'fat slut'. She so wanted to fit in and be popular and a part of the pack. Amy said they were 'catty' and mean, but she still wanted to belong instead of being their target of ridicule, their victim. Amy was asexual and said she feared the idea of hooking up. She laughed uncomfortably at their calling her a slut.

During this time, her mother was very busy working and was too occupied with all the family's needs to notice Amy's sadness, her suffering. No one noticed her obsession with thinness and social media. Amy hid her body under extra jumpers, so her mother didn't notice her weight loss. She didn't even notice Amy was no longer having menstrual periods, a consequence of having an eating disorder. Amy's father worked at a university and was too busy with his other family, his students. Amy's depression and acting out was a sign to me that she had developmentally regressed. She was attempting to avoid adolescence. It was a sign that Amy was unconsciously rejecting sexuality and attempting to stay in the latency stage, the stage before adolescence, saying, 'I want to stay being in control.' To move forward, Amy needed to let go.

Amy said the clique of girls were just like the kittens who had ripped her apart. Amy, too, was bleeding. Amy said she felt neglected, unsupported, and attacked in the same way the kittens were. 'Where was the mother cat?' she asked sadly. The mother was not giving enough food and love; she was starving her kitten. The kitten was neglected. She was treated badly and didn't know how to get control. Amy was developing some insight into how her dream was about her. Amy said she felt boxed in by life and by this situation. She had unknowingly painted herself into a corner. The dream had shown her how she was in a precarious and dangerous position.

Gradually, we understood that Amy was attacking her actual self by starving herself. This had resulted in the disconnect between her head and her heart. She was separated from her inner femininity, her intuitive self. The dream had also shown us she was full of repressed rage. Healthy anger helps define us, but rage has the capacity to destroy us. We worked together on this emotion that Amy couldn't digest or stomach. While working with Amy's hostile feelings that she was now becoming aware of, she had a brief disturbing nightmare.

I'm being forcibly put in a white straitjacket and taken to an asylum, a loony bin. I am trapped. I try to move my arms and legs, but I can't.

She shared that being taken away by force was a real fear she had never spoken. Tears flooded from deep inside her. This opened a window for us to discuss her fear of being hospitalised. As she was an adolescent, she had been admitted to the eating disorder ward at the children's hospital. She said, 'At least it wasn't the loony bin, but the *children's hospital.* Surely, I am more adult than a child!' These words hung heavily in the air like storm clouds. Amy was terrified of madness. Her nightmare of being placed in a white straitjacket also symbolised for me how her eating disorder had kept her virginal, innocent, trapped, unable to move forward developmentally in her body, sexuality, and sensuality. Amy was trapped. Had she contributed to her own madness? This I held in my mind.

A couple of months before seeing me, Amy was admitted to the children's hospital as she continued to refuse to eat. She would only sip water occasionally. It sounded like a real stand-off, an unconscious attempt at suicide. The situation was obviously serious. Amy had been diagnosed as failing to thrive as a consequence of anorexia nervosa. Amy said she was restrained just like in the movie *One Flew Over the Cuckoo's Nest*, as if she was crazy. The nurse passed a nasogastric tube into her stomach, and she was force-fed. I was thinking, 'Just like a baby needing to be fed, a baby unformed, a baby rejecting her mother's milk.'

I was mindful that what was happening externally symbolised what was happening within. With time, Amy understood that being tube-fed was needed to keep her alive. She hated the sensation of the hard, plastic tube being inserted into her nose. Amy had no memory or history of sexual abuse. I wondered about the rigidity of her defenses that were in place, allowing for no flexibility or fluidity.

Amy practised listening to her inner voice, making sense and playing with her animal instinct, her intuition. We talked about the strengths of a cat. Amy loved how they were true to themselves. She was now becoming true to herself. Amy was also becoming more adept at soothing herself when angry or disappointed. She was now back at school and had made a friend she described as 'gentle'. Amy was no longer the target of the cool girls; in fact, they no longer noticed her. (Perhaps they could see Amy was taking responsibility for her changing self.) Her appearance was now less androgynous. Amy was less fearful of moving away from childhood into adolescence, then finally towards adulthood. She was still thin, but she did share that she now had a healthier relationship with food. Amy was also now menstruating. There now seemed to be more to Amy than she had realised.

I had recommended to her doctor that Amy's parents seek some guidance about how to support her in her healing. This had occurred, and Amy now felt they were now more demonstrative in their love towards her. She felt her mother was now available for her.

Amy's response had shown psychotherapy can be the go-to for healing. The decapitated kitten of her dream was being put together again. Amy's dreams provided a course for the therapy in which we could both share and I could work. The outcome of the therapy had facilitated connection between Amy and her family.

INGE

Inge was referred to me by her GP, who had diagnosed her with clinical depression. She was thirty-two years old, attractive, European, a dentist, and lived with her long-term female partner. I noticed she held her head to one side, like an infant who couldn't control her head. Or was she having difficulty holding her head high? I wondered if she was experiencing shame at seeing me as she appeared uncomfortable.

Inge was born in Switzerland, where her father and mother were both well-regarded medical specialists. She described herself as the black sheep of the family. In her family, she felt unloved and uncared for. She believed her life was predestined. There was no room to move in it, and she was expected to be in the medical field. There was so much pressure placed on her to succeed. Her two brothers became doctors and, much to the parents' pleasure, were successful in their chosen fields. Inge was attempting to pass her postgraduate examinations and said this was her final effort. She said she felt sad and lonely, unsupported by her profession and unloved by her family. Her love relationship was at times troubled. She said, 'I'm not always present. I can be difficult and distant.'

Inge was challenging to form an attachment with as she was cool, distant, and defensive, and I wondered about her relationship with her mother. Then she shared this nightmare.

> *I am in our childhood home in Switzerland. I have just woken up in my old bedroom. I am a young girl, and I wander downstairs. It seems a very long and difficult journey to climb down the stairs. Finally, I arrive in the cold and dark basement. I turn on the light, and surprisingly, I am now in the family kitchen. Only my mother is present. She doesn't look up when I arrive as she is preoccupied. In front of her is a glass box. I look at it, and I think it is a microwave oven. I peer in through the glass door. There is a tiny baby, naked and screaming. It is going round and round. The baby is being cooked! The baby is going to die.*

Inge said she woke up suddenly, feeling terrified and distressed. Her immediate association was that many of her mother's patients were in humidicribs, and the microwave looked just like a hospital crib to her. Inge softly sobbed as she told me how she always felt her mother hated her, and that she would happily destroy her. Even the au pairs who brought her up favoured the other children, as they were much more likeable. Her father was physically unavailable and emotionally unreachable. He looked to Inge like he was trapped inside his head with no access to his heart. She felt like the baby in the oven, that no one was present to protect her or connect with her. We talked about how it felt to be this vulnerable and helpless child who was screaming for attention. We talked of how this dream was an internal image of a small, unloved, and unnurtured part of her infant self.

Inge expressed how amazed she was by how meaningful the dream felt and how comforted she felt working with a story that came from within her, even though, as she said, 'It is a shocking story.' We worked through her repressed rage and fear using the dream image. She felt she had been trapped within the glass box, unable to think or feel anything but fear. Her defenses that hid this damaged, vulnerable, and unformed infant part had kept her afraid, alone, and lonely.

I asked her to imagine being the infant in the microwave. 'What does your mother look like from in there?'

She said, 'She appears cold, mechanical, all tubes and wires. Like a robot, certainly not a human.'

She was fearful she had been dependent on a psychologically sick and mechanical mother. It was important I was an alive and robust therapist and yet still allow her freedom to move, play, and dream. We worked on the vulnerable part of her that was still alive. It began as pre-verbal, but Inge gradually found language to describe her feelings and her relationships that she no longer needed to attack or kill off.

We worked together twice weekly for more than a year, and during this time, attachment gradually became safe. Inge now felt she had the mental space for feeling and reflection, for being open and available to others and experiences. She felt less confined and restricted, more expansive.

Inge described one last dream.

> *I am happily travelling in an elevator with a middle-aged woman in uniform. She is motherly, and I think she's a midwife. I express some concern to her that we might be trapped together in the lift. It makes me a little anxious. The woman says it is fine. She says she knows that it is safe, and she knows how we can get out easily if needed. I press the buttons that determine which level we're going to, and I see the door of the elevator opens and closes easily. I just need to press the right button. I feel much better knowing this.*

Here we have an image of a care-giving mother who had facilitated the birth of an infantile part of Inge. I was able to contain her anxiety and distress in a healthy therapeutic container. Inge now had her own feminine internal mother to safely travel with her through life to every level she chose. She loved that this part of her was a midwife. 'I will be able to deliver new parts of myself when they are ready to be born.'

How different she felt in the elevator compared to how she had felt trapped in the microwave in the first dream. There she had been unable to grow as she was disconnected from the outside world, unable to communicate, trapped. In that space, she was dying. Here, she was in control and able to choose her destiny. Inge felt content and safe in her newfound self-knowledge. She was able to trust herself and others and accept that she now had a voice and could communicate what she wanted and be heard.

She abandoned her study, and she and her partner returned to live and work in Europe. At first, she felt it was a lot to ask of her partner, though she shared that it now felt safe to make demands on someone she loved. This certainly was new for her. In the past, she would have been dismissive, distant, and unavailable. Too afraid to feel, to risk rejection and the possibility of loss. Inge now was a much easier and more thoughtful young woman to be with in the room.

Sometimes, our ego defenses are rigid in an attempt to keep our vulnerable self safe from being seen or known. These defenses inhibit us from seeking attachment with self or another, making connection and giving or receiving love nearly impossible.

I will introduce Patrick to demonstrate how a dream can want to push through the unconscious into awareness. He was resistant to forming a relationship with me as he was fearful that if I managed to get close to him, his flaws may be seen and exposed, and he may suffer rejection and humiliation. This made him oppose change.

PATRICK

Patrick was a tall, strong-looking, immaculately groomed man in his early forties. He arrived wearing a colourful floral shirt. He had an air of self-sufficiency and superiority. Patrick was successful in his chosen field and appeared intellectually intelligent. He came to psychotherapy as his GP thought the process may be useful and that talking may be good medicine. It was Freud who coined the phrase 'the talking cure'. This was an unusual referral as Patrick wasn't anxious or depressed, so he didn't come with any obvious or problematic symptoms causing distress.

When he came into my office, the room was overpowered by a strong floral after-shave. I wanted to immediately fling open the window, but I couldn't do that without the risk of offending him. The aroma was so strong, it started to give me a headache. It made it challenging to stay present. Patrick told me he only wanted to talk about his recurring dream. He said he didn't need psychotherapy. That was his doctor's idea. Already I was wondering if I was going to be able to help Patrick develop an insight into his ability to see and get a gut feeling about his impact on others. He clearly said he didn't need therapy, but that is what

I offer. Would he have the desire to understand and value his inner life? Did he have a part that was aware and could be an 'observing ego' that would feel what unfolded in our work together?

He began to tell me his recurring dream.

> *I am continually dreaming of polishing this large, occasionally distorted, shiny, black car. The act of polishing is exhausting me. I look around me. There are blurry outlines of people in the background of my dream, but they are more like reflections than real people. I can hardly notice them, but I have a feeling these people would like to get closer to me, but I'm not interested in them. I have no desire to be distracted from my task at hand. I will know when the job is done by being able to see myself mirrored in the panels I'm polishing. I wake up tired, irritable, and with a sense of dissatisfaction.*

I asked, 'How are you feeling during the dream?'

'Not much. Maybe a bit frustrated that I am getting tired of polishing and not making any progress.'

'Is there anyone inside the car?'

'No, it's empty.'

'Do you know how it is to feel empty?'

'Yep. Everyone does.'

Patrick managed to shut the flow of connection and energy down with his brief answers.

'Can you verbally paint me a picture of the car?'

'Well, it's black, shiny, and a funny shape. It is a big car with a huge body, small wheels, and not really a normal car shape.'

'Does the car like being cared for, being polished?'

'It's a car. Of course not!'

'Can you tell me about the dream landscape? What can you see around you?'

'There's only outlines of people in the dream, without any definition. Everything is grey, or in sepia tones, like in a very old photo.'

I wondered if there was no space for another in the dream or in Patrick's life. It took Patrick much time, strength, and energy to polish his vehicle, but it was never quite reflective enough. He could tell when he was close to achieving perfection when he could see himself, mirrored back to him. Patrick was trapped and self-absorbed by this image. There was only space for himself, with no space for another. His unconscious task was to restore and keep his ego stable. I suspected that the car was a powerful symbol, given by Patrick's unconscious, of his ego and his life drive. He had no one to share this energy with. We were given an image of his internal world, and he was having to work very hard at maintaining this image. In the dream, the car was an unnatural shape, and Patrick said he was concerned about this. We worked on the image of the car, and slowly, Patrick became aware that the car was a part representation of himself.

In life, Patrick said his anger tripped him up. It erupted like a volcano. It seemed Patrick was filled with an unconscious rage that broke into his awareness, and this was getting in the way of him forming lasting and meaningful relationships. 'Eventually, everyone makes me angry.' As in the dream, Patrick was not that curious about others or interested in others becoming real. He felt no desire, or real need, to relate to other people.

'I'm a pretty self-sufficient sort of bloke. I find people just let you down.'

'Who has let you down in life?'

'Everyone.'

'I wonder if I will let you down.'

'Probably.'

When I attempted to explore his family history, Patrick would cleverly change the subject.

'Perhaps you have some old sepia photos of your family?'

'Don't think so.'

I was wondering about the lack of mother–child mirroring as Patrick was so resistant to my efforts to engage meaningfully with him unless I was agreeing and mirroring him. He said he came to therapy to talk. I did wonder what he really wanted to talk about. When I asked, he said he didn't really know. That was my job to find out! I was wondering if he would ever trust me enough to share. Would he risk getting close to me?

Luckily, he did seem somewhat comfortable to talk about the positive aspects of himself. I felt some anxiety and was relieved we could attempt to connect and maybe work with his dreams. I wondered if the anxiety I was feeling was anxiety that Patrick was unable to feel and process. I decided to be reflective in my work with Patrick. I planned in my mind how this could work. I had a sense that he was planning how to retreat and escape engaging in inner work. I understood that Patrick couldn't connect with me directly, so we connected via his after-shave, with an effect that was unconscious, meaning Patrick had no idea of it. We made another appointment. Gently, I asked if he could please not wear after-shave as I seemed to be somewhat allergic to it. He was surprised. 'Really?'

At our next appointment, we focused on the repeated dream image of the car. Patrick admitted to feeling shame that the car was occasionally distorted and out of shape. As a child, there was no space for imperfection. To his father, this was a sign of weakness and inferiority. This was a disclosure he seemed to regret sharing with me. I sensed the work becoming dangerous for Patrick. His arms were now crossed protectively over his body, and the discussion abruptly ended. Silence filled the room. Now I was getting a sense of how inferior he felt. It was destroying. It was isolating. It was humiliating. We were at an impasse. Patrick was not interested in expressing his feelings. I shared I understood how this must feel. He was surprised. Again, I asked how this felt as a child. As a little boy who wanted to be loved. Loved unconditionally. He couldn't remember.

Patrick's recurring dreams of his black car were in symbolic language in an attempt to break into his consciousness, his awareness. He seemed to have no real need to feel connected, or none that he would admit to. I was aware that behind the persona of grandiosity, there was a hiding, self-conscious, and shame-faced child. Patrick needed his defense to prevent his suffering, to protect himself against intrusion. But he was so heavily defended against not being able to maintain this internal ego image of the big black car, his unconscious fear of being imperfect and his ego falling apart and fragmenting, that getting close to me was going to be difficult.

I held in my mind the possibility of a therapeutic alliance in which I would go gently. Would he want a relationship? With me, with another? Would he have the capacity to maintain a relationship? There were times when I felt like an untethered boat lost at sea, adrift without a compass, nearly like I didn't exist. It was no surprise that Patrick had to work so hard at being reflected. I kept gently reflecting him. Patrick came to understand that his self-absorption was repetition of his childhood experience.

Gradually over the next year, Patrick started to change. In outer and inner ways. His dream did not reappear. He was much less defended and more available to engage in our therapeutic relationship. Patrick was becoming reflective and thoughtful, softer, as if the tough defenses that defined him were no longer needed. His sense of self was softening. His ego softening. This ceased our work together.

Nearly every client who comes to therapy is suffering. It is this suffering that weighs them down and prevents engagement in the flow of life. Clients who have suffered trauma, violence, or sexual abuse present with psychological symptoms and often also have underlying physical health issues. Unresolved and unprocessed trauma also locates itself in the physical body.

When a child grows up in an unsafe, traumatic, and abusive environment, the body's stress response is constantly activated and doesn't manage to return to the baseline of balance, or homeostasis. The brain's fear centre, the amygdala, remains lit up and the body stays in fight, flight, or freeze mode. This stress response tells the body it is under attack, and its only goal is survival. This response is constant and persistent. The body responds by the adrenal glands releasing cortisol and other hormones like adrenaline continuously. This is overwhelming, and other systems are suppressed. There is much research and literature published on these consequences. Dr Bessel van der Kolk wrote in *The Body Keeps the Score: Brain, Mind, and Body in the Healing of Trauma*, 'As long as the trauma is not resolved, the stress hormones that the body secretes to protect itself keep circulating.'

The following client presented with internal chaos as a result of early childhood trauma. If you have suffered trauma or sexual abuse, the weight of this material may be disturbing.

OLIVIA

Olivia had experienced child sexual abuse and was referred by her female GP, who had been treating her with an antidepressant and a mood stabiliser for three years with success. She came to see me when she was twenty years old. Her skin was olive, and her hair was brown, curly, and unkept. She was noticeably overweight. Immediately, I could tell she was physically and emotionally fragile and extremely withdrawn. She presented as being very young, timid, and deer-like with large, dark brown eyes like marbles, and she had the appearance of being caught in the headlights. She was cautious, anxious, and afraid, and her large eyes constantly scanned the room for our first couple of sessions.

Olivia was wary of being in this new environment and began therapy with some trepidation. Once we had slowly formed our therapeutic alliance, her eyes rarely left my face. This was a safe experience of attachment, and she was reluctant to let go. At times, this intense gaze felt uncomfortable. We worked together weekly for more than two years. It was my role to listen and bear witness to her pain, the abuse, cruelty, and suffering no human should have to endure. A theoretical framework based on my studies and training is where I placed and thought about the unimaginable. Olivia needed me to have this facility available as she was an innocent child without emotional or intellectual capacity and without a mother to process her thoughts and experiences and protect her.

Olivia grew up in a remote country town in eastern Australia with younger siblings. The four children were poorly home-schooled, and the family managed to fly under the radar of the authorities. Fortunately, Olivia had seen clinical psychologists for cognitive behaviour therapy (CBT) for many years, from the time she first sought help at the age of thirteen, when she ran away from home. The work she undertook was incredibly helpful in assisting her to deal with grief and PTSD. She said she felt too much shame to talk about all the aspects of her abuse in any detail, and it was still not safe to revisit. Olivia felt she was not ready, but recurring nightmares were now coming violently into her world and destabilising it, so she knew it was time to deal with her traumatic sexual abuse.

Olivia gradually shared her dreams as she started to trust me and the relationship. She commenced writing a dream journal. Her dreams were often nightmares, and she said her dreams now were relentless. It was easier for her to talk about her dreams than her actual lived experiences. I was apprehensive to repeat and expose her too early to her actual memories and re-traumatise her. I was grateful we had dream stories as a way into her inner world. I needed and wanted to be protective and nurturing.

In our first session, I talked about how all babies are born innocent and vulnerable. It is the role of the parent to nurture and protect them. Soon I was to discover that never happened for Olivia. She never had the attachment between mother and child essential for healthy development. This attachment allows the child to feel safe and secure knowing the parent serves as a secure base, enabling the child to explore, roam, and play, and to grow in the family, community, and the world at large.

Once Olivia felt secure enough in our relationship, she began to share her dreams. This was her first dream, a nightmare.

> *There is a broken and tiny girl doll called Barbie. She has two heads; one is stuck to her body, and the other head can easily disconnect and leave when she wants to. She's pretty weird. Chasing Barbie is a hard, broken, rubber-like, mean, and bad monster doll. I am screaming at him to leave her alone. No one hears me cry out. These dolls are not human. Barbie has soft, white, see-through wings that flap like a butterfly's. The male doll is strong and nasty and is magically powered by both the moon and the sun. Barbie is never safe and is always searching for tiny spaces in the vast universe in which to hide. All Barbie can do is try to hide or run. Luckily, Barbie is hard and looks much older than she really is.*

Initially, it was difficult for Olivia to share her nightmares with me. On the telling of this dream, she was curled up in a foetal position on my couch, huddled under a throw that was rarely used. She was visibly scared. The nightmare expressed what she was unable to feel or speak, as she had limited language for this narrative. Her experience of abuse was unspeakable. The nightmare was the psyche's way of processing these painful and unbearable experiences. The dream story was her story. She was Barbie, and her father was the chaser, the persecutor, the sexual abuser.

I suggested maybe she was like Barbie wrapped in her wings, having found a safe space on my couch. Slowly, Olivia could share some of the dream story. Just as Barbie found a crack in the ceiling in her bedroom that she could slip into, so too could Olivia. This gave her some momentary escape. The psyche had split and divided itself. One part of her stayed in her body, suffering, and the other part found a safe space in which to hide and observe the abuse.

'Just like the two heads in your dream. One part stays attached to the body, and the other part easily splits off and escapes,' I said.

'But I feel ashamed I left her there to suffer. So unfair,' sobbed Olivia.

'You were just trying to survive.' I reassured her. 'You were a vulnerable little child ill-equipped to process trauma, and no one protected you, no one heard your cries for help.'

Even though Olivia's family moved house often, she said she could always find a crack she could hide in. Here a part of her felt safe and no longer anxious. Yet she said she was still aware of a tiny, scared feeling in her body. Olivia found this safe space again in the therapeutic space. This space was the therapeutic container. Olivia said in her world as a child she could either run, hide, or die. That was what she believed. She said to feel was far too dangerous.

'Where was your mother?' I asked.

'My mother never knew what was going on, yet my mother always knew what was going on,' she spat. 'My mother chose not to see, feel, or act. I hate my mother! All she was good for was making pretty little children for him. Girl or boy, no child was safe.'

When Olivia was nearly thirteen, she found the strength to run away from home. She ran to safety. She located appropriate authorities who helped her move from the east coast, and she was taken into care. She changed her identity. When they accessed her scattered medical history, they realised she had 'fallen through the cracks'.

Olivia was never able to communicate her distress, which is a natural survival mechanism. Everything was shutdown. I knew it was so important for me to empathetically listen, to really hear her distress, and contain her suffering. Once in the session, I could feel myself start to split off, but I consciously worked at staying grounded and present. With time, both Barbie and the monster as the attacker were now whole figures as opposed to much earlier dream images that all seemed scattered and fragmented. Olivia remained terrified of the magical male monster. As he was made of hard rubber, she believed he was invincible as he could bend in any direction like a 'sort of transformer'.

After about six months of weekly therapy, Olivia had a dream.

> *An angel has appeared. She comes down into the room in a shaft of light. The angel can see him controlling everything. She can see he has such powers and that he can swing from a trapeze and then disappear into thin air. Just like a strong, magical acrobat. The angel tries to use her powers, but they don't seem to work. He just keeps chasing Barbie. She's getting stronger, but he still wins and hurts her.*

When that occurred and he hurt her, Olivia felt she had no memory. She had fallen into the terrifying and dark abyss.

Our work around the image of the angel helped enable Olivia's survival. The hardened male had become internalised. Olivia realised she had hardened herself so that it would keep others away from her, especially males. She saw them as hard also. Hard and dangerous. She also was becoming aware this hiding was keeping her alone and fearful.

I recalled a psychoanalyst in a lecture explaining when the client is being terrorised by an inner hostile presence that is the tyrant, you must always remember there is a frightened child present.

In her dreams, the demonic figure was getting smaller, but he was ever-present. He was the abuser, the persecutor in her nightmare. This was now the internalised part that was demonising her in the form of shame. Olivia believed she was a bad person, and she had held the secret of her abuse for many years. She was afraid if she told, she would not be believed and that she would be judged for being a bad person and humiliated. Maybe it was her fault? He always said it was her fault. Olivia had not learned to socialise at school, as they kept moving house.

She had no experience of normal ways of behaving and interacting. The children were supposedly home-schooled, but their education was minimal. Nobody noticed. Nobody cared. This also contributed to her feelings of shame.

There were many stories. Too many and too challenging to repeat. Olivia carried horrific secrets that she could not reconcile alone. The words of both her abuser and her internal demonic persecutor filled her with fear and self-loathing. That was the work of our therapeutic relationship. I was an empathetic listener who could hear, process, and bear her suffering. When it was safe, the terrorised child could appear. Slowly, she emerged.

But Olivia shared she was reluctant to be a grown-up. 'They lie, harm, and do bad things,' she said. Her father totally undermined her confidence, her ability to use her own voice, or have thoughts or feelings of her own. She felt unseen, unloved, and unworthy. But Olivia also hated this inner neglected, needy, and wounded child. She believed it was her fault and had learned to turn this hate and anger back upon herself. Olivia had engaged in self-harm. She began to eat for comfort. It changed her body shape. It helped her hide. It protected her. This felt powerful. She could cushion her feelings; she could also no longer look desirable.

With time, we used the image of the magical acrobat who could be invincible and dramatically transform. He was being given by her dream stage where, through creative visualisation, magical transformations occur. Olivia liked us using this as a playground for her imagination. She could now participate in the drama and safely be playful like a child. She felt the acrobat could be her, very strong and even graceful. Together, we made and placed a huge safety net beneath her, around her, just in case.

She suggested I could be the ringmaster as I could apparently control all the actors and the animals. I don't actively perform, but by my being there, she felt safe. I said I was happy just to sit ringside, observing, aware I had become one of the players on her stage. She invited the fierce fire-eater into the arena. He could be a silly clown and then transform into a powerful and masterful participant. We used the dream images in a creative and playful way. We played with safety. After being in therapy for about two years, Olivia had an illuminating dream.

> *I am in a dirty country; it's primitive, and all the children are starving. I am starving. Then a procession comes to town. There's music and juggling, and I'm hoping it's a circus. 'Will they let us poor kids watch?' I wonder. Then I realise I'm on the outside. I can't get close, even though I really want to. It is passing me by. 'Wait for me,' I cry out. The procession has passed me by.*

Olivia woke feeling sad but joyful that, at last, her dream was normal. Her dream had people in it rather than dolls. The dream was showing me there was still much work to be done together. She was wanting connection, desiring to be a part of the flow of life. She was hungry for it. There was still much loss to mourn, still so many emotions to feel and process. We did this by consciously engaging with the grown-up part of herself who could ask for help and seek protection, while still being aware of the presence of the wounded and vulnerable child. Olivia was learning to advocate for herself and push against the urge to stay small.

Towards the end of our work, Olivia went to Legal Aid. She asked for help as a young adult. She was now twenty-three. Once again, someone listened. They heard her, retrieved data, and, importantly, not judge her. They showed compassion and empathy. Together, with the help of others, they brought about change. It was not an easy process. Her father was finally imprisoned. Olivia told me a few years later he had died in prison.

An important part of my work was to be predictable and maintain scaffolding with structure and clear boundaries. Olivia had never experienced boundaries that were safe in her family. We had a safety net in place. Unpredictability lies at the very foundation of trauma. I needed to be predictable for her.

During the course of the therapy, I had a dream.

> *I am sitting with a young girl who seems vaguely like Olivia, and I am dressed in what looks like a uniform. There is an enchanting, coloured butterfly on my shoulder, flapping its filmy wings. My attention is taken by its beauty.*

I woke and thought about how invested I was in Olivia's healing. Perhaps overly invested. In my notes, I wrote I was hopeful the butterfly was an image describing Olivia's transformation, and that she had emerged safely from her cocoon. Because the winged butterfly emerges as a result of a transformation, it may symbolise rebirth or resurrection. I also wondered if this was my own transformation, as this work was expanding my own process. This dream brought some joy and lightness into Olivia's dark world and our work. It also indicated my creativity and insight into her case.

Olivia's experience of our work together showed her we are not alone, that one can be safe in a relationship, and that mankind is not all evil. It took years for us to achieve this sense of safety so she could understand herself, her own boundaries, and something as simple as her own needs. More than ten years later, at the age of thirty-five, Olivia returned for a 'check-in'. She was embarking on a new relationship, and she had encountered difficulties in being intimate. Despite this, she approached the situation with openness and maturity, feeling no shame in discussing it openly. Long ago, she had decided never to have children, but her goal was to safely engage in a relationship. She knew we could work it out together, as she had trust in me and the process. She had long since stopped running away.

Marie Curie said something relevant to this case and probably the majority of other cases, that 'nothing in life is to be feared; it is only to be understood. Now is the time to understand more, so that we may fear less.'

5

Dreams and Cancer

There had been a synchronisation between cancer and my life journey. I first encountered cancer when my best girlfriend's mother died of a brain tumour when she was just fifteen. This was devastating as I loved her like a second mother. My girlfriend silently grieved as her world fell apart. My mother believed funerals were no place for women, especially girls, so I was not permitted to go, and this I have always regretted.

As a nurse, I encountered cancer in many forms. In those days, leukaemia was not curable, and we had to watch children suffer and die and their families shatter. Our task with the child hovering between worlds was to remain calm, reassure the child and the parent, and be present as the medical staff worked towards alleviating their pain. My last position as a nursing sister was at a private hospital, caring for both oncology and psychiatric patients. This was very fulfilling, but I wanted to look after my own babies and be a mother, so after ten years of nursing, I left the profession.

For fifteen years, I was a volunteer with Canteen (an Australia-wide not-for-profit organisation offering support, development, and empowerment for people aged between twelve and twenty-five affected by cancer), then a volunteer with the Cancer Support Association. It wasn't long before I was employed part-time with them.

In my private practice as a psychotherapist, cancer patients found me. Having been a nurse, I had always been at ease with death. And then it happened to me. I was diagnosed with an invasive and aggressive breast cancer. Mastectomy, chemotherapy, and IV infusions every three weeks for a year, and hormone therapy for ten years.

When I worked with clients with cancer, it was particularly important I remained detached, paradoxically while being fully present and available. This took discipline and an internal stamina as I facilitated an objective and empathetic therapeutic alliance. I could not show them how my heart was often breaking for them. To them, I offered gentle calmness and concern. I knew I could be of no value if it became a real, normal relationship. That would be a friendship. Friends and family can offer that kind of support, a cup of tea, a comforting touch or hug.

This position was often tested at every level. My desire for a positive outcome was challenged. I always sat with hope and compassion in my heart. But these clients were terminal. Death and fear were in the air. With awareness, I would hold the client in my mind as a whole, working towards integration and individuation, and keeping a grip on Eros, the life instinct that holds all living things together, and having to hold the tension of the opposite, that of the inevitable death and the pull of Thanatos, the death drive.

These clients were suffering physically, emotionally, and spiritually. They often felt lonely, isolated, exposed, and vulnerable. I accepted their reality. Psychotherapy offered words and symbols for emotions as yet unknown, as yet unexpressed. Working with their dreams enabled finding these words through the presented dream symbols and language, now able to be spoken without fear or distress. This facilitated their journey, as the dreams offered an internal world that presented important insights into a place not connected to being controlled by their conscious mind, their doctors, or their cancer. The dreams were also a way of expressing what couldn't be said or felt and, importantly, a way of sitting with what came up in peace and stillness. The symbols and language, spoken or unspoken, came from within. Interpretations were not always required or wanted.

The following dreams are from my clients who were terminally ill with cancer.

LUKE

Luke and I worked together weekly from his diagnosis of prostate cancer to his physical death a year later. I wrote an article called 'Endings: A Year of Psychotherapy with a Dying Man', published in *Psychotherapy Australia* in 2005. This article was about Luke. Working with clients with a cancer diagnosis is different to working with mainstream clients. We get down to deep work immediately. Our relationship develops quickly and with intensity. Life and death, living and dying are in the room from the first moment. To die well is a challenge, a challenge that can be supported within the therapeutic framework and the therapeutic relationship.

Luke came to therapy as he said he now faced a problem he felt ill-equipped to deal with. He was a plasterer, a tall, strong-looking man in his early forties. He had come to his appointment wearing his work clothes and boots that were covered in a fine, white dust. Luke had just received a diagnosis of prostate cancer, which had spread throughout his body. His specialist could offer no treatment, no hope, and he suggested Luke get his life in order. He predicted he had approximately three months to live. Luke was anxious and felt shattered by the prognosis, at this stage more for his loved ones than himself. He enjoyed a long, loving, and happy marriage and dearly loved his little five-year-old son.

Luke was a strong man, practical, unafraid of hard work, but unaccustomed to talking about his feelings. He was ill at ease with sharing his vulnerability with me. The anxiety in the room was palpable. He began to share never-experienced feelings that he found overwhelming:

desperation, fear, and anger. I knew how important it was that I remain grounded and realistic in providing a secure frame that would safely hold life and death issues of Luke's conscious and unconscious self, his internal and external world. Luke's dream material provided insights into his experience and revealed a rich variety of images and underlying anxieties of an inner struggle that enabled us to make sense of this major transition in his life. Our work together began with intensity. Time was precious and the room was filled with a sense of urgency.

Luke recalled a dream in which we can see poignantly the key issue and associated feelings he wished to resolve.

> *I am in the kitchen at my parents' house, sitting at the kitchen table with a mate I've known for twenty years. We are eating and drinking, and we are happy.*
>
> *There is a new, white fridge, and I notice the door is not painted properly. I touch it. It is tacky, and I say I'll call and complain to the manufacturers. I look inside, and the fridge is nearly empty, and the food that is there is going off. I feel really anxious. I know that I must sort it out.*

Luke was engaging in psychotherapy to sort it out. His associations around the fridge were that it was cold, solid, and contained and held things in. It preserved food, but the food inside eventually went off. We talked about the fridge as being a metaphor for the self, and that it was conceivable that both the inside and the outside needed attention. Luke so wanted to contain and preserve his past, which the fridge promised to do, so he could live a healthy and happy future with his loved ones. Luke felt cold and useless, as if he had lost his identity. He felt that now in his life there was a part inside himself that was already dead, and if not dead, certainly there was nothing growing. This was rich material for us to work with.

Luke left our first session feeling relieved that he could explore his world with me and somewhat shaken by the realisation that his dream was so meaningful. It was not long before the metaphor of the fridge became a reality. His life and body quickly began to fall apart. His fate had been hidden from him by the plain white fridge door. Luke was surprised by how his decision to face the ending of his life in this way led him to discover the beginning of another life within, a life he had no knowledge of. Paradoxically, it was as if death was bringing him a gift of the beginning of life. Cancer had given him the key, and our psychotherapeutic relationship had allowed us to access this world.

Luke's psyche then offered the following dream as an indicator that things had changed for him.

> *I am on a building site, eating breakfast at the canteen. I ask my boss if I can join the workers. The job is at sea, and I am on a ship. I don't really want to work.*
>
> *I want to go fishing off the back of the ship. I have to explain my illness to my boss and fellow workers. I feel afraid as I share my reality.*

Luke was scared of what lay ahead, the unknown. The dream also echoed his reluctance to do the work required, and there was work to be done, inner work, even though he wanted to join the others. He wanted to play, go fishing, and be free of all that limited him. But we were fishing for insights about the self. He felt at sea and extremely vulnerable as he drifted towards his fate, towards his death. Such an adventure is destined to instil great fear in the adventurer, although Luke was clearly ready to 'go fishing', if not particularly keen on doing the work involved. Our building site that we were constructing through the creative process of the therapeutic relationship was strenuous and at times difficult work. It was often overwhelming for Luke. At times, it was nearly overwhelming for me. I would just trust the vessel's holding capacity and trust the process.

In Luke's dream, we see how the ocean can hold the archetypal image of embarking on the 'night sea journey' into death. In this journey, we had set out to do soul work together. So we sat with the reality of just what that is, like two people in a vessel, a three-dimensional concept of a vessel with a holding and containing capacity. Luke expressed his fear of letting go of his defenses and just being with his emotions. In the countertransference, I felt helpless and often at sea as to how to navigate our way through this. Often, I struggled with not knowing the answer to Luke's question, 'Why me?'

My knowing was that we might never arrive at a destination point other than his death yet could still move forward towards Luke just being himself. Looking back at my diary entries, I can see I was feeling isolated and occasionally lonely for some of this time, while paradoxically engaging in deeply emotional therapeutic relationships like the one with Luke.

A month passed, and a shift occurred, and Luke pushed through his resistance. Using ideas from Buddhism, he opened his heart and mind, and we set sail on a new course. Through awareness, he attempted to turn his thoughts inwards, to trust in the process, and seek clarity in the stillness and let go. Luke was finding a way to travel towards his death by discovering a different way of being. We engaged in the therapeutic process together, holding Luke's desire for attachment, his resistance to letting go, and at the same time, holding the opposite, his desire for freedom from attachment to achieve peace and solitude.

When I did sessions during the last few months of his life at his bedside at his family home, he asked me to read a few words from my book *The Tibetan Book of Living and Dying* by Sogyal Rinpoche. He found the words comforting. Luke was practised in following the golden light through meditation and visualisation, which we believed would help him on his crossing. One poem that gave shape to our work, and Luke particularly liked, was by William Blake.

> *He who binds himself to a joy*
> *Doth the winged life destroy;*
> *But he who kisses the joy as it flies*
> *Lives in Eternity's sunrise.*

Then came a dream.

> *I am standing at a workbench in a factory, a factory I am unfamiliar with. I am marking little squares on a big sheet of cardboard with a pencil and then drilling holes in the squares. In the room there are dozens of people watching me. There is no one I recognise, but I feel good about what I am doing.*

Luke said he felt empowered by the dream and the idea he could do the work while he was marking time and create something with precision with what was left of his life. He believed the unfamiliar people in his dream were his family that he was now seeing in a different light.

We thought about life after death and how Luke could contribute to fathering his little boy. I suggested we create a gift for his son, taking a hint from his dream. As he was now unable to write, he dictated letters as I wrote a diary to his son, with entries for special milestones that lay ahead, when Luke would not be physically present. It was a moving, beautiful, healing process. Luke finally told his son how he would form his own identity and he hoped his son would not be afraid to journey inwards and onwards. He spoke to him in a most poetic and beautiful way of his love for him and how this would never die. It was so difficult for Luke, but he pushed through the pain once again, and this dream came.

> *I am at the beach. I want to fly my kite. I can't move. I'm trapped in my body. It is so heavy, dead. I am very anxious.*

Here we see the articulation of feeling trapped in a dead body. Confined to his bed, Luke was not able to fly his kite, play, or move about freely. This sense of finality reawakened deep fears and anxieties within, as Luke could feel the heaviness he had embodied. He said he could now feel the power and the weight of death. We wondered if this was a preparatory dream for dying. Death felt close. Dreams came of feeling trapped and unable to free himself. In one dream, his brothers had to carry him as he was too tired to go on. Finally, he commenced having dreams of being in or passing through a tunnel or dark tube. This sometimes felt like a birth canal.

His doctor wanted him to take antidepressant medication, which Luke refused. He now knew it was time to stop fighting. He was exhausted, tired, and depleted of resources, but he didn't want the medication to carry him. He wanted to do it alone. After the deep meditation that day, Luke's eyes filled with tears as he said, 'The blue water of the ocean, it looked so beautiful. I wanted to go for a swim. I could see the gold rays, the light in the sky. I am nearly ready. I can feel the stillness.'

As in a dream image that calls the dreamer to a better place or way of being, we can see the water of a different journey. No longer the 'night sea journey' into the depths of the soul, the ocean was now offering gentle stillness and comfort, a spiritual container. It was now Luke's desire to enter the oceanic phase that would carry him through the transition between spaces and places, between the conscious and the unconscious, and between life and death. Luke was calm; the water was ready for his crossing.

Luke's bloated body was finally failing. He was taken to hospital, where he had another dream. Luke was ready to cross from the world he knew into the unknown. He was no longer connected to the nourishment of Mother Earth. He was no longer afraid. His spirit was already leaving his body. This was the dream he had the night before our last session.

> *I am floating above the hospital bed. I can see as I look down a body disconnected from its head. It is not whole. I am not anxious or afraid. I am accepting.*
>
> *I recognise it is my body, but I feel very separate from it. I feel released.*

Luke told me he was without anxiety or fear; he felt only freedom and acceptance. He smiled as he said quietly he hoped to soon go fishing off the back of the ship. We smiled together in a shared understanding.

Luke was ready to face his final breath, his crossing over from this world to the world of the unknown, and perhaps of nothing, from being to not being. Preparation had been done for this moment with me through dialogue, his dreamwork, his visualisation and meditation, and he was ready for his final hero's journey. Luke told me he planned to cross when his wife went to pick up their beautiful little boy from school, which he did successfully. Such a gift of kindness and love right to the end. At the end of this session, we said goodbye. I find it hard to articulate how I felt, other than to say it was agape, compassionate love.

DAISY

> *Faces she has three:*
> *The first inscrutable, for the outer world;*
> *The second shrouded in self-contemplation;*
> *The third, her face of love,*
> *Once for an endless moment turned on me.*
>
> – Robert Graves, *The Three-Faced*

Daisy made her own appointment and arrived alone. I expected a teenager attached to headphones, mobile, etc., although she carried a handbag. 'Seventeen going on twenty-seven,' I thought, yet she reminded me of a girl playing dress-ups in her mother's clothes. Daisy was tall and thin, her skin flawless and as pale as her cream jumper. She looked ethereal, like Audrey Hepburn dressed as an angel. Her hair was fashioned in a long brunette bob, a wig, I later discovered. Her face was flat and expressionless, and methodically, she told me her story. She had cancer of the ovaries, and it had metastasised. Her ovaries had been removed. She had completed chemotherapy and was halfway through her course of radiotherapy.

'I have no ovaries, no hair. I have mouth ulcers, and I'm seventeen. But I didn't really come about having cancer. I really need to talk about my mother.'

Daisy had been composed, delivering data in a surprising adult, linear way. I wondered if she was re-experiencing her diagnosis with emotional numbing. I asked about her mother, watching her hands become fists and seeing the blood drain out of them. White knuckles were pressed tight against her thighs. 'She doesn't care. She's not doing enough. My white cell count and platelets are dropping before our eyes, and she does nothing. I feel so alone.'

'I can see,' I said. 'It's happening in your hands. The colour is disappearing. Your hands are bloodless.'

She looked down at her white fists, and sobs slowly erupted from within. Finally, she was feeling seen and was having her reality validated. Her fear, the burden of her suffering, was able to be expressed. Before my eyes, she became childlike, vulnerable, and full of grief. 'I need to talk to someone as I feel scared and alone.'

I suggested Daisy keep a journal to express her feelings, thoughts, and dreams between sessions. She was concerned her mother would read it. Daisy felt her mother constantly invaded her privacy, just like her cancer. It occurred to me her mother's vigilance was an indicator of her desire, and as one insight often leads to another, I also was not without desire; I was aware I did not want her to die.

At the session, she shared this dream.

Dreams and Cancer

I am aiming a gun at this man who is going to kill me.

He is big and threatening. I am so scared. I shoot him. His body seems to absorb the bullets. I shoot again. Nothing happens. He won't die.

She said she awoke terrified and clammy with sweat. Daisy wanted me to talk about her dream. I explained that dreams had many layers. I felt the first was about the developmental process of separation, which, as a teenager, she was attempting to navigate. The parent was a formidable force, big and threatening, just like the man in her dream, who would give up their power only when they believed the teenager was capable of claiming it. The inner world perceived this force as demonic and holding her back.

I felt that there may be a battle ahead, as in the dream Daisy was already defending herself against this perceived force. I shared that another level of the dream was about her attempt to kill the cancer. As in the dream, she was in a dangerous situation. Daisy was being confronted with having to face the magnitude of a life-and-death situation. Cancer cells were trying to kill her, and chemotherapy and radiotherapy were trying to kill the cancer cells. So much death and destruction in the hope of healing and survival. The dream was showing us the collision of both the situation of a teenager attempting separation and the fight against the disease of cancer, and she was feeling powerless.

'Who would you like to kill?' I casually enquired.

'Oh, everyone, especially my mother. But, honestly, I'd really like to kill the cancer. It won't seem to die.'

I asked Daisy if it was common for her to feel afraid and alone as she did in the dream.

'Oh, yes, and especially lately,' she replied.

I asked her associations about the image of the gun.

'I wish my dad had a gun.'

When I asked what he would do with this gun, there was a long silence.

'Nothing, I suppose. He wouldn't hurt a fly.'

Daisy wanted her father to protect her as she felt there was no one to look after her and keep her safe. She said she felt alone, vulnerable, and unprotected. My mind was suddenly racing at an extraordinary pace. The urgency of my thoughts made me wonder how much time we had. Or was this busy mind a defense against sitting in the silence of the life-and-death crisis that we faced? Daisy said this man in her dream was a stranger, as was her internal masculinity, which up till now was unrecognised, though she played with this in her language when she was telling me her medical story.

I asked her how it would have been if the desired outcome had been realised, if she had shot this man, and she looked me straight in the eye and said, 'Well, it would be such relief. I'd be safe. But then I'd be trapped again as I'd be put in jail for murder. I can't win. And I am trapped. I want to leave home, but I have a death sentence. I have cancer.'

Towards the end of the session, Daisy voiced concern that her mother probably would not agree to her coming for more sessions. 'She is so annoying.'

I suggested she make use of the masculine energy expressed in her dream as a conscious tool to assist her to speak out for what she wanted, which she clearly stated was to engage in therapy. The next day, Daisy's mother phoned me. She sounded defensive and expressionless, as if she was withholding her feelings from me. Her words and sentences were short and clipped. She said the issue for her was the money and she didn't want to pay for a service she believed was unnecessary. Of course, she was angry and suffering. She must have been beside herself. Her position was unimaginable. We negotiated a reduced fee so Daisy could keep coming.

In the next session, Daisy spoke about her father being absent as he spent a lot of time at work, his habits unchanged since her diagnosis. He was very quiet, and Daisy said he lacked self-confidence. 'Mum seems to rob us both of that,' she said sadly. He also was grieving his mother, who had died about six months earlier. Here was a family in grief, and their individual way of processing this deep emotion accentuated their isolation. When Daisy spoke about her father, her voice and face became soft and reflective. She loved her father, and even though he was not demonstrative in his affection for her, Daisy said she knew he loved her.

But when she spoke about her mother, she became angry and was often reluctant to look at me. Their relationship had never been close, and Daisy wondered if her mother was afraid to get close to her. She wondered what a normal family unit looked like. I explained that for many, the ideal family was like connective tissue; it contained, gave support and cohesion, gave definition and, importantly, bound people together. It also formed scar tissue when damaged.

Daisy said she saw herself as outside of her family and that it was defined without her. 'I think Mum was disappointed when I was born. I was bald, pale, skinny, and very plain. Mum had no milk for me. I thought all mothers loved their babies!'

I found myself wondering if seeing Daisy bald, pale, and thin was reverberating deep within her mother. Daisy felt she was deprived of her mother's breast, which she had interpreted as being deprived of her mother's love. Fundamentally, love expressed itself in physical terms. 'Mum had plenty of milk for my brother.'

I was intrigued that she had a whole birth fantasy and story that was fixed firmly in her mind. In her story, Daisy had little substance and held little space in her mother's mind. We had much unravelling ahead of us of this personal myth she had created and continued to live. Daisy said she was always thin and sickly, and she had entered a world of secret fears where there was some relief in withdrawal. She said she was eleven years old when she realised she was alone and lonely. Daisy had become quiet and was now aware she had regressed back into the fantasy of the safety of infancy. She told me she secretly sucked her thumb to soothe and settle herself to sleep.

Here she was at seventeen with cancer cells relentlessly attacking her female organs. Hormones and disease were assaulting her body. The adolescent task of identifying with and separating from her mother seemed too threatening. I was attempting to carry the hope for both of us. We had many sessions dealing with her attachment anxiety with her mother, and then she had the following dream.

I look down. I have a sore, a wound on my leg. It won't heal.

I go to all levels of the hospital, I see many different doctors and nurses, but they can't help. I go to an office building, like where Dad works. I go to each level and see many different people, but no one can help. I am alone and scared.

Daisy's dream demonstrated that the psyche knew at an unconscious level that her body had a serious physical disease. I was also wondering about her internal capacity for healing. The dream brought Daisy's cancer back into the room, and it brought our relationship back into the room. She felt alone and afraid. The actuality of the sore on her leg was the cancer, but it was also a representation of her mother and their relationship, which was resistant but desperately required healing. Her radiotherapy was completed, and the reality of her struggle was now between life and death.

I was beginning to feel in tune with Daisy, and she was becoming more secure within our relationship, but the dream presented a symbolic psychic wound that resources seemed helpless to heal. How could she make the transition in life alone, afraid, and feeling she had no one to help her heal? At every level—the physical, emotional, and intellectual—she believed there was no one to help. Her internal world was devoid of resources. She believed neither her mother nor father were emotionally available.

Daisy expressed her dread of being alone, and she was sick of this old familiar feeling. Her associations around the hospital in the dream expressed the ambivalence she felt. She was always visible in hospital, but she said it came at a price. She also said once again she couldn't ask for what she wanted; she felt helpless, just like in her family. The hospital never seemed to be able to cure her. She then had this third dream.

It's as if I am living in a cartoon. There is a little elephant.

I become aware I am the elephant, and I am drinking from the pond. I am so thirsty. There are these fluffy little puppies going off to school. Then Fergie appears in a blue dress with a little brown clutch bag.

She woke up suddenly and thought, 'I must go shopping and see if I can find that blue dress. I so want that dress.'

Daisy's life was similar to the representation of the dream. It had the 'as if', two-dimensional quality. The dream was showing she had not yet acquired a fully coherent structure of reality, and her imaginary world, like that of all teenagers, was active. The boundaries between her sexuality and her identity, reality and fantasy, and the ambiguity between child and parental roles were in fluctuation, in process. We talked about the little elephant being Daisy, coming to therapy and drinking from the pond, where she gained nurturing and reflection. She was thirsty to be replenished. The pond was offering her the ability to be projected into the subjective world, yet it was a cartoon world, an imaginary world. Here in my office, she existed in a three-dimensional, real world, even though it was only once a week for an hour.

Daisy was attempting to grow up (though at home, she and her brother are the fluffy little pet puppies), and Fergie, the sexy teenage singer, had entered her internal landscape. Eros was here and was leading to her wanting, desiring. Daisy was expressing an unconscious desire to inhabit her own life, and the dream was empowering the Fergie, an unknown part of her, to become known. She associated Fergie with fame and being seen and being sexy. 'Everyone knows Fergie. She's hot,' she said.

Daisy was beginning to feel the power of being a young woman, which up till now, she had repressed, and her mother, probably terrified and paralysed by fear, had forbidden. She was in the process of developing her own sexual identity, feminine in a blue dress. She was now eighteen and had deferred going to university due to her cancer. All her hopes and daydreams centred around leaving home and family, which would enable her to find freedom, happiness, and a new beginning. This newly acquired desire for independence had fallen flat as fate had cruelly intervened. Having cancer had necessitated a reliance on her parents and had inhibited her ability to meet and make friends. Into this gap, Daisy had fallen, and she said she was desperate to climb out and begin her life. Daisy's newfound self-awareness from our work together was creating conflict. As her physical health deteriorated, her mother was becoming more smothering.

'It's not love; it's control. Always breathing down my neck, looking over my shoulder.'

I suggested that this was her mum's currency for love.

'Is that love? I hadn't thought of it like that.'

We sat quietly as Daisy processed and began to feel this idea of her mother's love for her. We then talked and imagined how it was for her mother. Unimaginable. How was Daisy going to take control if her mother would not relinquish it and if her immune system continued to offer little resistance to the cancer? Her body was becoming more dependent on adult input as her psyche demanded freedom and independence. The push and pull were dynamic and palpable. We were experiencing the clash of adolescence versus disease. We went back to the dream with the cartoon as there was now an elephant in the room. We talked about the possibility of her death. Daisy realised her body was struggling.

'I don't want to die, but I mostly find it so hard to live. And only you have any idea. At home, we don't talk about anything. Life or death.'

I attempted to reassure her that her family did not know how to show or express their concern or love. This was new to them, and they were not equipped. They, too, wanted to protect her from the inevitability of her death. This was an expression and gift of love. Somehow, I found the words to reassure her of their love for her. I have found that talking about and reflecting upon impending death eases the actual process of dying. I also found that parents may talk to each other, but not to the adolescent. Daisy asked about what I knew about death. Had I been with someone as they died?

Softly, I spoke of the mystery of death, how it may be the end of life or the beginning of another—I certainly didn't know. Today, still, it remains a mystery. I explained how I had always naively and intuitively called it a crossing-over. From my experience as a nurse, I was always present physically and emotionally with my patient, offering the comfort of presence and gentleness. There seemed to be an actual lack of suffering as the life force, Eros, chi, commenced its pathway out of the body. It was peaceful. Daisy was drinking from the pond, gaining some form of nourishment.

Daisy cancelled her next session by text message. She had never missed an appointment before. A family member had organised an alternative medicine consultation, and Daisy's text was laden with hope. Our next and final session was consumed with her hope of not just remission but of recovery. She was buzzing with adrenaline and anxiety. A healing holistic hospital overseas was recommended, and she was to leave as soon as possible. A family member was going to accompany her and had offered to finance this expensive venture. I was filled with dread. Daisy was not physically strong enough to travel; her immune system surely would not cope. Our therapeutic relationship was going well, and I did not want it intruded or impinged upon. I did not want to lose her.

Towards the end of our session, Daisy threw me a rope to anchor to. 'Last night, I had an awful dream. It is still very fresh in my mind.' This was the final dream she shared.

> *I am going through Grandma's house after her death. It is really dark, empty, and sad, and I am alone. I go to the fridge, and it is empty. On the shelf in the pantry, I find and open a jar of Vegemite. It is nearly empty. Shall I throw it out or not? I do not know what to do. I feel really scared and very anxious.*

Daisy's psyche was giving us a landscape image of her internal world. Here lay the mythology of her soul. Her internal resources depleted, the fridge that contained and preserved was empty, the Vegemite nearly empty, and the house, the metaphor for self, was full of grief. Death was in the air. My hands and feet felt cold, bloodless. It felt like no time to be travelling afar while there was little comfort or resources available, as the fridge was empty. I was trying to hold on to hope. Daisy was torn between going and staying; she did not know what to do. The tension—keep it or throw it out? The jar was nearly empty.

We entered the dream. Her association around her grandma was that she used to be very poor, though she was wealthy when she died. Her grandma lived her life as if she was still poor. She couldn't spend her money and enjoy the benefits. This was just like her mum and dad. Daisy did not understand their restraint, their frugality. I felt sadness at their lack of generosity and their inability to express their love. Daisy looked at me with longing. I wish I could have given her what she so desperately needed to stock up her pantry. But I could not, and that was not my role.

The next day, I received a text message to say she was leaving for overseas. 'Wish you were coming with me.' Her next text informed me she had arrived at the clinic, but she was not permitted to use her phone. Four weeks later, I had a phone call from a social worker at the hospital oncology ward. Daisy had returned home seriously ill. She had been admitted directly to hospital, and her immune system had collapsed. Her family would not allow anyone into the unit to visit. I spoke with the oncology nurse, who said Daisy was curled up in the foetal position until her death. She had regressed to infancy, and she had failed to thrive. The intensity of this moment I shall never forget. Daisy would never cross the bridge into adulthood and into the life she so longed for.

MARCUS

Marcus, a forty-five-year-old man, was facing death with grace. He asked me to help him with his short yet powerful dream, which he sensed was important, but he didn't understand why. Marcus had a loving wife, and a son and daughter who had both moved out of the family home. He had been a hard-working scientist until a couple of months before when he was diagnosed with an aggressive prostate cancer. Marcus said he had never looked inwards; he was always focused on his future as a researcher and a family man. Up until now, he had valued wealth as something one accumulated outside of oneself. Certainly, he had never paid any attention to his dreams as he believed they were unimportant. Lying on his daybed in the family home, he told me the following dream.

> *I am at sea. The sea is blue and wide. I am in a small sailing boat, similar to a dinghy known as a 'mirror', a small yacht I sailed in my childhood. I can see no other boats on the horizon. I am in the boat with my twenty-year-old son, Andre. We are alone. I am struggling to pull the ropes to adjust the sails, so without saying*

anything, I hand the ropes over to Andre. I notice that he is much stronger than I am. For the first time, I am aware of this as I watch him easily pull in the mainsail. I can see his muscle definition. It is so obvious in comparison to mine. In the past, I would always do this, you know, take control, be the bigger man. This time, it is different. We sail along on the flat sea in peace.

I let Marcus talk about his dream, giving him space to be reflective. He shared that he did hold some anxiety that he was not being 'the man' in the dream, not being the strong one for his family, especially his son. Losing his potency as a man and father had caused him suffering, and he found this very confronting. His whole life had been based on this premise of the patriarchy. Up till now, he had viewed vulnerability as an emotion for children.

Marcus let his son show his strength to him. I could see he felt confident his son could manage without him. He found great comfort in this as his body was failing him. He could hand over the ropes and let his son sail his own boat, to oversee his own journey and his own destiny. The sea was calm and wide for this transition. He shared he could feel this letting go, especially in his shoulders. Physically and emotionally, he understood he no longer needed to shoulder responsibility for his son. What a gift this dream was from the psyche. It held up a mirror for Marcus to see, feel, and be able to take action to let go. Marcus understood this with both his head and his heart. He was now accepting that it was the perfect time to let go, so now he could die in peace. In his life, he had been such a successful, powerful man, but he now was happy to be free of that pressure. It was as if the dream's awareness had given him permission to relinquish this responsibility. He now felt his son was able to cope without him. Tears were now free to flow.

Marcus said he was pleased he asked me to help him understand his dream. It illuminated his own journey and that of his relationship with his son. It was a joy for me to be involved in the process of helping Marcus find peace. Both he and his son were now free to move on. Marcus could fully let go. Andre had already set sail in his own boat into his own wide ocean of life.

Marcus asked if there was anything he could do to assist in his dying. I assured him his work was done but suggested he could do some gentle meditations of following the light for his final crossing. I suggested he could use the dreamscape image of the calm blue sea as the landscape for finding the natural radiance of light and following it as a guiding light. There was nothing to do here, just be relaxed, free of any activity or distraction. Breathe deeply and follow this light of compassion with love and gratitude. We said goodbye. A week later, Marcus died.

KATHLEEN

Kathleen sat quietly in my waiting room. She was early for her appointment, and I noticed she was studiously reading a book called *On Death and Dying* by Swiss American psychiatrist Elizabeth Kubler-Ross. This was an ominous beginning. She was a thin and attractive fifty-year-old. Her thinning grey hair was pulled back in a neat topknot, which seemed to leave her face exposed. Sleepy green eyes peered at me as we went into my room. A patient she met in the chemo room suggested she come and see me as she was concerned when Kathleen said she still hadn't been able to cry.

Six months ago, she was diagnosed with terminal ovarian cancer. It had metastasised, and her oncologist had run out of treatments to offer her. It was too late for surgery, and the six rounds of chemotherapy hadn't shrunk the cancer, and her tumour marker was still rapidly rising. Kathleen bravely told me she was dying.

'I understand I am dying. I've done the denial. I've done the anger, briefly visited the bargaining, but now I've fallen deeply into depression. And I'm so scared. I don't want to die depressed. I've read this bloody book from cover to cover. But I'm afraid. I'm afraid of this black hole I'm in. It's like I've stumbled, lost my footing, and tumbled over the edge into a deep hole of darkness.'

As Kathleen was telling me this, my eyes were stinging and burning, and I was afraid I was going to cry. I shared this reaction. I never cry in therapy. Her eyes glassed over with tears, and at last, she could let go. She sat and cried for a good half of the session. She said it felt such a relief.

Kathleen started to tell me her story. She grew up on a farm in country Victoria. Her mother and father lived on a large and lush property, and she was their only child. They grazed cows and grew beautiful roses that won awards in the rural show most years. Her grandmother lived in a dark and smelly room off the back veranda. Granny had dementia, was unable to communicate, and often made howling noises. Her father seemed to be responsible for her. 'She's your damn mother,' her mother reminded him constantly, but he was at work all day, so Granny was neglected. Kathleen was terrified of her, and she died when Kathleen went away to school. It was Granny's house; she owned it. Her parents were waiting for her to die so it would be theirs. 'So that should have made them happy, but that would have taken a miracle,' she said sadly.

Kathleen described the farm as being green for a lot of the year, providing perfect grazing for their cows, yet there was a darkness to it that she couldn't articulate. Her father worked in town as a bank manager, so they employed a farm manager who looked after the running of the property. Her mother was always depressed and stayed in her semi-dark bedroom most of the time. 'Go outside. Go and play. Leave me alone. You're making me sick.' Kathleen felt unloved, rejected, and lonely. Finally, she was sent away to boarding school. There, too, she felt unloved and lonely.

Academically, school was easy for her. She spent a lot of time in the library and found comfort in books and learning. Socially, she felt alone, different to the other girls, and she said she pretended not to care. She hid her wounded self. Her strategy was to go to university in another state so she never had to return home again. This she did. She studied medicine and in her final year fell in love with one of her lecturers. It turned out he was married and abusive towards her. Kathleen was heartbroken, became depressed, and never completed her degree. Her sense of self, her feminine identity, and her relation to masculinity were damaged. There was so much grief and rejection in her story. I was now realising depression was a familiar place for her to land in.

I asked if she had any recent dreams, and she shared a dream that troubled her, yet she didn't know why.

> *There's a little girl playing in the old and dusty woodshed. There are cobwebs everywhere, and they're sticking to her face, but I can see there are no spiders. I'm thinking they must be hiding because you can't have webs without spiders. The sticky web is getting in her eyes and her mouth. She can't see or yell out. I then become the little girl, and I'm really scared because I can't see or yell for help and I know there's a big, dangerous spider somewhere.*
>
> *Then I'm at university, and it's exam time. I'm just a child. Can't they see I'm too young to be here? It's some sort of mistake. I try to tell them, but then I realise if I stand up, everyone will see I have no underpants on. I'll be exposed. I remember I have forgotten to put them on. I was in such a hurry to get ready. My face is bright red as I'm feeling ashamed and I'm feeling very sad.*

I asked Kathleen how she was feeling on telling me the dream, and she felt very anxious and concerned for the little girl. I asked her to share her concerns with me. 'I can't really find the words; I'm now just feeling very sad.' Kathleen once again was crying.

'I'm wondering how this dream relates to your life at the moment?' I asked.

'I guess I feel like I've failed again. I can't heal from this cancer. I can't hide, or yell for help, or even clearly see what is going on inside me. I'm constantly exposed at the hospital. I'm scared, ashamed, and embarrassed, just like in the dream. I'm a failure. I don't trust anyone, and I don't trust myself.'

The dream had been brought up at the end of the session. I was wanting to go deeper into the dream and eventually take another perspective, another angle. The dream was mirroring her feelings and how she was dealing with the cancer, but I wanted to explore the woodshed and the danger lurking there. We needed to unravel the web she was caught up in. It held memories that needed to be cleared out.

Kathleen had a nightmare the night before our next session.

> *I am going on a journey. You are coming with me. I feel really comforted by knowing that. I am packing my suitcase. It's the case I used to take to boarding school. It's brown and flat and held together by a wide strap. I really want to go away on this journey. You suggest we take the case apart and repack it. I start taking the clothes and bags and shoes out, and I feel around deep inside and get a creepy feeling. It's so deep in there. I look in, and it's pitch-black. I can just see there's a pile of old-fashioned sepia photos of Granny's in one corner, some objects I don't recognise, and I dive my hand in deeper, and I grab hold of a huge slippery snake that's thrashing around trying to get away. I try to scream, but no words come out of my mouth, just spiders and their sticky web.*

Kathleen woke up terrified and was grateful she had our session the next morning. When she was telling me her dream, I noticed she was now sitting on the edge of her chair. I felt we were on the edge of something, something that had to be unpacked, revealed, and acknowledged. This was her depression. It lay deep in this dark void, packed away with old memories.

Dreams and Cancer

We were running out of time. Her oncologist suggested she get her affairs in order and think about palliative care because he predicted she had only a couple of months to live.

Gently, quietly, I asked. 'What happened in the woodshed to little Kathleen?' She started to sob. Deep, body-wrenching sobs erupted from her thin body as she remembered the farm manager.

'He was hiding in there, waiting for me. I was only little. It started when I was about five. I thought he was being kind. I thought this touching was loving. Nobody ever touched me. But soon he hurt me. It was dirty. He was dirty. He smelled of the stinking cows. But she kept sending me outside. The smell of his dirty fingernails and rough elbows. He made me touch it. I would scrub myself till my skin was raw; I didn't understand what was happening. I was scared, and no words would come out of my mouth. I hated him and wished he would die. I wanted to die too. He was old, I was young, and now I am going to die. So unfair. He stopped when I was about ten. I was starting to develop physically, and perhaps it could be dangerous for him. Then I went to boarding school. Thank God! I told no one. I've never told anyone. I've been ashamed about this dirty secret, the shame. Such raw shame. And then I come here, and you want to unpack my life. I now want to unpack my life. I can see now how it's there in the dreams, just like you said. So much danger has been lurking in the dark. Darkness in the woodshed, and darkness in me. I've been trapped my whole life by this dark shame.'

Kathleen was now sitting back in the chair. She was at ease. I suggested the snake was also in the dream as a symbol of transformation, as I felt the discovery of the abuse, seeing it, naming it, and acknowledging it would help lift her depression and move her closer towards the acceptance of her death. The spider had spun its web, and we had cleared it out. Now Kathleen could speak her truth and, importantly, be heard.

Kathleen's depression did lift. She started to engage in some visualisation and meditation with me in preparation for her crossing. She had an unusual request of me. 'Could you please come to my funeral? There will be no one there who really knows and understands me. I will feel so blessed if you come on my final journey, just like in the dream.' I said I would be there. This was so against my usual position, but I could see how important this was for Kathleen.

Kathleen had a last dream before her death.

> *I'm in a garden. It's green and vaguely familiar. It is quite beautiful, and I am feeling peaceful and joyful. I notice the large tree in the centre of the paddock has exposed roots. Its trunk is strong, and it has a small canopy of green leaves. The leaves are starting to fall. It isn't growing in the ground. It's close but not connected.*

We smiled at the message from the psyche to Kathleen. She was feeling joy. She was no longer depressed. The tree of life was no longer connected to Mother Earth. Her journey towards her death was beginning.

I went, as asked, to Kathleen's funeral. It was small and subdued. I walked at the rear of the people following the hearse. One woman approached me and asked if I knew Kathleen well. She remarked that none of her friends really knew her at all and assumed I didn't either. How sad I felt. Kathleen's abuse and carrying the secret had kept her shutdown and closed off to others. She could not trust another or allow herself to be close to another, so she was alone. How blessed I felt to have had the opportunity to share her secret inner world with her.

RAVI

I have found that men who are aware and have a relationship with their anima, their inner feminine, are open to the spiritual that lies deep in their psyche. Ravi was one such client. This was an end-of-life dream of wholeness. Ravi was nearly fifty years old. He was a small, frail man with lovely olive skin and was dressed in blue jeans and a neatly ironed shirt. He was not partnered and was without children.

Ravi was in the process of physically dying. He had terminal pancreatic cancer and came to therapy to talk. His medical team had suggested he get his affairs in order as he was expected to live only another three months. Ravi had been to a lawyer and made a final will, and he felt a visit to see me would assist in tying up loose ends. He shared he had lived a peaceful life. He presented as being without anxiety. He was born in Sydney to Indian migrant parents who had converted to Christianity.

Ravi said throughout his life he had attempted to live mindfully. He sadly admitted that he was not sure if he had ever experienced true happiness, though he often experienced inner peace. Since studying and practising Tibetan Buddhism, Ravi had become more familiar with his internal life. He said previously he had only focused on his external life. This, he discovered, brought him limited and transient joy. He wept silently behind his hands after telling me.

Ravi and I worked together for only ten sessions. I recall these sessions were tranquil and calm. Time in his physical body was running out. He was accepting of his diagnosis. He had not struggled against his fate. A daily practice of meditation helped clear his mind and open it to a truthful self-understanding and a detachment from fear and anxiety. We quietly talked of the parallels between Buddhism and psychotherapy, especially around attachment.

In the very beginning of our first session, Ravi remembered an ending of a dream he'd had at least a year ago. He felt it was significant on waking but only thought of it again on entering my office.

> *Some people, mostly women, are gathering together in a group at the side of a rocky mountain. I can see they are trying to tie a naked man with a thick rope onto a large, brown, wooden structure. He is bohemian, thin with untidy, long, brown hair and a beard.*

Is he Christ? One of these women in the group is my pregnant wife. He is not struggling but letting them do this to him. I feel that I somehow have been roped into being in this position, as if I am this man. My body feels stretched, thin, exposed, and vulnerable. Finally, he is now on what is clearly a cross and still not struggling. He is resigned. I look up and am shocked to see that it is my pregnant wife on the cross! She has now become Christ-like. The dream wakes me, but it doesn't disturb me.

I asked Ravi how he felt about the dream. He said he felt cross and annoyed as he wondered if the dream may have been prophetic. Then he smiled and said he might have been able to change the outcome of his diagnosis, as Christ surely becomes God. We smiled together. I was wondering about the word 'cross'. Why wasn't Ravi angry? He was outwardly so at ease with this fate, being crucified in the dream and in life with an early and approaching death. I was feeling cross that this lovely spiritual man was having to soon surrender to death. I asked about his associations around the cross. He suggested maybe he was at a crossroad. Ready to move on to the next life. Perhaps the cross was an internal compass, or maybe symbolic of his destiny. Ravi's wife in the dream, pregnant with possibilities, was his inner bride, his anima figure. How could I explain this to Ravi when we had such limited time?

I said I wondered if his inner feminine figure as expressed in the dream, was Christ-like by experiencing her own sense of spirituality. This was being assisted by other feminine figures. The process was arduous yet meaningful. It was stretching him and leaving him feeling vulnerable. We talked of how this figure was tied, not nailed to the cross, as in the biblical story. The feeling of being vulnerable was more important than the experience of crucifixion. By Ravi becoming aware of his significant, pregnant, feminine side, he was able to deepen his spiritual calling. As a practising Buddhist, Ravi said this had certainly occurred over the past year. For this, he was very grateful. This dream became especially significant to me in the telling and processing of Ravi's final dream.

> *A middle-aged man and a younger woman are in a double bed together. I can't see my body, but I am looking down on them from above the bed. I am feeling love for them, especially the woman, as I am watching them. The couple are lying quietly together and without any sexual desire for each other. They seem to be happy together. I am feeling content as I look at them.*

He said he woke feeling peaceful.

Ravi and I talked about the dream. The man, the masculine, he felt was a middle-aged man similar in colouring to his father, and the slightly younger woman, representing the feminine, or anima, looked vaguely like his mother. They were both brown-skinned and equal. The opposite internal figures were in balance and content. Ravi said he, too, felt content and in balance. He felt light yet had a sense of wholeness in his body and emotional self.

We talked of his parents in relation to the dream. He realised they were not his actual parents but their imago; that is, the residual traces of his original parents. Ravi felt gratitude, tenderness, and love towards them both. He became teary when he recalled how his father would gently hold his hand as a little boy and guide him through his young life. Ravi could feel his father's gentle presence within him throughout his life. As we drew attention to this feeling, Ravi could feel this connection of love nestled in his hands and his heart as we sat together. His father would travel with him for the remainder of his journey.

As a Buddhist, his spiritual beliefs helped soothe his natural fear of death. Ravi shared a vision he had during a meditation. It was set in the first flat he'd had as a young man. The flat in his dream was built on the banks of a flowing river. Ravi said he emotionally felt flat, flattened by life, so I felt the flat represented his inner world. The river was symbolic as it represented the flow of life that would return to the greater source with the cycle of life. This vision that had gently erupted from his unconscious also had a biblical feel, as did his first dream. This vision showed the now-perfect balance of his inner figures, so he could now let go, follow the light, and cross over in peace.

Ravi was not afraid of his imminent death. He was resigned, like in the first dream. There was no inner or outer struggle. He had lived his life as given to him. He was with death, not fighting it. He had fulfilled and completed his individuation and was ready to go. Because he was looking down from above in his second dream as he observed the couple, it made me feel that perhaps his soul was already getting ready to leave his earthly body to embark on his crossing. He needed nothing.

Ravi brought to this final session a piece of wisdom that resonated within him from the Diamond Sutra as he wanted to share it with me. It was an exchange between the Buddha and one of his students, Subhuti. The Buddha asked Subhuti, 'Does one who has immersed himself in the stream that flows to enlightenment say of himself, "I have entered the stream"? Subhuti replied, 'No, Buddha. He is called a stream-enterer because he has attained nothing. If he thought "I have attained the state of entering the stream" were to occur to him, then he would be clutching to a personality or soul or some idea of a separate self.' Ravi felt huge relief that the burden of himself had now become the stream-enterer and was simply just being.

After I learnt of Ravi's crossing, I came across this wisdom. On reading it, I thought fondly of Ravi. Tibetan Buddhist Pema Chodron said, 'Somehow in the process of trying to deny that things are always changing, we lose our sense of the sacredness of life. We tend to forget that we are part of the natural scheme of things.' Ravi had lived his life fully in the sacredness of life.

6

Dreams and Healing: The Map of My Journey through Dreaming with Breast Cancer

In his book *An Imaginary Life*, David Malouf writes, 'What else should our lives be but a continual series of beginnings, of painful settings out into the unknown, pushing off from the edges of consciousness into the mystery of what we have not yet become?'

Recalling and working with my dreams gave me a story and images in which to feel, understand, and acknowledge my emotional and physical journey and experience. During the cancer journey, I had a series of dreams over a period of a year. These offered a fresco of images and stories, a sequence, a map that guided and assisted me. The dreams were a reassuring reflection of the journey; they kept me connected at a deep and healing level.

I invite you to engage with the dream sequence as you would if you were viewing them in an art gallery. Just as life on earth has seasons, my dreams each have their own season, time, and beauty. Each, individually, is a relevant reflection of where I was at that time; collectively, they hang together as a process. Walk around each dream, each symbol, accept each layer as a work of art, each an individual healing gift from the psyche, each integral to the body of the dream story, the experience. Together, they form wholeness, which is the cycle of life. This cycle was the transformation from illness back into life. There was an unconscious tenacity, a reassuring life force. Like the newly born baby that instinctively latches onto the breast, the drive to survive is strong.

After each dream, I would write it in my journal, and then I would randomly select one tarot card reading from my Raider-Waite deck. I have included the card at the end of each dream. This was done to provide me with an image that would offer a direction in understanding an interpretation of the dream and where I was at in my illness. It suggested an interesting starting point for the analysis rather than a magical 'This is what it all means.' A pictorial image in the chosen card seemed to resonate, offering a creative wisdom. There has been profound synchronicity with these cards being revealed at the necessary time as they were surprisingly insightful.

DREAM 1: A Warning. A Daughter's Dream

The first dream was that of one of my daughters. It was a brief nightmare.

She dreamt I had cancer and I was going to die. She was distressed as she shared this dream with me. Death dreams are difficult for the dreamer to accept. We humans cling on to the past and resist mourning this loss, so the psyche gives us a shock, and a death dream of the mother will facilitate this transition. I assumed this was a classic separation dream. This was a psychic death, not a physical death, and this interpretation settled her. She was now in her early twenties and no longer a child. Death dreams assist the dreamer to let go and allow a different relationship with the dream person. My daughter was on her own journey, living and studying in another state, in a new love relationship, with parents who were now divorced. She was busy making changes in her life, outward changes as well as inward changes. She was developing her own sense of self and individual identity.

Our relationship was shifting like sand; it was changing. She accepted this symbolic death and came alive to her new self and the radiance of her new life while engaged in the process of individuation. She was still in tune with my inner world when she had this dream. This was available to her as she was not fully separated psychically from me. Only briefly did I wonder if her dream was prophetic. Was there a message for me? Sometime later, my cancer was diagnosed.

DREAM 2: Urgency

I am walking happily along a winding path. I walk through a fertile, green, and grassy field. This is bucolic, I think to myself. I can smell the freshness, the fragrance. It feels familiar, and I am content, yet I know I must keep walking. I can feel the strength in my legs as I continue walking.

Quickly, the path changes. It becomes dusty and dry. No longer green and lush, but yellow like sand. I am in the desert. There are dusty pebbles and small rocks I crunch on as I walk. I try to turn back, to see where I have been, but I cannot move my head. I desperately want to go back.

I rub my gritty eyes and cannot believe where I am. The street is like a stage set, saloon doors that are slowly swinging back and forth, leading into a pub. Old and dusty coloured lights that are hanging between the posts swing gently and move in the breeze. I wonder if this is Dodge City as in the old TV show Gunsmoke of my childhood. It sure feels and looks to me like I am in a Western movie.

My body is suddenly cold with fear. There are three men ahead, swarthy, aggressive, menacing men leering at me. They are cowboys. The men are like hungry wild animals, ready to pounce. My heart is crashing about in my chest.

Suddenly, my old girlfriend Hannah appears. There she is sitting across the road having coffee, reading a book, oblivious to what is happening to me.

I scream to her for help. 'Hannah! Help me!'

'No,' she yells back. 'I won't help you. Sort this yourself.' She returns to her reading. Totally detached from my situation. I can't believe she won't help me.

The men now chase me. We are running, fast, furiously. I know violence is coming. My legs are getting heavier, my body covered in sweat. I'm running forever, until I can run no more. I turn and face them.

Then I feel the sudden and sharp pain as a bullet hits my left breast. They got me. Dead centre. My breast that sits in front of my heart.

I woke, gasping for breath, clutching my damp breast. It was 2 am. I wrote down my dream, managed to settle myself, and eventually return to sleep. The next morning, the dream was forefront in my mind. I was curious and needed to understand its meaning. There was a message within the dream. The dream had shaken me. It prompted me to take action.

MY ANALYSIS

At the time, I interpreted the anxiety dream as being about my relationship with Hannah, a woman with whom I had been close but who now seemed to have no time for me. I was upset as I missed her friendship. She had taught me a lot, especially about myself.

Later meditating on the dream, I wondered if Hannah was possibly a shadow part of my self, the disinterested, unhelpful part that I had been unwilling to acknowledge. The part that did not have my back. At some stage in my early development, I would have realised that being unhelpful and self-pleasing would never gain me love or friendship. The part of my personality that Hannah represented was repressed so she only dwelled deep in my personal unconscious. Perhaps she was shadow.

Now I was thinking differently about Hannah. She was not rejecting. Hannah was another side of me. She was the quiet aspect within that can stay calm. Detached from the drama. She was an aspect of the positive feminine within me. She had been present the whole journey. Quietly grounded, calm, able to make intelligent, unemotive decisions, non-reactive, positive, present but without anxiety. Hannah within was always there, being objective rather than subjective and a positive addition to my feminine self-confidence. (I will need her to be detached from the drama that lies ahead. She can go to chemo, read her book, stay grounded, and not react.)

I looked at the geography of the landscape. The green, fragrant, and lush life I was enjoying. It was about to change. My calm and peaceful life was behind me. I had been living in the fullness of life. Unbeknown to me, the battle with cancer was ahead. There the road was no longer nourishing and lush. It was desert, dry, rocky, and dusty. This was me going into the new world. A world from flourishing health to a world of sickness. I saw my body walking along this path. Then I was under attack.

My association with the barren landscape was my father. He loved *Gunsmoke*, a Western drama set in Kansas the 1870s in 'Pleasant Valley'.

It was his favourite TV program. There was always drama and conflict. Cowboys and Indians. His favourite character was Marshal Matt Dillon, a wayward cowboy who became a lawman and a caring sheriff. Like the actor John Wayne, my father was also a bit of a wayward cowboy; he was the Marshal in our home.

The menacing men, like cancer, were ready to attack. And I was attacked. Their menacing reinforced the power and aggressiveness of the cancer. The cowboys amplified the barrenness of the landscape and situation. I attempted to keep running. I was so afraid of these menacing men. I felt this fear in my body. My heart was crashing and pounding in my chest. My legs were heavy. I was anchored, where I stood, grounded in reality. I could run no more. My physical body was tired. So, I turned and faced the aggressor. Then I was wounded in my breast. My left breast where the cancer was silently dwelling. I did not dodge the bullet, here in Dodge City. It hit the dead centre of me, but it was not a death shot. I did not die. The shot had pierced my heart.

This dream was a prophetic dream; it was a warning. I did not heed the warning with urgency. It was some weeks before I sought medical help.

The Tarot Card

I chose the Three of Swords.

The Three of Swords signifies grief, tears, loss, and sorrow. The heart, the central symbol in the card, is pierced. My heart was pierced. I have been hurt to the core of my being. There are heavy clouds above. Rain was pouring down from within. My life was soon to be saturated with torrential rain, a downpour. I have cried tears, and I have caused tears. The swords are blue. Blue, the colour of sadness. Blue is also the colour of calmness and serenity. This was what I was needing.

The background of the card is grey; the sky and heavy clouds are grey. There is no light. There is no sun shining here. The heart in the card is red, the colour of health, courage, and passion, but also the colour of anger. There is heartache in this card. Possibly a broken heart. This may have been from a relationship, divorce, or death. I had recently experienced all three. My left breast that was wounded sits above my heart. I certainly have experienced a sword piercing my heart. There is an acute awareness, and there is heartache.

When I drew this card, it was in the upright position, offering hope. My question to myself, with compassion, was: 'What is the heart of this problem?'

I freely associated around the number three. Images of number three are found over and over in mythologies and religions.

The number three was Oedipal. Mother, father, and infant. I commented to myself: 'Surely this complex is fully resolved within myself.'

There was the maiden, mother, and crone. My favourite Gustav Klimt painting *The Three Ages of Women*, symbolising the cycle of life, hangs on my office wall.

Three can be religious. In the Holy Trinity, God is three in one, the Father, Son, and Holy Spirit. Jesus rose on the third day. There are three archangels, the Magi presents three gifts for the baby Jesus, and there are more to be found in the scriptures.

Three can be found in the Hindu tri-murti of creator-preserver-destroyer.

Three was the number of wisdom and harmony.

I was reminded of the prophecy from Simeon to Mary. In St Luke's Gospel 2:35, Simeon tells Mary that a sword would pierce her heart as she stood at the site of the crucifixion and that her motherhood would be mysterious and sorrowful. 'And a sword will pierce your own soul too.'

DREAM 3: Going Nowhere Fast

The following week, I was involved in an interstate training as an Executive Committee member of Canteen, a not-for-profit organisation that assists children and teenagers to deal with cancer, their own cancer or that of a loved one. I had been working with them as a volunteer for about twelve years. I loved my involvement with the young people and the organisation. I contributed and made a difference. Although unsure why, I was apprehensive about going interstate. Without taking time to explore this feeling, I decided to go anyway. During my first night away, I woke feeling unwell, even slightly fearful.

> *I am trying to take my dog Polly for a walk. But the lead has become wrapped tightly around her legs, holding her back. We are both unable to move forward.*

The dream had woken me. I felt unsettled. I wrote down the dream and fell back into a restless sleep. That morning, I woke with a high temperature. I had a virus and decided to return home early. On the flight home, I contemplated what Polly represented. She was strong, timid, loyal, unconditionally loving, protective, and incredibly instinctual. I loved Polly; she was our rescue dog.

I visited my GP and requested tests as I was unusually anxious since the 'wounding' in my first dream. I was also concerned about this dream. I had not been listening to my inner guide, my instinct, my intuition. All year, I had been feeling fatigued. My GP was adamant I had a virus. He, too, was certain my fatigue was due to an under-active thyroid. More thyroxine was prescribed, a decision not in accordance with my blood test results. Why did I accept this diagnosis? The medication was not helping. Why did this diagnosis soothe my fears of uncertainty?

MY ANALYSIS

I was the dream ego. I looked in the dream as I appear now. The dream image of Polly at one level represented my physical body. My body was not able to move forward. This I linked to my first dream of being caught up, stuck in the desert. Polly was being tied up by her lead. My desire to do good and contribute was thwarted. The theme of being unable to move ahead was powerful. Polly, at another level, represented my domestic intuitive and instinctual function and confirmed my decision to return home.

To dream of an animal was important as animals respond and react to their instincts, and instinct is the deep foundation of human nature. Instinct was to be recognised and integrated into one's conscious world. If not, the animal part of the self can become dangerous and menacing, especially if wounded. The dream also had a prophetic function, a warning. Something was stopping me from moving forward, preventing my body from physically moving. I was tied up by something.

The Tarot Card

I chose the Hanged Man, number twelve in the Major Arcana. Number twelve is a significant number and is thought of as a perfect number, the number of authority and symbolic of wholeness. There are twelve months in the year, twelve zodiac signs, and Jesus had twelve disciples. The hanged man card symbolises the paradox of pain and ecstasy. It embodies the surrender to a near-death experience, which can give us our life and inspire a deep devotion to the inner truth. This comes with spiritual insight, hence the yellow illumination around his head. When I chose the card, I had a sense of helplessness and curiosity as I had just returned home from the Canteen retreat feeling unwell. The hanged man was powerless to control his destiny or his life.

On close inspection of this card, the figure doesn't appear to be in any distress as he hangs himself in an act of self-sacrifice. He is in a yoga position, hanging precariously from the makeshift cross. He has a sparkling gold halo around his head, signifying a highly evolved figure. The hanged man is a reminder of the cost of the situation that lay ahead. His legs are red, the colour of passion, health, and courage but also the colour of anger. His body is blue, the colour of sadness, the colour of serenity. Yellow, the colour of the halo that surrounds his head, signifies an illumination. It also symbolises sunshine, hope, and happiness. Hanging upside down, one feels discomfort, even vertigo. Had I hanged myself? Was I to be sacrificed?

When I chose this card, I had been in a suspended space. I felt disempowered as I couldn't move forward, just like in the dream of Polly. His clothes are blue. 'Am I sad?' I wonder. I had vertigo while feeling unwell at the retreat. I knew there was a message here. My life was being turned upside down for a reason. This needed to be illuminated and was a call for action.

DREAM 4: A Mother's Gift

Visiting my GP on my return home was fortuitous. Unfortunately, he didn't take me seriously. Yet I knew something was wrong. I insisted, especially about the mammogram. 'But you look so well!' He just wanted to give me more thyroxine. Finally, he listened, and he ordered some investigations. After blood tests, mammogram, ultrasound, and then biopsies, I was suddenly afraid.

I was informed I had an aggressive carcinoma in my left breast. I asked the doctor if I could have felt the cancer bursting out of the duct, and she said it was possible. The pain felt during my first dream may well have been the physical invasion by the carcinoma as it erupted from the duct into the surrounding breast tissue. There was no palpable lump to be felt. My mammogram a year earlier was normal. There was an urgency to act. No more hanging around. I was to have my breast removed. My breast symbolic of being a woman. The feminine. My breasts were a part of my identity. A part of my being a sexual woman. It was a connection to my mother who nursed me and to my daughters who I nursed and nurtured. It was a connection to intimacy and to sexual pleasure.

I underwent a left mastectomy with reconstruction. The nurses were kind and efficient. My surgeons were wonderful. They showed compassion as I faced the loss of a breast that I was reluctant to lose. My breast was laden with meaning and emotion. I needed to let go and surrender to the situation that I was facing.

The night before my surgery, I dreamt of my mother and her good friend Joy.

> *I am in the kitchen in the home of my childhood. There is a long corridor that runs up to my parents' bedroom. My mother and her good friend Joy are calling me. They are smiling at me. 'Come with us. We have a lovely gift for you, a gift you may need.' I skip and follow them.*

> *They are both young, attractive, and vibrant, as they were when I was a child. In the home of my childhood, they take me to my parents' bedroom. They are both so happy. Joy hands me a delicate old-fashioned tin of talcum powder she has taken from the cupboard that held my mother's underwear. It is a pretty paper-covered tin in a soft pastel floral design. It feels like a healing balm and a blessing in one. I feel the warmth of love and pleasure in the dream at receiving this gift. This I feel in my body, and my eyes are awash with tears of joy.*

The dream woke me. I felt peaceful, contained, and nourished, though teary.

I recalled my mother had one of these pretty floral tins in her bedroom cupboard. I loved to occasionally play with it and smell the delicate perfume. I could smell its gentle fragrant perfume in the dream. It was just how it was when I was a child. My mother never used the powder. It belonged to her mother, who died when my mother was a teenager. She cherished this tin of powder. In the dream, I was so pleased she was gifting me this, and I felt love, joy, and gratitude.

I also felt their calling me was helping me accept what was happening now and to step forward to face whatever lay ahead of me. This was a place beyond an attachment to the outcome. It was a place of freedom rather than fear. I experienced a paradox: the less we are attached to life, the more alive we can become.

MY ANALYSIS

This was a beautiful, healing dream. I had a realisation, a confirmation, that love and support were all around. I was feeling the freedom in this gift. The dream said I was going to survive, even though as I knew from the earlier wounding dream, it would be a desert experience.

I felt the natural healing of the psyche taking place, and with time, much joy was born. I so love the way the psyche plays with language. Joy Bourne was my mother's friend's name! I love that my internal mother was so close and available to me. I felt so connected to her and thrilled that she was reaching out to me at this difficult time. It was as if a part of her was within, travelling with me. This was very affirming, nourishing my soul.

There was an awareness of the intergenerational feminine: grandmother to mother, mother to daughter. The gentle fragrance of the perfumed powder represented the fragrance of life, and the beauty of life. I was looking at the loveliness of life. This came through the feminine. This beauty reinforced the shooting, the wounding of my breast, but I did the journey on my own. I carried the tin of perfumed powder through the desert, through the wasteland. The perfume that came distilled from the lush green land. My mother had not been alive for many years. It is at times of fear and uncertainty one craves the comfort of the mother. There is nothing as powerful as presence.

The dream offered gifts while I was facing the unknown. I had discovered a new relationship with joy. I had always associated joy with happiness. Now I saw and felt it was synonymous with unconditional love, for self and others. For life. Now I was able to be free of any attachment to the outcome of my life, of this journey. This felt very much alive and joyful. I had a sense of freedom. This freedom was life-affirming. Such a healing gift. Like a good-enough mother, the internal mother gathered me in, contained me, thus reducing anxiety and tension, providing love, emotional nourishment, and emotional truth.

From this dream arose an abundance of love from my husband, my daughters, my family, and my friends. They were a source of strength, and I was surprised at how freely they showed their love for me. At the same time, I was trying to hold, process, and make sense of my loss and grief.

I was invited to join the Winners Club. This group of women formed when a few women who knew each other began to meet over coffee to share their ordinary and extraordinary experiences of being a cancer sufferer. Wisdom emerged from the sharing, together and individually, as they were facing the unknown. At a time of feeling separate and often alone, the sharing enabled a connection that transcended this isolation. I experienced so much kindness from others.

My husband felt helpless. He started making sourdough bread. This was great medicine for us both. His gift to me and a distraction for him. Men struggle when there is nothing they can physically do to help. He couldn't fix me. My daughters and family and friends gifted me knitted beanies, books to read, vanilla slices that I love, fresh fruit and veggies from the markets, fruit bread, flowers and indoor plants. Phone calls of love and support. I was truly blessed.

I commenced chemotherapy.

Before I started chemotherapy, I had a strong desire to talk intimately to my local minister. He was a special man and a special friend. I needed to talk about meditation and prayer. I was struggling to connect to something greater than myself, perhaps to God. I phoned and explained briefly I needed to chat. 'Come around.' I called into his house at the boys' school where he was chaplain. While we talked and shared afternoon tea, the heavens opened. Torrential rain pounded the roof. The large glass windows shook. Hailstones the size of golf balls pelted down from the heavens. The view of the river from the window became a wall of white.

Eventually, it passed. Then there was stillness. I was quietly crying. Eventually, I, too, had no more to say, to feel. He loaned me a book and quietly said goodbye. I paddled out along the wet walkway. All the cars in the car park were dented and dimpled with hail damage. My car was untouched. It was a miracle.

I saw there was widespread devastation. Birds were killed, found dead under the trees. Once again, I felt, as I did in my earlier dream, there had been a shooting, yet I had survived. Everyone got dented, except me. It was a miracle that seemed beyond myself. Maybe there was a God, and He was on my team. The storm seemed a life-giving force. I would survive. I brought to my life a positive attitude. A deep knowing. Prayer and meditation now came easily. I just needed to be still. Be silent. Just quietly be.

The Tarot Card

I chose the tarot card the Ace of Pentacles. The suit of Pentacles relates to materialism, and with hard work and practicality, good fortune will be provided. This card held much promise emotionally, spiritually, and physically. It was an ace card, always welcomed as it indicates much hope. In the tarot deck, there are four ace cards, all positive, promising, and representing good fortune. A windfall. Everything was 'coming up roses'. This card indicated the potential for growth, stability, and success. My life's future was fragrant. This card presented a new beginning. It presented the cycle of life.

I often feel when this card appears that fate has a hand in the gift, as the gift appears from seemingly nowhere, out of the blue. This card represents my fate of good fortune.

I felt immense gratitude when this card was revealed.

DREAM 5: Emerging Through Chemotherapy

After my fourth chemotherapy infusion, I spent what seemed like hours in the dark of night crouching over the toilet bowl. This racked my body and my soul. The anti-nausea medication was not working. I was in the thick of it. I looked in the bathroom mirror. A pale, thin alien. An object, afraid at this moment of being the subject. In this moment, I felt so alone. Not one hair left, anywhere. I searched frantically. Nothing. Consciously, I kept fear at bay. If death awaited me, it would be okay. I would not make a story in my mind of the unknown. I was being challenged. I chose life.

I had been up to the hills to see Michelle for a therapeutic massage.

She was an amazing, gentle, spiritual woman. She told me all she could see was grey. Chemical grey. But there was light coming. She seemed to move the grey heaviness around within me, and finally out from within me.

I heard a baby crying throughout the session. 'How can you bear it?' I asked her. The baby was distressed.

'No, there's no baby crying,' said Michelle quietly.

Really?

It was my internal baby. Crying.

Our dog Polly never left my side. She knew I was suffering. She could smell the chemicals. She showed me unconditional love.

I wrote in my diary how cancer was like a war zone, a seemingly appropriate military metaphor. I was attacked, my disease was invasive, aggressive, unpredictable, and then my body was bombarded by chemical warfare. But I would survive. I was strong. I had my defenses in place. I would become stronger while under attack. Just like in my early childhood, I was building an internal resilience.

That night, I had this dream.

> *The need to leave where I am overwhelms me. It drives me forward, even though my body feels weary. I see the distant road ahead, and a heavy vehicle awaits. It could be military; I'm not sure. I just know I need to get to it.*
>
> *I have two options, as there are two paths. One easy, one difficult. One familiar, one unknown. The easy way is clear to see. There stands a beautiful shop, and I can see through big glass windows inside. It has shelves, layered, with compartments and objects that are all colour-coded. The objects are all the same. Vases and bowls that are pastels, blue, pink, soft purple. It is very ordered. There, by the far door, stand my girlfriend and colleague Britt's parents with their arms crossed. They do not look very*

welcoming. I don't want to go that way, even though it is an easy route to the vehicle.

My cousin's husband is with me. He is a strong, muscular man, larger than life. I say to him clearly, 'I'm not going that way. I will take the other route.' He says, 'Okay, if you must.' Yes, I will swim through it.

Ahead of me is a dark, deep, muddy, grey river with long reeds and rocks on the far banks. I immerse myself in the water, which is thick like soup. The mud is getting deeper. I start to sink. The more I'm being dragged down, the more I feel in touch with some powerful force within. It is a long, difficult, and dirty swim. I feel in my body each difficult stroke. There is grit and slime in my eyes as I try to look ahead. It is hideous. My arms and legs ache with exertion and fatigue. I am in this state for such a long time before I emerge. It feels endless.

Finally, the struggle is over. I come to the surface. Eventually, I feel my feet touch the slimy riverbank. I am so cold, cold to the core. I feel my body shivering.

There is no one around, and yet sense I am not alone. I slowly pull myself out of the river onto the bank. It takes great effort. I am exhausted.

There is the new road and the car ahead. The relief I feel in my body is extraordinary.

I wake anxious and pleased it was just a dream. I know in my heart I have been, and am still, swimming through the mud of chemotherapy and darkness. But I am through the worst of it.

MY ANALYSIS

The dream provided me with a picture of where and how I was journeying and had shown me a freeing path, both physically and emotionally. The dream was classical baptism imagery. I had to choose to go into the deep. Deep into the unconscious. Once we venture into the water in a dream, a change of consciousness is inevitable.

In Alchemy, I was in the stage of *nigredo*. As Christopher Perry describes: 'The cleansing, purification, the *nigredo*, is the process of individuation. It is blackness, darkness, the darkest time, the time of despair, disillusionment.' I had been deep within my internal world and had come through an inner and outer journey. Through the desert, a wounding, a hailstorm, now mud, grit, and slime. Hideous.

I had emerged as a new, stronger, more resilient self. It appeared I had a choice, yet I had no choice. I just had to choose this path, the path towards life.

This was a turning point. I can't choose the easy road as I can't be waylaid. It will be a distraction. It will be beige. This was life. Challenging me. I knew at a deep level that without change, there would be no growth. This dream was an expansion of my original dream. A different death experience that I must go through. Enabling a transformation in my own life.

The car or vehicle was a metaphor for the self. I needed to get to the self that awaited me. It was solid, offering protection and a way to move along a different road on the journey. My life as I knew it had gone. I had chosen a pathway that was not boring, ordered, and predictable. No longer a trace of beige! I had emerged changed for the ordeal. I had to face the dark night of the soul. My life needed to be lived fully at a deeper, less superficial, more profound, authentic level.

I was no longer afraid.

There is an Indian parable called *The Devil and the Pilgrim*.

One day, the devil met a pilgrim walking along the roadside. The devil was rubbing his hands together, singing and very happy.

The pilgrim asked him, 'Devil, why are you so happy?'

The devil replied, 'Well, today, I am going to kill ten thousand people.'

'That's a tall order,' said the pilgrim. 'How could you possibly do that?'

'Oh, it's very easy if you know how,' was the devil's reply. 'All I have to do is kill one with cholera, and the rest will die of fear!'

Fear would feed disease. Fear of disease and death is part of the fabric of our Western society. I was a thin thread that was a part of this fabric. I had felt fear and had chosen to take another route. An unfamiliar route. Even though it was in a desert, it would not kill me. It would not keep me from love. Love for myself and love for others. It was this love that would set me free.

The power of the imagery of being in the mud was now cradled in my consciousness. I could access this place so easily and now without fear. As in dreams set around water, I had been deep within my unconscious. Becoming numb to my suffering through fear would not bring me joy. It was the exact same part of me that felt in touch with suffering that felt and experienced joy. The dream facilitated transformative work carried out in the depths of the psyche. The inner work of becoming conscious. Joy was born.

The Tarot Card

I chose the Strength card. Perfect. I was getting stronger. I was getting stronger by accessing my inner world, rather than from my outer world.

The Strength card is number eight in the Major Arcana. I was so happy when this card appeared. It was the perfect antidote to my last dream and my suffering. This card represented my ability to confront, overcome, and conquer all that was challenging me physically and emotionally. How peaceful and intimately the beings in the card are interacting with each other. She appears to be taming the lion.

There is a real relationship here, and this was a possibility. This was a different type of strength I was needing. A more powerful, courageous strength. A courageous and personal strength without any fear. The lion is, after all, the king of the jungle.

I was gaining physical strength from swimming, and emotional strength from Reiki, reflexology, remedial massage, and seeing a psychotherapist, which helped me process my grief. The untamed primitive part of my self was wanting to be related to. It was untamed and relating to it could lead to further growth, freedom, and transformation. But without the connection between the woman and the lion, and if she doesn't feed and attend to him, he can devour her body and soul. My strength was to come from their relationship.

I knew I was just an ordinary woman, as was the woman in the card, but that I, too, was beast, wild and courageous. I was not afraid as I stroked the lion, taming the beast within. My lion was enormous, and it was a part of my psyche, being my feminine, my instinctual nature, intuition, wisdom, and it needed to have a relationship within. It was to be a relationship being directed and mediated by the feminine. I had dreams and plans, as there was still much to explore in discovering real freedom through consciousness. The number eight sign was about balance, equilibrium, and steadiness. I recalled a Chinese client who dreamed of number eight, and she was thrilled. A very lucky number, especially for a woman, she informed me. The number eight was also the sign of infinity, a mathematical symbol, being limitless and endless in possibility. My pathway ahead was full of possibility.

I loved that the earth was green and fertile. My inner growth was being fed by this fertile terrain. I felt more grounded after seeing this card.

DREAM 6: Celebrating a New Phase of Life

I am planning to give my daughters a party, a celebration for them both. They are becoming women.

I know I must travel down deep into the dark recesses of the Underworld, as I really want the party to be special. I start the journey. It is long, onerous, and arduous. The road is dark and gloomy. Finally, I have arrived at my destination. Here I am in the Underworld, and I meet a strong, dark man in leather pants with heavy silver chains attached. This man lives here. His chest is bare, head bald, and his arms are very muscular. He frightens me, as I wonder if he is part-animal.

He is carrying a bright and powerful torch light, which he shines to show me the way.

We are getting ready for the celebration. I am showing my husband around before the party starts. Fairy lights are strung up and glittering around the rows of pristine white tents. It is still very dark outside. Together, we go and look inside one of the tents. It is perfect.

We enter the next tent, and there is a beautiful, naked, young woman lying on a bed covered in a white sheet. The young woman is pale and blonde and lying very still. Both my husband and I look at her longingly. Her body is curvaceous and lithe, sexual, beautiful. I tell him he can lie on top of her but cannot kiss her mouth. He can only kiss her forehead. My husband doesn't want to leave the tent. He wants to stay with this gorgeous, sensual woman, but we must move on. I, too, want to stay. I want to kiss her.

The muscled guide shines the torch to where we need to go next.

My husband and I go to get into the train, like a ghost train, but he wants to delay. He suggests I go ahead. But I don't. I watch him go back to the tent, and I see him lying on top of the girl, kissing her mouth. Sadly, I go up to him and say we must go. I sense this is because we both want her so much. We both acknowledge it is best that we leave.

I woke up feeling sad and aware of some deep loss within. I was aware I missed being a sexually alive and attractive woman. A part of me just wanted to go back in time and feel like a complete woman again. A woman with real breasts, breasts I could feel, not silicone ones. I wanted to be the young, available woman on the bed. Also, I wanted to embrace this part of myself I was having to let go of. This was a realisation that came from having this dream. I was left feeling the potential for an expansion of a part of myself.

MY ANALYSIS

In my life, my two daughters were beautiful young women. Their lives were on track, and their transformation into womanhood had been a delight to observe and be a part of. In this dream, I was wanting to celebrate them. They had effortlessly transitioned into womanhood. I felt there was a deeper level to this dream, especially as I was once again having to go into the Underworld. I needed to pass through the gates being manned by my guide, the muscular and frightening man with animal drives. He held the powerful light. The light of consciousness. He guided me, showing the way down to where I was left longing. Longing for my lost youth and womanhood, and yet here I was planning the celebrating of my daughters coming into theirs!

I recognised and felt my discomfort of again having to visit and confront the dark Underworld within, and the frightening man who was in charge. How chained he was to his world. This dark man represented my inner masculine or animus who was the mediator between my conscious ego and my unconscious inner world. He was now an important help to me, a part of my inner world. I was afraid of him in this form as up till now he had been unconscious. So I needed to summon him, call him up to engage in the outer world. He could liaise or mediate between my inner and outer worlds. He was strong and directed and depicted the rite of passage that I was undertaking. He was Earth Man, my Earth Animus, who lived in the depths.

It was anxiety-provoking to move from the light of consciousness into the dark of the unconscious, from height into the deep. The Underworld represented my unconscious inner world, a world removed from my reality, my real world. My animus man was the carrier of the light, the symbol of consciousness. The light pointed me in the direction of transformation and the journey I was choosing to take to achieve this.

When working with the psyche, the dream is often placed right where the dreamer would rather not visit and presents emotions the ego would rather not feel. Psyche offered me a fresh imaginative perspective that had emotionally moved me. The dream had revealed itself, and I had uncovered a truth I had not fully allowed myself to acknowledge.

Initially on waking, I thought the dream was about my husband. Was he wanting another? Perhaps a younger, more vulnerable, sexy, and fully available woman quietly and patiently waiting for him? The ego would probably be much happier with that interpretation. Let's make it about him and not me! Now I could reflect and feel that loss of my youth and still be able to plan the celebration for the next generation. I was passing on the inter-generational feminine to my girls, who had been passed on to me by my mother and grandmother. This had been shown to me in my earlier dreams. It is the cycle of life.

My journey on the train of life was to share a different relationship within myself and with my husband. I was facing this relationship with an acceptance and a celebration. We didn't need to feel alone as we longed for love and intimacy. This now had come fully to my awareness. The dream allowed for a celebration of the emotional and physical intimacy we shared. It had also presented me with a flashback of myself in the tent. She was a symbolic feminine figure depicting youth and sexuality. I was able to have a new celebration of my daughters as women. I had all of them symbolically within me. We could have a party for all. I could embrace this sexual energy, this life force, in others and in myself.

I engaged in creative visualisation between the young woman and the strong, muscular man holding the light. She stirred and was re-energised. I invited her to the party, to help get the show on the road. She offered me a fullness the cancer treatment had challenged. I thanked them both for opening a new aspect within. They were helping me to jazz up my life, my intimate life.

In mythology, Psyche's final task as a woman could only be embarked upon when her work was done and her earlier tasks had been accomplished. My role as mother was to be finally celebrated by my daughters giving up their innocence (the white tents, white sheet covering the young woman's body symbolic of their virginity) and their coming into womanhood. I, too, was coming into the next phase of my life as a woman. I grieved the loss and accepted the change. I also accepted the challenge to awaken parts of myself and call them to the outer world. My induction into the Underworld had also given me an infusion of instinctual power and intuition.

The Tarot Card

I chose the Three of Wands, an upright card from the Minor Arcana. Wands represent energy. Number three is about taking positive action, using passion and communication. This card is also about standing and looking into the future. My future. The figure looks out across the land and finally to the sea as he plans to broaden his horizon. For a successful outcome or future, the card is showing me the need to stay grounded with my feet firmly planted in reality. My growth and security are not to be compromised. I felt secure within myself. The three sprouting wands are also firmly planted and are not to be uprooted. I have a place in the world as I look to the horizon. The red of his cloak symbolises passion, health, and love. The dream was showing the importance of passion in relationships.

This card also invited me to blend my heart and mind with further action that would help shape my future. I could use the interplay of intuition blended with passion and creativity. This I undertook with creative visualisation as I invited my internal figures to dialogue with each other and with me. This was very fruitful as I remastered myself as a sexual and sensual woman. I have always felt there was so much potential for new growth and change when this card appears. All the little new green shoots on the wands are a sign of new growth, hope, and fertility. My dream and my response to it had enlivened me and encouraged my willingness to communicate with my internal figures and my external love relationship.

DREAM 7: Going into the Underworld and the Realisation of Loss

I receive a message. It is clear I need to travel. I am going on a pilgrimage. There is no choosing this pilgrimage. I somehow know it has been chosen for me. I travel deep into the Underworld. It is dark and dangerous. There is no road to follow, and there is no guide to lead me. The path is well-trodden, though not well-cared for. I feel reassured others have been here before me. 'Do they come back?' I ask myself.

I am at a gate. There is the gatekeeper who is cool, detached, but he lets me enter. 'You are wounded,' he says.

'I cannot feed my babies,' I tell him.

'You have done that. Your babies are fed. Your work is done. It is time to cross.'

'Cross? I am not ready to cross.'

I keep travelling. I am going deeper, but I know how to return. I will get back to the gates.

I am trying on a bikini. My girlfriend is with me. She is keen on the bikini. I'm only interested in a skirt, a colourful and flowing skirt. A hippy skirt that makes me smile. I look into the mirror to see the skirt. I see the guru. It is Buddha. His face is glowing. He has chubby cheeks, pink and round. He is up on a platform, draped in wedding veils. He has just married. The groom is Neil. He looks so happy. Everyone assumes Neil is enlightened in the dream, but I know he is just my hairdresser. Neil and I hug. We laugh that we knew each other in another lifetime. On earth. I am sitting talking. I am an Indian hippy, wearing my bright skirt, and some people are listening.

I talk to the people:

'I am sitting here so you can hear me. I am just like you. We are all connected. We are all one. We are sentient beings.'

I walk along a pathway. There is blue wisteria. The colour is vivid and very beautiful. I know I am at one with the universe.

I woke up feeling sad, aware of some deep loss, a symbolic death. This was my story. It was very relevant to where I was, and where I was not. There was wisdom, perhaps enlightenment, and joy.

A year later, my husband and I embarked on a six-week pilgrimage. We visited the holy city of Jerusalem. A holy city for Jews, Christians, and Muslims. Tears continually streamed from a reservoir deep within me. My face was awash with tears of joy, some sadness, but brimming with love. The limestone colour, washed from tears, from blood, was breathtaking. The sunset, a golden hue, washed the country with warmth. We met many New York Jews on a pilgrimage to the city. I helped a woman with her dreams. It was a powerful sharing experience.

MY ANALYSIS

Travelling into the Underworld was going deep into the unconscious. The Underworld, mythologically and metaphorically, was dark, mysterious, and elusive. These stories and their accompanying imagery, like dreams, provided relief and understanding to internal disharmony or conflict, and with this came self-knowledge.

In classical mythology, Persephone was the first living visitor to the Underworld. She was the daughter of Demeter, the goddess of agriculture and fertility. She was a virgin and an innocent maiden. Hades, the god and ruler of the Underworld, wanted Persephone, so he abducted her. The Underworld was known as the World of the Dead.

There are similarities to the myth in the dream. As a mother, I had to go into the Underworld to say goodbye, to fully feel the grief of no longer having my own breasts. Even though I was past being able to feed my babies, there was sadness in coming to the acceptance of this poignant loss. I needed to go past the gatekeeper. I was going deep into the land of the dead. Something had to die. My way of life had to die.

I was with my girlfriend, a part of the feminine that had to die. I gave up the bikini, as the youthful erotic had to be let go. I was to welcome a new kind of feminine. The colourful, hippy-skirted, free feminine.

Neil, the natural therapist (as are all hairdressers), was to wed. It was Buddha who took the wedding veil, the feminine. There was a spiritual, profound depth as they entered a soul marriage. This hadn't come out of a pilgrimage. Neil came to my house and cut off my ponytail and shaved my head before I commenced chemotherapy. We shared much together over the years, secrets, sadness, and mostly joy. The paradox was that it was Buddha who was enlightened.

There was a part of me that had to stay and dwell in the depths. I had to make this journey. I was now back at the same level and had become fully human. Here I was in the dream, and now, sharing the fruit of it with others. I was taking in the fragrant blue wisteria. As in the Garden of Eden, it blossomed spiritually for me.

To move on, grieving and feeling the loss was required. Suffering to transform came from within. It was the doorway to physical, emotional, and spiritual healing and transformation. I had undertaken the journey. The feminine blossomed within as I wore my skirt of the feminine as I visited the Mount of Olives in Jerusalem.

The Tarot Card

I chose the card The Lovers, an upright card from the Major Arcana. This card is number six, a number symbolic of love, harmony, and balance. Love is our being, our essence. It is experienced through relationships, with others, with ourselves, and with our internal God. I have found in life that the source of true fulfilment lies within, in our soul.

I looked up to see the angel wings of The Beloved. A triangle. The couple are human figures who seek communion not only with their fellow man but with a higher power. This source offers wisdom, a reminder of something much greater than myself. The Garden of Eden. Adam and Eve. The two trees: the tree of life, and the tree of knowledge of good and evil. The beginning of original sin. The appearance of the serpent. The eating of the forbidden fruit from the tree of knowledge. There was a tension here of conflicting desires. The card has many levels.

I looked at the couple and imagined a story about them. He looked so young and tender; she so fertile and nourishing. Were they Adam and Eve? Were they at a crossroads? The lover must always free himself and his youthful ego to find a new relationship and harmony within, to connect with his emotional and spiritual self. He was the hero on his journey. But what interpretation was I to take from this card?

I couldn't have the lover any longer. The lover I have is the spiritual union with the beloved within. I was also being prompted about my internal balance of the duality of masculine and feminine. Beautifully, I received another message from my glorious husband as to how healthy and happy we were in our relationship.

DREAM 8: Transformation and a New Beginning

I had a mammogram of my other breast. There were some potentially pre-carcinogenic changes in the pathology. I was to have more surgery. I knew in my heart this was for the best. But before taking this next step, my husband and I took a cruise through the Red Sea that finished in Rome to celebrate the end of twelve months of chemotherapy.

Finally, I did not feel like a cancer patient. My hair was growing. My hairdresser and I decided to bleach it blonde. It was new and exciting. I had eyelashes and some eyebrows! New growth, new beginnings, were truly joyful. I was conscious of new growth around me in nature and within myself. I was gaining strength physically, emotionally, and spiritually.

Jerusalem once again filled my reservoir, providing food and nourishment for my soul. I left a powerful letter tucked into the solid Wailing Wall made of thick cream stone in the old city. I also delivered one for a particular long-term client. It was a special place for prayer and worship. The experience of being in this country was profound. I returned home to have my mastectomy and reconstruction.

The night before surgery, I had this dream.

> *I am in a foreign country that is unfamiliar. It is uninhabitable and non-fertile. The colour is like that in Israel, the colour of limestone.*
>
> *There is a valley, and I look way down. The rockface is a rich orange and brown, like the Kimberley landscape. I am surprised. It is like looking into an abyss.*
>
> *My friend John is standing next to me. He gives me a gift. It is an envelope, a certain piece of land. I tell him I'm fine. I don't need it as I have everything I require in my life. He insists.*

We look around, and we are in my granny's backyard. Green and fertile with poppies, gerberas, all the flowers she grew are in bloom. Her large conch shells hold blue water that supports floating poppy cups, the seed pods from the poppy seeds. We floated them as children. A place for creative play for the child's spirit. There is the strong sense that my granny is about.

I felt joyful and peaceful at being given such a beautiful gift.

This dream reassured me as I was on the trolley going to the operating theatre. All would be fine. I visualised the garden of so much happiness, harmony, and change. I felt the love from my life with my family, especially my granny, my granny who was strongly connected to Mother Earth as she paddled around it in her wide bare feet, her garden always fertile as she tended it with care and joy. Being in nature helped me heal. I had the blue sky in my eyes. The cycle of life was always present, in every breathing moment. I just needed to look around me, outside of me, and listen to the humming of sleepy bees and happiness, the chirping of birds. I was being given another intergenerational gift from the feminine.

All did go well, and my recovery was on track and uneventful. Chemotherapy was completed, surgery was completed, and I was getting stronger in every way.

MY ANALYSIS

The dreamscape once again held the opposites, the infertile desert and unknown land transforming to the fertile and the known, just as in my first dream. I had never experienced fear like this. During this time, I had attempted to overcome my anxiety around dying, which was very much like looking into an abyss. It was unknown; it was the unknowable. The existential realities of death seemed without much hope, yet this came with an unwanted, unexpected gift. I was gifted an envelope, an envelope of fertile land. John, my animus figure, had suffered. He was the positive masculine. A man who was well-acquainted with grief in his life.

The land at first appeared barren. It held the ancient, the eternal rocks that got worn down too. They represented the divine, the ancient days. There was Father God in the rocks offered by the Mother Goddess. The garden was fertile, blooming, and resplendent with love and new growth. Persephone's fragrant blossoms. A good prognosis. My internal grandmother was offering love, wisdom, and comfort. My granny was the great keeper of the earth, and through our lineage, I was the inheritor of this image and of this love. Life was about personal and spiritual growth, finding meaningful ways to connect within, with others and to the world around us. Offering kindness to the self, others, and Mother Earth. Life had been the ultimate teacher. This experience had taught me so much. All these gifts I have received by being present and having an open heart.

The Tarot Card

I chose The Empress. Number three in the Major Arcana. Once again, number three was presented. This time, it was the maternal energy of the glorious Mother Goddess. The Empress. She symbolised creation, creativity, and harvest abundance. She offered love of self and others. She was the keeper of the earth and sky. I was thrilled to see her again, as she offered growth, abundance, and beauty. The ripe yellow wheat in the foreground and the bright yellow sun-filled sky, symbolic of hope. She wore a crown of stars as she sat regally on her red velvet throne.

The Empress symbolises the feminine Mother Earth/God that made the world blossom and bloom in full flower, no longer just buds with potential. She embodies the feminine principle: formation, preservation, nourishment, and transformation. She sits in a lush fertile and creative garden of rich vegetation. This card was reassuring. It offered me nurturing, protection, containment, security, and reassurance that my world would go on. The Empress invited me to embrace the beauty of life and cultivate a sense of harmony and balance in all aspects of my being.

DREAM 9: Looking Straight Ahead. A Guide for the Future

THE FINAL DREAM

I am travelling with my mother-in-law, Joan. We are getting ready. A woman has a collection of long, hand-knitted jumpers. Would I like one? Gosh, they would keep me warm. But I don't think I will have room. Joan said I won't need one where we're going. There is a cream one I like, but we three women smile together as I say I will take it another time. I pack my small suitcase as we are going on a journey to see this sacred site I've been searching for. It is high on a mountain.

I am in an open-top funicular slow train with a group of children. It is one seat wide, and I am in the front seat. On the rockface, we see deep carvings and painted frescos all the way to the top. It is so beautiful. I reach out and feel its coolness. Eventually, we arrive at our destination. It is a spiritual temple or church. I know it is exactly what I have been searching for.

There we see the wise man, the spiritual leader. The spiritual man is dressed in white robes, and with him is a large, dark brown, muscular labrador dog. The dog appears gentle and is untethered, as he seems to live there on the mountain. His coat is shiny. The dog is slowly going towards the edge of the mountain. I call for the dog to come back! The terrain is dangerous. He still goes close to the edge, and as he effortlessly starts to ease himself over, the wise man grabs the dog's hind legs and supports him. I grab his hand and hold onto the railing with my other hand, and together, we ease the dog back to safety. I feel the strength and tension in my body and between us, all the while strongly aware as to how connected we all are. Happy and relieved that the dog is safe, I let go. We are smiling.

I turn and notice the children are afraid. I reassure them. Everything is okay. We return in the train carriages, and on the journey down the mountainside, I clearly say to them: 'Don't look back, and don't look down. Look straight ahead, and you will be fine.'

They are reassured and no longer vulnerable or anxious. I am feeling compassion and courage. These feelings happily co-exist. The journey is over, and we are all fine after the experience. I feel as if I have found that which I had been searching for.

I woke from this epic dream and felt secure and unafraid. It had been a long journey. I had faced the edge, the edge of the world, the edge of the abyss, and the edge of the unknown.

I had found strength from the spiritual aspect within and frequently found myself in silent prayer or in touch with my God. My mantra was one of gratitude every three weeks as I entered the chemo room for one year. 'Thank you. I thank you with love, kindness, and gratitude. I give this to my heart, my body, and to others.' I was also able to calm and settle my inner child with these words.

Much beauty was revealed along the way of this journey, carved deep within the walls of life and psyche. This was a dream on which I occasionally chose to meditate and engage in creative visualisation to assist in the healing process of my body and soul. The dream's use of imagery, story, and language assisted me to gain emotional wisdom and understanding of my internal and external world. The dream also gave me a glimpse of life's basic lesson plan: 'To not look back, or down, but to look straight ahead, and all will be fine.'

MY ANALYSIS

This long journey was showing me how I have had to leave the old behind me. I was well-equipped for the journey ahead. The green and fertile and the barren had been perfectly poised in the fresco of dreams leading to this final dream, providing me with a map. There was much wisdom from the feminine lineage, of which I was the inheritor. My lovely mother-in-law, Joan, was with me on the final leg of my journey, another link in the inter-generational feminine, my granny being the great keeper of Mother Earth.

Elijah learned that God was not in the wind, the earthquake, or the fire on Mt Horeb, but in the silence. I had been searching for the God within, the silence within.

Being on the funicular railway train, as in my cancer journey, was like being on a rollercoaster ride. There I touched and felt the depth of the eternal rockface of the mountain. On the mountaintop, I met the dog that dwells there and could go over the edge at any time. When I was there, it inched its way over the edge. While pulling his body back to safety, I had an encounter with the divine. I had looked into the face of death. All the parts of me pulled together to safety and looked to eternity. I had calmed the little children. I can calm others, as I do in my work as a therapist. I had settled the child within. I now have a mantra that is soothing. I have a dream that I can revisit and re-use to settle.

During my journey, I had noticed the pattern of the dog or animal imagery being present. In this dream, the dog was brown and muscular. It felt like the dog represented my body. The dog also symbolised instinct and intuition, and often went close to the edge, even towards death, as it had been a quality that was undervalued and even repressed. I was now conscious of my intuitive capacity, and by paying attention, I would do and be as the dream instructed, and I would be fine.

My search for meaning gave my life another positive aspect. The spiritual had helped pull me back. Back from the edge. Back towards life. The dream even provided a clear blueprint for a meaningful life, a guide for my future. I was acutely aware of how connected we are to one another and also to the spiritual, to the God within, and how we need each other to survive, to pull together. I had made the pilgrimage to the top. I had travelled from the depths to the heights.

The Tarot Card

Randomly, I chose The World, number twenty-one of the Major Arcana. This card signifies freedom, wisdom, independence, and creativity. Tears washed my face with joy as I held this joyful and meaningful image. This card assured me I had come full circle. I started out on a long journey I didn't choose to take. A journey I had consciously embraced. This card is all about completion and freedom. The sky is blue. With this freedom came a change in perspective. I understood there was no end to the journey.

Looking at the card, I realise the dancing figure in the centre is the feminine. She is free. Free to dance, while still being contained. She holds the two wands, two poles of the opposites: masculine and feminine, positive, and negative, consciousness and unconsciousness, light and dark, heaven and earth. The energy in the card is dynamic, as represented by the flowing scarf, an ever-present moving spirit and the ever-present feminine. There are the four elements, the images of the four evangelists—the lion for St Mark, the ox for St Luke, the human head for St Matthew, and the eagle for St John—to square the circle as she is embraced by the tightly woven wreath of being human. This wreath contained and protected her newly emerged self. She was dancing with joy. I was dancing with joy.

The cycle had ended, and a new beginning awaited. I had survived. I was now free to enjoy the prospect of a new chapter. I had the power and wisdom to understand the wholeness of the world. I had completed one of the journeys. The card also shows there is no ending. Now I had experienced the extraordinary, and it was there I found solitude. Today, my life is happily ordinary, and I am filled with gratitude.

The Winners Group

When I started chemotherapy, I was invited to join a small group of women with whom to share the cancer experience. It was affirming how having cancer immediately enabled us to form a strong bond. The group was known as 'the group no one wants to join', but we renamed it the 'Winners Group'. We were, and still are, certainly winners. This group is part of our healing experience.

Together, we share. We share food, our stories, our experiences, our feelings, our remedies, helpful advice or suggestions, our ideas. We offer our trust. Often, we share our fears. These we mostly could not share with others. It is a place to listen, to speak freely, truthfully, and be heard. We all understand. We offer comfort, an unconditional unspoken love and kindness. We tell our stories without fear of being judged, criticised, or abandoned. We give; we receive. We are there for each other through life and death. We are not afraid. We met each other at the beginning of our cancer journey. We also go to the funerals of those of us who have passed, but these beautiful women live on in our hearts. We emerge from each challenge presented to our body and spirit along the way. Together, we suffer, sometimes cry. Together, we laugh. Suffering can be a doorway to transformation. Together, we heal. We know we are not alone at a time when we are most vulnerable to feelings of isolation, as we engage at a deep and meaningful level.

JOSEPHINE

Josephine, a member of the Winners Group, provided the following. This encapsulates the attitude of the whole group and resonates with my own experience. 'At forty-seven, I didn't really believe the lump in my breast would be cancer, but sure enough, it was. All the usual treatments left me tired and weak, but eventually, I was up and running back into life again.' The Winners Group was and is a wonderful group of women all facing tremendous hurdles. Somehow all walls were broken down between us, and everything was on the table to talk, laugh, and cry over. These times were precious and healing and gave great insights into other people's struggles, grace, and humility. Though we lost some beautiful people, their spirits carry on and show us how to be grateful for the lives we have.

These are some of the blessings that arose from my cancer challenge. I learnt to embrace some things and let others go.

I learned to:

- Embrace my family and friends and let go of the ones who bring me down.
- Embrace going with the flow and let go of trying to be in control.
- Embrace my true self and let go of the judgement of others.
- Embrace nature and let go of making my home look too perfect.
- Embrace what is happening here and now and let go of what has gone before.

During chemotherapy, one day when I was in my living room, I could strongly feel the presence of my mum who died in 1989 at the age of fifty-six. She seemed to be asking me to go with her, but I couldn't commit. My brother rang not long after to see how I was, and I started to cry for the first time since it had all begun because, although I missed my mum so much, I wasn't ready to go, and I felt like I was letting her down. However, life itself was calling me.

MELISSA

Melissa, who was a member of the Winners Group, shared an insight into her lived experience with breast cancer. Though not a dream, her experience in the guided meditation was equivalent. 'I was in the chapel with the school chaplain, who used to instruct a group of interested mothers in meditation classes. We were all quietly sitting in a group following our breath. In this guided meditation, he took us through many terrains before arriving at a small running stream. Following his gentle voice, my imagination was stirred. On the other side of the stream, the terrain was quite barren except for a few bushes, about man-height, and rather prickly looking, like you would find in a desert. There stood a man in the loose robes often depicted in biblical stories.

'I quickly realised this was my father, who had died when I was twenty-four and he was fifty-six. He was holding out his hand to me as if to help me across the stream to join him. I was terribly upset because I was not ready to die and couldn't understand why he wanted me to go so early. I was fifty at the time. This image was very vivid. Six months later, I shopped for some new clothes, and as I was hanging them in my wardrobe, a very clear thought went through my mind asking, "Why are you buying new clothes when you know you have breast cancer?" It was like a thunderbolt holding me to the earth.

'The first week of December, the same year, I discovered a lump in my breast, my GP sent me off for tests and a biopsy. He rang me to say he wanted to see me first thing the next morning. I just knew.

My husband said, 'Let's go out for a coffee at a coffee shop close to the beach.' As I walked in, I noticed my meditation teacher sitting at a table all by himself in the middle of the café. My memory has the sun shining in on him, illuminating him. This was interesting as I hadn't seen him for about nine months, as he had left the school.

'I walked up to him to say hello, and when he asked how I was, I explained. We were both taken aback by this incident as he had only just become free of all obligations and had no commitments. I believe I was sent to him for guidance. He was wonderful, and he did some spiritual healing on me. This I know worked because when they removed all my lymph nodes from under my left arm, they were all negative, which was a very surprising outcome, as I had two lumps, one which had already broken free as it was invasive, and a large pre-cancerous area. I felt that it was a miracle. When he did the healing, he said there were lots of angels helping him. I find it hard to believe this but impossible to ignore, and it had the best possible outcome.'

Maybe the first part was a creative visualisation and the rest was just unexplainable serendipity.

7

Dream Motifs

A LITTLE HISTORY OF DREAMS

In the historic library at Nineveh in Babylonia, there have been references found on clay tablets regarding dream theory and the meaning of certain dreams. These were found in the library of the Assyrian king Ashurbanipal, who reigned between 669 and 626 BCE. It is thought that Ashurbanipal's dream book was used by the Roman soothsayer Artemi Dorus (circa 140 CE).

In early history, the Egyptians built temples known as 'Serapeum' (named after Serapis, the god of dreams) and practised dream 'incubation'. The high priest and priestess prepared with the ritual of meditation and prayer on entering their sleep chambers. They did this to receive divine guidance and inspiration through their dreams. The Egyptians, Greeks, and Romans all believed dreams had healing powers.

In biblical times, dreams were thought of as divine messages. In the Bible, there are twenty-one dreams recorded. These dreams are believed to be a message from God. Mohammed, the Prophet said, 'Now Allah has created the dream not only as a means of guidance and instruction. I refer to the dream, but he has made it a window to the World of the Unseen.'

For centuries, indigenous tribes around the world relied on

internal guidance. Where to hunt and sleep, for example. The Naskapi people of North Canada developed a relationship with the Great Spirit, which they believed gave them insightful dreams. They created rituals and art based on their dreams, which gave the people an ability to find their way in life, in their inner world, and in the outer world in nature, particularly the hunt. As a people, they were obliged to follow their dream instructions. The Inuit Indians believed we dream when asleep as that is when our soul would go wandering. The dream is thus referred to as the soul's journey.

The Indigenous Australians from Arnhem Land known as the Yolngu people believed the '*mali*' or soul or shadow part of the dreamer leaves the physical body during the dream and travels to actual places in the spiritual and physical world. The transcultural psychiatrist John Cawte explained how the *mali* could be dreaming outside the body, so the dreamer is to awaken slowly, giving the *mali* time to return to the body. Indigenous legends, which are rich in symbolism, talk of the creation of life as the Dreaming or Dreamtime. These legends describe how the power of the great spirits emerging from the earth, sky, and sea took on mostly animal forms. Each individual has their own Dreamtime forebear, linked to a certain creature.

DIFFERENT TYPES OF DREAMS

MYTHS

Dreams may be mythological. Our descent when we dream takes us below our consciousness into what is known in mythology as the Underworld, a place we journey to and from. In classic Greek myths, the stories of Theseus and Orpheus, as well as the long journey of Odysseus, all embody the theme of descent. Myths give voice to the truths of our unconscious selves, so they reveal rather than hide these essential underlying truths.

Dream Motifs

The appearance of myth in a dream evokes emotions that are usually immediate. The mythical dream story manages to convey richness and an ease in translation we can easily feel without the need for it to be explained. Myths can teach us the values we need to live our lives by and can provide a framework for these skills.

Our dreams introduce us to mythological figures and modern legends who play out in dreaming, like superheroes Superman, Robin Hood, and Wonder Woman. They all pursue the hero's journey and appear in our dreams to help the dreamer on their own journey. The hero myth is where the hero goes within to bring back treasure to share with his tribe, community, and the world. He is required to undergo battles, hardship, and trials, face and slay the dragon, and then attain the treasure. It is a symbolic death and rebirth experience, a pattern of growth and transformation.

Our work as therapists is to accompany our clients on archetypal journeys into the underworld and bring them back. We cross rivers; we visit dream landscapes, biblical, mythological, surreal. We journey into the unconscious and seek to discover fragments of the psyche, process them, and bring them to consciousness, contributing to a sense of wholeness.

NIGHTMARES

All children experience nightmares, and they often occur at times of fear and anxiety and when situations or emotions are incomprehensible to them. All the feelings associated with the nightmare are given a vehicle of release. Nightmares for us all are nearly pure emotion, releasing the tension that has built up in the unconscious. There is a need to feel these powerful emotions more than we need to understand the story. We may also experience these emotions physically while dreaming the nightmare and bring these feelings and the images that terrify the dreamer into awareness. It is as if the unconscious wants to direct the dreamer into expanding their consciousness.

The dreamer is having to face a painful unknown aspect about themselves in a nightmare. They often serve as a red flag signalling an unresolved problem or issue and the associated feelings that promptly need attending to. There is often a fear needing to be faced and brought into consciousness, into waking life. This fear is possibly related to facing a painful, perhaps unknown aspect of themselves.

We have nightmares to shock us out of a deep unconscious behaviour or situation. We are unaware and need to become conscious, so our unconscious attempts to rouse us, saying, 'Wake up and pay attention!' It is important the dreamer deals with this. The nightmare will keep recurring until it is integrated into awareness.

The dream story expressed in a nightmare is like watching and experiencing a horror story. The nightmare is physically and emotionally terrifying, as the dreamer experiences fear, panic, and anxiety. Nightmare images are vampires, ghosts, giants, or monsters. The dreamer feels like they have been visited by an evil spirit. The dreamer often wakes before the dream is over.

The dreamer may go on to experience night terrors. They will experience a bodily response to the dream. Their heart rate increases as does their breathing and blood pressure. They may experience a night-time psychosis, hallucinations and disorientation, and be delusional. The dreamer may scream, yell, walk, and experience an overwhelming panic, a little like a magnified panic attack. Night terrors may be a sign of an undiagnosed anxiety disorder. In adults, this may be triggered by stress, alcohol, fever, or insomnia. It may also be a symptom of PTSD. It is as if there is no relief or release in the dreamer's waking life. Perhaps something is unbearable, something too painful to be registered.

The dreamer may also have the terrifying experience of sleep paralysis. The physical body feels trapped and is unable to move. This is a very frightening sensation. The brain is slow to release the body but has an awareness the body is in lockdown.

It can be helpful to work on a resolution of the nightmare so it may be completed and resolved. This helps to settle the anxiety that travels with the nightmare.

It is the emotions that I am really interested in while working with a nightmare. The images and the story are secondary to the raw emotions that are needing to be processed. When worked with therapeutically, the feelings that are released during the nightmare can correct a situation in the dreamer's living world.

The nightmare will reoccur until the dreamer has become aware and until the message has been received. If we acknowledge the issue and take action to resolve it, the psyche has done her work. If we don't get the meaning of the nightmare, the psyche will resend the dream in a different story or form. The effect of a nightmare or a 'bad dream' can be the catalyst for change. A correction or change in conscious attitude is the result of the wake-up call. If a client has a nightmare the night before our session, this is a very important signal to me, and I need to hold this in my mind.

LUCID DREAMS

Sometimes, we are aware that we are dreaming during the act of dreaming. This lucid dream state can be a magical and freeing experience. The rational part of our brain, the pre-frontal cortex, is active, and it feels like the mind is expanding as we fall or climb into this lucid state. As there is no distraction from the physical body, the lucid dreamer just dissolves into a deep state of being. Some dreamers experience lucid dreams when they have a daytime nap.

One can even manipulate the dream story in this lucid dream state. The dreamer can achieve the impossible, like flying, becoming invisible, or experiencing time travel. Through practising deep meditation, one can enter this hypnogogic state and discover creative solutions to problems or issues. One can gain control in the dream, be curious, and even ask questions. In normal REM sleep and dreaming, this is not the case.

Lucid dreams can be somewhat like a pleasurable sexual dream, with a heightened sense of awareness. The dream can be filled with excitement, vivid colours, and dream objects or symbols that are bright and luminous. There is a sense that our conscious mind is merged with our unconscious mind. Recalling a lucid dream makes it easier to analyse.

Firstly, ask yourself if you are dreaming. The dreamer can then ask what the dream is trying to convey. It has an intensity about it, a freshness. There is an awareness not dissimilar to being awake and conscious. This may come and go during the dream, so while experiencing awareness is a great time to be active and take control of the dream. You can change the narrative. If the dream is upsetting or unpleasant, this is the time to dive in and change the ending.

I had a client who was engaging in self-destructive behaviours. These became a very confronting part of her dreams. She managed to experience lucid dreaming and attempted to change her acting out of these stories while immersed in the dream. She started by waking herself up, washing her hands, and re-entering the same dream. Lucid dreaming helped her confront the issue of harming herself and allowed her to feel her emotions physically and emotionally. Journaling about your lucid dreaming experience will connect you to your dreaming mind.

Once in a lucid dream, I felt like a young child playfully sliding down a rabbit hole. I had to leave the dream to go to the bathroom, so on my return, I re-entered the dream by visualising going back down the rabbit hole again. It was just as magical. The next day, I booked myself into a float tank and meditated on the dream while floating in the dark, quiet, contained space. I attained a sense of oneness and an inner and outer experience of peace, but I was not able to fall into a dream state. It was a meditative hypnogogic state.

SEXUAL DREAMS

Sexual dreams may indicate the beginning of a transformative process in the unconscious. This is where ideas are conceived, nurtured, and finally birthed when fully formed. It is not uncommon to experience an orgasm while enjoying a sexual dream. The dream may be an erotic experience. It may coincide with dreaming of an oceanic wave. It is best to not judge or analyse it too deeply. Just accept it as pleasure.

We can think of a sexual dream expressing the desire to connect with a part of the self not yet fully conscious in the pursuit of wholeness. There may be a desire to merge with another, then getting lost in that merging, losing definition as an individual. There is a natural attraction and desire for merging and union with another. This leads to a feeling of wholeness, a psychological completion. It also may be showing the opposite, for example, towards an attraction that hinders psychological development, wholeness, or a genuine relationship or relatedness. It may indicate a lack of intimate connection.

The dream may raise an issue that is needing to be dealt with. An attraction to another, being unfaithful to something, or someone who is unavailable may lead the dreamer to explore a change within, or perhaps in their lived world. This is the psyche's way of creating a connection between the inner masculine and feminine to create balance. The dream may be accompanied by a feeling of longing and loneliness. Or the sexual dream may speak to the dreamer's actual waking sexual life, sex being a natural quality, a natural urge.

Teenage boys quite often experience wet dreams, or nocturnal emissions. They can evoke shame in the dreamer as they are unexpected and unexplainable. They may or may not be in response to an erotic dream. Wet dreams are not usually associated with masturbation, but if so, this is often the young man's way of self-soothing. I recall a young adolescent telling me his wet dreams were about either his mother or his older sister. This gave him mixed feelings of being potent and even manly while being sexual in the dream, yet he was left with a feeling of being bad, ashamed, and powerless. The fact that he was unable to direct his feelings and control these bodily emissions left him having to be secretive. He would try to hide his pyjamas, sheets, or pants, and his associated memories of bed-wetting as a small child left him confused, ashamed, and depressed. Sharing with me proved freeing.

Females also can experience a wet dream, though the emission is miniscule compared to that of the male. Biologically, wet dreams are developmentally normal. It is important that parents talk openly about these dreams with their teenagers so it is normalised and not seen as an imperfection or an issue of shame for the dreamer. Dreams of masturbation may occur. This is about self-arousal, literally. Maybe the capacity to be self-loving is evident or missing.

Sadistic sexual dreams can show the unconscious need or urge for control, dominance, or assertiveness. There may be pleasure by the psyche of 'fucking over' another or a part of the self. Masochistic images may be a call for awareness in a relationship. There may be an unconscious glorification of being in the position of a victim. There is no sense of being free or able to be assertive. Sexual perversions are passionate attempts to connect with the dream image. Vampirism depicts the thirst for 'lifeblood'. The dreamer may be sucking the life drive out of another, or the self. They have the capacity to drain the vitality of another. Fetish dreams or voyeurism direct one to an over-involvement or over-fascination in a certain object or body part, for example, a shoe, a standpoint, or panties that hide feminine secret parts.

Oral sex dreams often depict the desire for phallic energy. Body openings, mostly the mouth or vagina, eyes, nose, and ears are common dream images. They are the entry point for the external world. In the sexual act in a dream, it is interesting to note:

- Is this an act of making love?
- Does the act feel loving and intimate?
- Is there a feeling of longing?
- Is there a desire to merge with another?
- Do you know the person you are being sexual with?
- Is the person of the same or opposite gender?

- Are you exposed while having sex?
- Who is on top? Who is dominant?
- Is there violence, perhaps even rape?
- What is going on in your life?

Look for any hidden inhibitions, desires, or erotic defenses. Can you link the dream to a real-life situation? Can you find a bridge with the emotion you are feeling in the dream? Is there a solution?

To be raped feels passive, defenseless. Dreams of rape are very disturbing, whether in the role of victim or aggressor. The dream usually wakes the dreamer as it is very often graphic and confronting. It may be a nightmare, saying, 'Do pay attention.' Rape is a power struggle. It may be in the workplace or in a relationship. Being controlled, pushed around, bullied, volatile behaviour, criticism, violent outbursts, all perceived as attacking or being attacked. The dreamer is powerless. Control is being given to another.

The dreamer may be being confronted by a new unknown part of herself, for which she is unfamiliar and unaccepting. It feels wrong, strange even. It may take a rape to bring about a death of a part of the dreamer. As Marie-Louise von Franz said, 'Constantly in dreams, parts of our personalities undergo deaths and births.'

Collectively, women may feel raped by hostile men of having their own emotions. This dream usually points to a negative relationship with the feminine. In my work, I have not heard a dream of a female raping a male. The dream is urging the dreamer to confront his relationship with the feminine, to confront the dreamer's internal and the external feminine relationships. These relationships need to be positive, as the feminine will enhance feelings and emotions, as opposed to the out-of-balance masculine who is acting aggressively. He is turning this aggression inwards towards himself, causing pain. He is 'doing violence' to himself, though it is directed onto another in the dream story. The dreamer is being asked to be respectful as opposed to being aggressive.

Or assertive rather than aggressive. If the dreamer is the victim in the rape, then her (or perhaps his) inner world is also out of balance.

It is good to ask:

- Are you afraid of being in control and assertive?
- Or are you unaware of taking away another's freedom of choice?
- Is this happening in your love relationship?
- Are you being 'screwed over' in life?
- How are your emotional and physical boundaries?
- Is the perpetrator familiar to you?
- Does this person represent a part of you that is causing harm?
- Are you in the victim position and thus feeling powerless?
- How old are you in the dream?

It takes a lot of energy to keep a part of the self unknown and repressed. Eventually, it will erupt in a dream or nightmare, and if the part is not integrated, it may become an overwhelming emotion. It may feel like an assault. Often a dreamer is afraid that he may be about to enact an actual rape, which, of course, in his waking life, he would never do. It is not uncommon for women to dream of same-sex sexual interaction. These dreams are often very pleasurable as the feminine is longing for connection. Female sex is less intrusive or invasive than having sex with a male. This may be a fantasy that the dreamer is afraid to act out in life. Or it may speak to the dreamer's actual waking sexual life or indicate a lack of intimate connection.

ANXIETY DREAMS

Anxiety dreams are common dreams, and often present as a nightmare. The nightmare is often short and sharp, getting directly to the point. Often the dreamer feels young and childlike in the dream, and these dreams are unsettling as they are always charged with emotion.

Dreaming of being naked is associated with feeling exposed,

embarrassed, and possibly publicly humiliated. These dreams are often set at school or university, indicative of there being a lesson to be learned. The dreamer is being shown there is no boundary or protection in place. This results in an anxiety or vulnerability, usually felt in the body. Another common anxiety dream set at school or university is being unprepared for a test or exam, showing possibly that we are unprepared for what lies ahead. It is time to stay conscious. A fear of social judgement or rejection causes anxiety and indicates insecurities and a fragile sense of self.

We can feel anxiety when we dream of being in a foreign land or around people of a different race. We are being shown that we are in new or unfamiliar territory. The foreigner or stranger that the psyche is presenting to you may be a shadow figure that to date is denied by your conscious self. This person may well be masked or their faces may be hidden. Try to identify the emotions that you're experiencing in the dream. Often the person is so unfamiliar, they speak a foreign language.

A common anxiety dream is of the dreamer trying to run through thick mud and going nowhere. They are 'stuck' in a situation, or a relationship dynamic, unable to move forward. The dreamer may be sinking, drowning, falling, being trapped, or being arrested.

Another anxiety nightmare is being chased by strange or dangerous men or a wild animal. It is good to ask, 'What or who am I running from?' This may be a real situation in your daily life or it may be a shadow part of your self or needs that you are denying exist. When this is identified, it is easier to find that strength from within and stand firm or stand your ground. There is then an acceptance that there is no need to run.

One client would attempt to fly after trying to run away but was unable to take off. This caused even more anxiety as her fight-or-flight response was triggered. Her usual method of dealing with anxiety was to go into flight mode rather than stay and fight. The dream was pointing her in the direction of staying put and dealing in a grounded and effective manner with the situation.

A similar theme is swimming against the tide or trying to keep your head above water and not drown. If you're swimming, this may represent your immersion in your unconscious mind or your emotions. Perhaps there is someone or something that is holding you back? Therefore, you are unable to live to your full potential. You may well be doing this unconsciously to yourself. Or perhaps you are feeling afraid in your daily life. Try to identify who or what situation you are fearful of. Then you can ask for assistance or just deal with it alone.

When working with anxiety, the healthy emotion that is revealed is vulnerability. I am quick to reassure that vulnerability builds connection, whereas anxiety does the opposite; it distances one from connection. Anxiety is infectious as it attaches itself to others. This makes it challenging to remain connected.

TRAUMA

Trauma or violence interrupts our trajectory through life. We are learning to navigate our way in the world, and this interruption immediately alters and destroys our sense of security. It results in feeling insecure and an inability to put our trust in our self and others. Questions are constantly asked. Steps are always taken with caution, hypervigilance, fear, and anxiety.

A secure therapeutic alliance—perhaps incorporating trauma-focused cognitive behaviour therapy (CBT) with a trauma-narrative focus and eye movement desensitisation and reprocessing (EMDR)—is healing, enabling the client to process and manage emotions and relationships. The work also helps the client tolerate traumatic memories, dissociation experiences, and sleep difficulties. Work is also done around triggers that invoke memories of the abuse or trauma. This can only be embarked upon when there is a secure therapeutic alliance, where trust, boundaries, and understanding have been established.

Trauma that to our adult self doesn't seem all that painful can still have a lasting and serious impact on our development. This may come out in anxiety dreams. Nightmares are part of experiencing and processing PTSD or any traumatic or abusive event. This is the psyche's way of processing that which is painful, unbearable, and mostly unspeakable. These are feelings and experiences that can't consciously be contained and metabolised and are then symbolised in the psyche. These memories are fragmented and may be held within the physical body. Trauma disturbs our capacity to relate to self and others.

Severely wounded clients are split from their emotional associations and unable to process symbolic material. The therapist needs to be mindful to refer on to suitably qualified trauma specialists when dream images, for example, have destructive archetypal and chaotic imagery that clearly point to psychopathology in the dreamer.

Melanie Klein studied and identified the process of splitting, a deep-seated human tendency. On experiencing trauma, the ego struggles to organise and deal with this overwhelming capacity to cope. Children are certainly not equipped to process trauma. This can occur as early as pre-verbal development. The immature ego responds to trauma by 'splitting', resulting in the defense of dissociation, a normal reaction to trauma. When trauma reoccurs, young children may unconsciously split off as their habitual response to stress. It can become their 'go-to' place. Splitting, like dissociation, is an effective defense as it puts an end to the actual experiencing of pain, horror, terror, even the threat of death. Clients occasionally call this split-off space their 'safe space' once they have become aware of this happening.

I have noticed that clients who have experienced early trauma have difficulty in identifying their emotions and find it challenging to self-soothe. Of course, when splitting occurs, sensation often ceases. Jungian analyst Donald Kalsched has undertaken much research in this area. It seems there is a tearing of the psychic membrane or skin in early trauma that contains our mind. This leads to a lack of cohesion in the psyche and a splitting as a survival measure. Psychologist Heinz Kohut describes the 'utter chaos and lack of self-cohesion' that may be depicted in dreams. This tearing explains why dreams I have worked on in early trauma or abuse clients have been explained as alien, as having an 'other world' quality.

Psychotherapy helps by providing a contained and boundaried space where it is safe to share feelings, memories, and fears. Dreaming helps with the processing of these experiences. I am always mindful in noticing and sitting with emotions that are present in the dream, emotions that emerge from the dreamwork, and emotions that linger within the client between our sessions. I am also conscious when these emotions linger within my mind.

Creative visualisation can be useful in trauma work. It can help free up the untold story and help free the secret that can't be thought—containing, metabolising, and integrating. This potentially makes life more bearable. This is the step taken after the dream has been explored. It can only occur when the therapeutic relationship is safe; only then can the ending of the trauma dream be reworked. This can then become a newly imagined, rewritten dream story that can be used to soothe when awoken from sleep. Together, we imagine this rewritten dream story. My client will write it, draw it, or memorise it so it becomes the 'go-to' rather than the nightmare, which otherwise is where our memory will take us. It can even become a mantra.

I have had a couple of trauma clients who have had strongly mystical experiences in their dreams. They also have experienced Godlike and angelic visions that are felt to be divine. One of these clients is now a psychic medium who contacts spirits. I recall when he came into my office for the first session, he said my dead grandmother was happily present in the room. (My grandmother had gifted me the money for me to purchase my office, and occasionally I felt her presence.)

MOURNING

Dreams allow us to experience mourning or the loss of another. Our loved ones appear as if alive and real in a visitation dream. These dreams help the dreamer reach acceptance of their loss, though they may be confronting. This usually occurs about six to nine months after a death. It is as if it takes a gestation period to be able to fully let go. Mourning was written about by Freud in his essay *Mourning and Melancholia*.

There are two ways of feeling sad. In mourning, we are aware that we are suffering loss. We constantly think of the lost person, and life seems pointless. Eventually, this feeling passes. Life is still worthwhile. Melancholia is much more difficult. It is also a sadness, but we are not actually conscious of what we have lost. A little like the dream of Harold in Part 3. The person suffering can feel numb and depressed. Helpless, hopeless, and without purpose. Dreams magnify this state. Sometimes, there is a hidden anger or rage that comes out in the dream, allowing a stage of grief to come to consciousness. This is healing. We work to find the forgotten past events and reunite them with the sadness.

DEATH

Life is a constant symbolic death and rebirth of the personality. The death of dream figures rarely refers to an actual physical death, though when we have death dreams, we wake up believing we may soon be going to face a literal death. These dreams are remembered with anxiety and fear as we feel sure this is a real indicator that we're approaching death. Such dreams occur during times of transformation. I recall a client once dreaming of the death of the baby she was holding in her arms. It was a long and troubling dream in which the dead baby gradually turned into a kitten! The cat is the archetype of the feminine. This was rather exciting as this woman was feeling disconnected from her nurturing and intuitive self.

Dreaming of a death is about endings, allowing new beginnings, letting go, and renewal. It is said as soon as we stop growing, we start dying. Life and death happen within us. Death is a dream symbol that holds our attention and leads us to awareness. Perhaps we haven't reached our potential. Here there is a message the psyche needs to impart. It can shock us into fully living our lives. There may even be murder involved in the dream. There may also be a fantasy of death due to feelings of being alone or being a victim isolated without support.

A death dream may also represent the end of a relationship, or a situation that no longer has life in it, thus, being disconnected from the life drive and attracted by the death drive. This is a pull shown and often felt in a dream towards a death. Dreaming of death may reflect a fear of loss, abandonment, or separation from family. This often occurs at times of feeling vulnerable or afraid.

When approaching physical death, we may dream of a journey or a marriage. Usually, these dreams are not so concerned with the physical body; rather, they are about the process of individuation. They also show how the body is becoming less grounded. At the time approaching death, the dream helps the dreamer come to terms with their mortality and offers comfort, reassurance, and inner peace.

Some Symbols and Images that Arise from the Unconscious

All dream symbols have specific relevance and associations to the dreamer, but many carry universal meaning. They contain a greater meaning than we know. I have identified and commented below on a few common symbols that appear in dreams.

The Greek word for dreams is *'oneiros'*, which means 'image'. Dreams use symbols rather than language. These often-incongruent images evoke an emotion or feeling as opposed to a thought. Only the dreamer has an inner understanding of the meaning of these symbols. They are personal to the dreamer. Dream symbols are metaphorical rather than literal. A metaphor is the 'application of a name or descriptive term to an object to which it is not literally applicable'. As with every symbol or metaphor, it is the dreamer's associations that direct us to the answer.

We then go back to the dream and the associations. The process of teasing out and exploring the dreamer's associations with the symbol is the work of the therapist. This can provide the basis on which the therapist and the dreamer can work together.

The dream symbol embodies a meaning that has yet to be discovered and understood by both the client and the therapist. The symbol is powerful as it stirs a response from our conscious self. Then an understanding comes as we link the symbol with meaning. The meaning comes alive when there is a relationship with the symbol. This then becomes a thought, and joyfully it is no longer an unconscious symbol. This brings what the symbol represents to consciousness.

Not all dreams require symbol interpretation. Any interpretation comes from the dreamer's own thoughts and feelings. I find it is important to keep going back to the dream images and associated feelings and to the dreamer's relationship with these symbols. As a therapist, I can be drawn into creating a context to place the dream symbol into, with a desire to make meaning. This is often best held rather than shared. It is the work of therapy to enable the dreamer to bridge and link this symbol. The dream symbols are the building blocks leading to the core of the self as well as the spiritual self. They are the way into the inner world.

HOUSES

Houses commonly appear in our dreams as images of the psyche. The house symbolises the dreamer. They have many similarities to our self, with doors to enter and exit, windows to see out of, a front and a rear. The house may represent the body of the dreamer or different levels of the mind. For Jung, building a house was a symbol of building a self. In dreams, houses may represent what you have created for yourself, your values, what you are 'at home' with, or a place to feel you can be yourself. Feelings associated by the dreamer are important.

Doors appear in dreams in different forms. They may be immovable or stuck, locked with or without a key, indicating that the dreamer may be open or closed or ready for self-exploration. The door and the threshold are symbols of a passage into our own interiors. The door may be heavy or prison-like with bars. It may be falling off its hinges or unhinged. A door is a barrier to what lies outside the self, outside the house. It is also a barrier to what lies within the self, inside the house.

It is common to hear in therapy of the dreamer anxiously searching for the key to the door. There may be a conscious and unconscious ambivalence of being exposed or revealed. If the key is found, then we have access to the dreamer's inner world, and we can see all the fears and fantasies that may cause disruption or even chaos to the conscious view of who we think we are. The dreamer wants to find the key, yet consciously, they may be sabotaging it being revealed to them.

The bedroom is an intimate room. It houses our intimate, private life. It is no place for intruders. A child's bedroom is often associated with feeling safe and snug. Occasionally, this can be a room for punishment, time-out, perhaps abuse.

Windows are important as they offer the opportunity for us to see out or for others to see in. Are we receptive to the outside world and the amount of light we let into this world? Do we have shutters as defenses on the window to block this view in or out?

To dream of altering, changing, or raising the roof of a house may indicate a raising of one's expectations. The roof offers protection and security. Notice the condition of the roof in the dream.

If the dream is set in a church or temple, the roof may represent the dome of heaven. Perhaps this place of worship may represent the spiritual side of the dreamer. Or a place for reflection and solitude, prayer, or wisdom.

To whitewash the house may signify wanting to cover up an embarrassment or feelings of guilt. The home is a place with soul; it is also a symbol of where we feel at home.

Dream Motifs

We frequently dream of the houses in which we spent our childhood. Places where we were innocent. Or perhaps where we were unhappy or lost our innocence. If so, this may be the origin of the issue that you are dreaming of. Perhaps it was here that a certain behaviour pattern began that is now troubling. The dream may unlock hidden memories. Mostly these memories have been hidden or repressed for a reason as they were possibly unbearable. Houses can also be the symbol of the place or occurrence of trauma. But also perhaps this is where you felt safe, loved, nurtured, and nourished. Where you felt secure, sheltered from all the elements, seen, and mirrored.

Jung talks about the many levels of consciousness within the dream symbol of a many-levelled house. Unknown rooms, cellars, or basements in the house indicate the unknown, unexplored areas of the self. They are a deep level of our unconscious.

The staircase links the different levels of the house. It may represent an emotional link between the different parts of the self, be they conscious or unconscious. The dream can sometimes involve the final descent into a cave cut into Mother Earth. This may appear in myths and dreams as the Underworld.

Dreams set in the attic or on a high level of a house may represent the intellect. Thinking or dwelling in the intellect can be a safe space far from the depths of the unconscious, far from the emotions. Here we think rather than feel. Dreams of a towering structure or a tall chimney may invite a Freudian interpretation of a phallic symbol. The appearance of the Paris landmark the Eiffel Tower may represent a powerful erotic symbol.

The state of the dream house may reflect the internal state of the dreamer. It may be impoverished, untidy, or requiring work or renovation. It may be unsafe. A large and impressive house may suggest the dreamer's potential for expansion.

Dreams set in museums may represent the past, a library a place of information and ideas, and a church or temple may represent a spiritual side of the dreamer. I recall a client's dream of being trapped in a very ornate and complex castle surrounded by a moat, making entry impossible. The castle was showing us the magnitude and strength of her defenses that were keeping her alone and lonely. It looked secure and beautiful on the outside, but inside was a different matter. Inside, it was empty, and the internal walls were cracked and fragmented. There was repair work to be done.

One client was continually dreaming of renovating his house. He was busy pulling it apart, demolishing it, and restoring parts that he valued. In therapy, he was consciously renovating himself. The dream gave us an internal image of the unconscious work that was underway, under construction.

An astrologist client's dream was set in a house, but surprisingly, her association with the house was the planetary house of her birth. This held meaning particular to her.

The thirteenth-century Sufi poet Rumi composed a symbolic picture of daily life in the coded language of dreams.

> *This being human is a guest house. Every morning a new arrival.*
> *A joy, a depression, a meanness, some momentary awareness comes*
> *as an unexpected visitor. Welcome and entertain them all! Even if*
> *they're a crowd of sorrows, who violently sweep your house empty*
> *of its furniture, still treat each guest honourably. He may be clearing*
> *you out for some new delight. The dark thought, the shame, the*
> *malice, meet them at the door laughing, and invite them in. Be*
> *grateful for whoever comes because each has been sent as a guide*
> *from beyond.*

BATHROOMS

Bathrooms frequently appear in dreams. They are for washing, cleansing, elimination, and letting go. Bathrooms require water. Dreams are like water—they are hard to hold, they run here and there, and it is difficult to make them solid. Water purification can occur in the symbolic bathroom.

It is quite common to dream of washing oneself, which may be about trying to get rid of a troubling situation or person. We so easily can be contaminated by touching dirt, bacteria, or a virus, as we have experienced in the COVID pandemic. This contamination is accompanied by fear, individually and collectively. There may also be some shame or embarrassment that needs to be erased, washed off. The washing may also be about the denying of a part of the self, perhaps a shameful or dirty part. Perhaps the presence of a compulsion.

There is also the biblical washing away of the sins of the world's contamination. There is the washing of the feet. Baptism symbolises a process of purification. The infant or adult is cloaked in white robes after the ceremony and instantly has a new and pure beginning.

In life and in our dreams, we can appear naked in our bathroom. This can be incredibly confronting as all is revealed and it is impossible to hide—we are forced to see the naked truth. Here we are unveiled and exposed.

Toilets can send us a message of being 'shitty' with someone or our self or being in trouble. It may also symbolise being blocked or stuck. The plumber's presence may be the therapist or the therapeutic process. The dreamer may be needing to get rid of something, or someone, that is no longer needed or of benefit. To defecate is a deliberate, assertive activity or expression. It is instinctual. It is a natural bodily function. If constipated, one is not willing or able to let go of an idea or behaviour. Conversely, the dream of diarrhoea may point to being out of control and running. Freud says this anal symbolism is about the desire to dominate or withhold. The two-year-old learns this from potty training. Do I give Mummy what she wants or do I withhold? It starts early. In German nursery language, the potty is known as the 'throne'.

There is often a lot of emotion involved in using the toilet. Maybe the need to relieve yourself. 'Taking the piss', being 'pissed off'. Both involve being angry. Both involve letting go. Feelings of shame, embarrassment, or discomfort about something or someone in the dreamer's waking life may be being reflected.

A client, Joe, dreamed of going to the toilet, but it was full of faeces. It wouldn't flush away. He tried and tried, but it all just overflowed into his family room. There was no place in Joe's life for self-expression. Everyone else had a place to get rid of their stuff, but he was at an impasse. Nothing seemed to be flowing, and when it did, it fouled his living space, his family room. The place of relationship was being contaminated.

Dreams of faeces are common, and the dreamer is often embarrassed to discuss this topic. But as they say, 'shit happens'. The alchemists believed that gold was to be processed from shit. This was because the highest is to be found in the lowest. Faeces represent potentially transformative activity, unlived assertive or creative possibilities.

WATER

Our dreams are like water—they are difficult to catch and hold and make a shape of. They are fluid, and they resist our efforts to make them concrete. Dreams come from the metaphoric and mysterious deep ocean, our unconscious. The sea, oceans, rivers, lakes, and ponds of water are universal dream images that symbolise the unconscious. The ocean is deep and unfathomable, as is the unconscious. It is the depth of our imagination and the source of creativity.

'The eternal stream' is a metaphor for the soul of man and for consciousness. It is also thought of as the great body representing unity and wholeness. Water is often associated with intuition and spirituality. It may point to a need to connect with your inner wisdom and listen to your intuition or it may symbolise enlightenment or spiritual growth.

Water is the symbolic purifier. It is a powerful symbol of cleansing and renewal.

It is essential for human life.

Water can be destructive. Powerful. Harmful. Floods cause drowning and damage.

Ask yourself: Are you at sea? Have you lost sight of land? Are you sailing too close to the shore, or the wind? Are you venturing on wider seas? If so, are you prepared? Do you have a compass, a map for navigation? Are you in uncharted waters?

There is a saying about being 'as mercurial as the sea'.

Water symbolises our emotions, our feelings. In the dream, are you in too deep? Out of your depth? Are you just keeping your head above water? Or are you drowning? If drowning, then this is likely showing the dreamer is in danger. The answer may be to get the dreamer's feet firmly on the ground. Swimming in water suggests that the dreamer is acquiring the ability to navigate safely through the waters of the unconscious. The more familiar we are with our inner world, the more likely we are to be swimming in our dreams. Calm water may symbolise tranquillity, while turbulent water could represent inner turmoil or uncertainty.

Water is essential to our external and internal life. It keeps us alive. All the cells in our body require water. Water is representative of our emotional world, our feelings. Our tears are made up of water. It is essential for growth in nature. Water is baptismal. It is thought to have the power to wash away the sins of the world. A river winds its way through our lives. It can be an image of the flow of time. It is a mysterious flow of energy. It may symbolise vitality, energy, and the flow of the life force.

A dream of water may be symbolic of life at present, and it may be helpful to ask:

- Is the water clear or murky?
- Can you see into the depths?
- Do you need to emotionally cleanse or do you have a desire to wash away negativity and start afresh?

- If you are in a vessel, is the vessel sound?
- Is the river meandering, static, or fast-flowing?
- Are you going through a period of change or transition in life?
- Do you need to adapt to this change?
- Is the river blocked? This may indicate you, too, are emotionally blocked. Perhaps physically blocked, either by yourself or by another.
- Do you feel you could cry a river?
- Are you floating on the water? If so, this tells us there is no connection to the earth and you are not being grounded. To dream of being on the edge of a body of water is to be on the edge of awareness or consciousness. A very exciting place to be. A river connects us, and it can divide us. It may carry us through life.

SHIPS OR BOATS

Ships appearing in dreams can have a deep significance. They sail on the ocean, our unconscious. When engaging in psychotherapy, it is not uncommon to dream of being on a voyage in a boat or ship at sea as we are exploring the unconscious. Look at how the boat is travelling. Is it drifting aimlessly or going full steam ahead? Is it lacking direction or aiming for a destination? Look to the surrounding conditions. Are the sea and sky tranquil or stormy and dangerous? Has the boat capsized? There are signs here of where the dreamer is at physically and emotionally and perhaps what lies ahead. If in a rowboat or canoe, much exertion is required to move ahead, and the dreamer is exposed to the elements.

Associations and descriptions of the conditions are vital. A ship symbolises what carries us through life, perhaps the body. To be in a good or solid ship suggests something solid is carrying the dreamer through life into the future. If the vessel is a barge, there is much weight that can slow progress. A ferry is an archetypal vessel associated with a journey from one stage of consciousness to another. The ferryman is the archetypal wise old man.

VEHICLES

Vehicles or cars are a symbol of one's life drive. They reflect our identity or self-image. Cars plus other modes of transportation show us how we move through various stages and experiences in our lives. Mechanically, cars can easily get out of control. Driving a vehicle takes a sense of control or autonomy in one's life. Perhaps the dreamer is feeling powerless or out of control. During the therapeutic process, one can dream of not being able to find one's car. This is because changes are happening and the new is unrecognisable. Perhaps the person has changed, and the dream is pointing to this.

If you are dreaming of a vehicle, it is good to ask:

- Who is driving the car?
- Who exactly is in the driver's seat?
- Why are you not driving the car?
- Where are you, as the dream ego, positioned?
- Are you inside or outside the vehicle?
- What are you carrying in the car?
- Is it visible or hidden in the boot?
- Are you in control? If not, who is in control?
- Are you going with or against the flow of traffic?
- Are there potholes, bumps, or curbs?
- Are the entrances and exits easy to navigate?
- Are the tyres inflated or flat?
- Has someone cut them and sabotaged the journey?
- Are you going somewhere with a purpose or just driving?
- Or are you perhaps trying to avoid or escape a certain life situation?
- Is someone stealing your car? If so, are you unconsciously doing it to yourself?

These details can be surprisingly significant.

If travelling in a bus, there is a distinction of the collective rather than the private. A bus is very public. A bus can carry plenty, like dreams. To dream of driving a motorcycle may represent the unprotected, maybe the dangerous. It can be masculine energy and perhaps adolescent. Noisy and powerful. Exciting.

A train can be a potent phallic symbol. The train has a defined route as it is destined to travel on tracks and there is no free will involved. To dream the car is out of control, the brakes fail, or we don't know where the brakes are points to a situation being enacted in our everyday life. These are anxiety dreams.

A young client dreamt she was in her car high on a mountain. The front half of the car was hanging over the edge. She wasn't worried, but she admitted that not being worried didn't fit the situation. She felt she needed to be worried! We talked about what she wasn't in touch with that could be dangerous. 'Perhaps my drug use,' she wondered aloud. Well, she was high (on the mountain), and she really could reach out for help to pull her back away from danger. The dream directed our work to the road we needed to be connected to. She was in the driver's seat, and she gradually was able to reverse away to safe ground.

A gothic teenager dreamt of two roads. One was dangerous and exciting, but it ended in flames of fire. The other was grey and pedestrian, boring. In her life, she was venturing along the dangerous road. It took an exploration of her dream for her to rethink her journey. She could still be a goth and express her identity on the predictable road. It was safe.

PREGNANCY

Dreams of being pregnant are very common and may evoke various symbolic meanings. These are dreams of new growth, new beginnings, and transformation. A therapist is often a witness to this change, and to the birth. If there is the birth of a baby, this could be a symbol of self, the inner child, or ego development.

The pregnancy may be a gestation of ideas, or a metaphorical baby that lies deep with the dreamer. It may be a story, a project, or a business venture. Only the dreamer knows what has been conceived, and what is growing and alive. What is soon to be birthed, soon to be let go and brought into consciousness and into the world. In birth, we come from darkness into the light. There is potential for a new life full of possibilities.

The dreamer may be needing to get in touch with her maternal, feminine nature. The pregnancy may awaken this impulse. It may awaken feelings of brooding, nesting, of following a natural rhythm, or it may awaken feelings of being controlled, trapped, pushed out of shape, being distorted, invaded, or overtaken. The dreamer may feel resentful and that their freedom has been impinged upon. There may be fear and anxiety about change and growth in the future.

FLYING AND FALLING

We have flying dreams often when we are ungrounded, unsupported by Mother Nature or by life. We are animals made to walk on earth, not fly. I have had clients who dreamed they were eagles, with expansive wings that enabled them to fly. To achieve this height usually takes much hard work and courage. The eagle is connected to the power within. The eagle is thought of as the king of the birds. In dreams, the eagle may represent a spiritual elation, which may be associated with soaring fantasies. The dream may be a warning of perhaps being elevated above the everyday, and the balance may need to be restored. Flying too high can have its perils.

When one dreams of flying too high, it is a good time to ask:

- Who is supporting you currently? Do you need to ask for support?
- Do you have your feet firmly on the ground?
- Are you on top of the situation you find yourself in?

If you like being in control in life, the dream may be showing you how the opposite feels. Or maybe it is suggesting you are not living in the real world and are out of touch with reality. Maybe you are even thinking magically, giving you a non-grounded perspective.

Or if you are enjoying this feeling of flying, maybe you are now on top of the issue that you needed to distance yourself from. Now you are being shown a different perspective.

Flying while asleep can enable us to experience how it feels to be truly free. It is our ego that prevents us from enjoying this freedom. If our ego is inflated, then we can be flying way too high.

Perhaps you are over-estimating a situation or being over-ambitious.

Are you observing from a distance rather than joining in?

Are you flying in the face of fortune?

Are you flying into a rage?

Native Americans, Tibetan Buddhists, and others claim that all people have a light body that can leave the physical body during sleep. This is shown when dreaming of flying low.

Then we may have a falling dream to counter this position.

Do we want to escape a situation or desire sexual freedom?

Falling dreams often occur when we're anxious or out of control in our waking life.

The falling dream may be a needed deflation if our ego is flying too high.

Maybe in falling, the dream is showing us that the dreamer's life is falling into place.

If we drop suddenly in our dream, it may reflect a sudden disappointment.

If we are climbing, this is usually a metaphor of our journey inwards. It can also be about climbing in search of truth or meaning.

I once had a client who kept climbing in his dreams to avoid his fear of falling into darkness. His darkness was his depression, which terrified him. He had been in the abyss before and only could emerge with medication. This time was different as he was dreaming. The dream gave him the courage to try a different and healthier approach.

GAMES

Dreams of card games, board games, or rolling the dice often reflect how the dreamer is performing within a group situation in their waking life. Decisions may need to be made strategically and carefully. Is this life solitary? Is the dreamer talking chances wisely or otherwise? Game playing may symbolise a competitive nature and a desire for achievement and success. Winning and losing can reflect feelings of confidence or insecurity. The dream may symbolise an inner conflict or struggle and may represent challenges faced in life.

Playing a game of chess had been a dream theme for two teenage boys who came to therapy. Neither played chess in their waking life. In the dream of one boy, the game was showing the struggle between the black and white pawns. The boy said the dream felt like a battleground. It revealed the conflict he was experiencing with his father and also the conflict of his internal figures. He hoped the dream would somehow magically reveal a strategy so he could win.

I explained how instead the dream was giving us a picture of the developmental battle he was undergoing. This client enjoyed the idea of a battle in which he could kill off his parents and take over their power. He imagined what this would look and feel like. It felt powerful. The dream helped him play and imagine a strategy with his dream game of chess. This game play became a way of resolving his struggles.

The dream of a game of chess can offer themes of intellect, strategy, control, and conflict both internally and externally. Feelings and thoughts around this dream can offer valuable insights.

ANIMALS

We have learned much from the animal kingdom, as animals have been our teachers throughout the years. Indigenous clans have passed down this learned wisdom over many generations. Shamans and healers continue to impart and use the wisdom and to use the connection between Mother Earth and all creatures.

Animals commonly appear in our dreams. They are a deep, primal, and primitive instinctual part of the self. The animal itself is familiar, but the emotion is often unfamiliar or hidden from us. Animals are protective of their young. Each animal has its own strength, its own essence. They may appear exotic.

Animal drives such as fear, lust, and anger can be felt on an instinctual level. Dream animals may symbolise instinctual gut feelings we have about another. Instinct is to be recognised and integrated into our conscious world or the animal part of the self can become menacing, especially if wounded. Animals are the beasts within. Being bitten or attacked by an animal may suggest the dreamer is feeling vulnerable or hunted, or perhaps doubting their own strength. If being chased by an animal, this may represent a way of coping with fear, anxiety, anger, or hate. This is a choice being taken rather than facing and confronting the situation in life. To gain an understanding and insight into the fear, it is best to explore who is chasing you.

Freud said animals appearing in dreams is a classic expression of repressed or unexpressed sexual and aggressive tendencies. Jung argued that animals in dreams were to be analysed individually, depending on the character they portray in the dream and the dreamer's associations. He also believed that animals may represent a 'divine' side of the human psyche.

Animals are closely connected to nature and may point the dreamer towards their desire to connect with their natural world. It is good to become familiar with your dream animal. Bring them into your conscious self by befriending them. Do this using your imagination—see the animal in your presence. There is power in unity. This animal has come from your inner dream story.

Look at the animal.

What does it look like?

Think about its personality.

Does it remind you of anyone you know? Or any part of yourself that resonates?

Does the animal speak to you in any way? What is its message to you? Perhaps it is offering guidance or insights.

If the animal is part of a pack, this may represent a sense of belonging, family, or community. If alone, it may symbolise feelings of isolation or independence.

DOGS

The dog is a frequent symbol that appears in our dreams. As pets, they are loyal and love their owners unconditionally. Dogs continue to enrich our lives with companionship and the gentleness of a best friend. Dreaming of a dog may represent a desire for an experience of love that is given without any expectations. Or it may represent feelings of attachment or dependency. Dogs represent our instincts and our natural intuitive urges. There may be a message about the need to trust one's instincts or to pay attention to intuitive insights. One needs to take care around domesticated dogs as they have the tendency to immediately revert to a wild state on provocation. Dogs are wild and dangerous; they can be hostile and attack the vulnerable. Depending on the behaviour of the dog in the dream, it may represent the need for assertiveness, aggression, or desire for protection, either emotionally or physically.

Dogs require training, boundaries, and care.

Dogs are used and trained as watchdogs, guard dogs, and guide dogs.

Black dogs suggest dark feelings of depression.

The dog may also represent the physical body.

Dogs are playful animals and bring joy and happiness to people's lives.

Early tribes would have half-wild dogs that would give warning of approaching danger, acting as valued protectors. The dogs helped them hunt and were a great source of warmth on long winter months, offering the half-wild intuitive, protective energy.

When the dog appears in our dream, it is an opportunity to reflect on these qualities and associated feelings and endeavour to bring them to consciousness.

HORSES

Like dogs, horses can express urges and passions in ourselves that we have learned to harness or need to harness. According to Freud, horses symbolise the sexual drive. Jung noted horse dreams may indicate health conditions. The horse is a strong and powerful animal that embodies childlike energy. It is free, chaotic, strong, and unrestrained, spirited, even wild. They are connected to nature and the outdoors, movement, or journeying, whether physically, emotionally, or spiritually. Often the horse represents passion, unbridled libido, and sexual energy. Horses are also keenly instinctual and intuitive.

If dreaming of a horse, it could be good to ask yourself:

- If riding a horse, notice your feelings and also those of the horse. Are you experiencing sexual pleasure while riding the horse?
- Is there a sense of freedom and independence?
- Or do you have an unconscious longing to harness your own inner power?
- Or do you long for a sense of being powerful?
- Are you inhibited and fearful of falling?
- Does this match your sexual experience?

The rider of the horse may represent the rider's ego.

To have a dynamic relationship with a horse requires cooperation and trust. Do you have this in your relationship with yourself or another?

Forty-year-old Marica dreamed of owning a very old horse.

Dream Motifs

I have a workhorse, and he is grazing in a large, green paddock at the rear of my farm. He is fair with a light brown mane and bushy tail. As I'm approaching him, I hear these words spoken: 'He is Neanderthal, somewhere in between.' This makes perfect sense in the dream. I notice that he has a huge scrotum, laden with seeds. He can hardly walk. I feel sorry that he is so weighed down with this physical condition. I can tell he is carrying such a burden.

Marica woke with a heavy feeling. She was working very hard in her own business, just like a good workhorse. Her business was successful but all-consuming. This was a pattern that was passed down from generation to generation. Because of the image of the seeds in the dream, I began thinking about her creative and playful self, a part that needed to be expressed. The large paddock where she worked was green and fertile, yet as a workhorse, she was feeling weighed down.

As Marica was an avid reader, I offered her *Women Who Run with the Wolves* by Clarissa Pinkola Estes from my bookshelf. In her next session, she shared having experienced a visceral response when reading the old Russian fairy tale of Vasilisa. It resonated within, and she was emotionally moved. Marica was keen to work with the myth of Vasilisa and her own little internal doll. The session was about giving expression to the seeds of creativity. This was a time to sit with this energy, walk with it, nurture it, talk to it. It was about treating it like a relationship. Marica was keen to get to know this unexpressed part of herself, this fertile part that was weighing her down.

We engaged in a meditation around the image of the horse. She wanted to be in touch with the young foal, the energetic foal who wanted to play and explore. The foal was libidinal and frisky. She wanted to belong to the pack, allowing the workhorse to just be and slowly and steadily do his work. It was time to redirect this energy into her creativity. Working with the myth of Vasilisa, she began to nurture and nourish her inner doll who also had the capacity to provide intuition and comfort. Gradually, Marica became more in balance, able to work, love, and play. Seeds had been sown for change. She now felt able to climb on the horse's back and experience the sensation of feeling light and as free as the wind.

BIRDS

Birds appear in dreams when we are undergoing spiritual growth. They are associated with the wind and can fly towards the heavens. They can 'transcend'. Birds are associated with nature and freedom and with transition and change. Migratory birds travel long distances and can adapt to new environments.

Birds are associated with the breath of life and the divine spirit. A very common association is that of the soul. They dwell in the space between heaven and earth. Birds are often seen as messengers of the divine and may be an expression of the dreamer's spiritual journey or connection to the divine. Birds can be thought of as protectors, messengers, or guides.

While on holiday, I visited Delphi on Mt Parnassus in Greece. It is the historic site of the fourth century BCE temple of the Greek god Apollo. It is a beautiful, spiritual place. The night I arrived, I had a vivid dream of a majestic eagle. I didn't know the myth of Zeus releasing two eagles into the air. One went east, one west, and they met in Delphi. Walking through the ancient stadium and temple was a very moving and emotional experience that I shall not forget. I sat quietly and did a meditation, which was powerful. It had the energy of the eagle, the power of the great spirit.

The eagle has a deadly beak and sharp talons. He is the emperor of the birds of prey. The eagle suggests dominance and supremacy. He is a noble and fierce bird with a powerful intellectual ability. This may represent the dreamer or another.

The owl comes alive at night and has huge eyes that see all. He embodies wisdom. He makes a mournful sound of moping. The image of the dove or nightingale suggests peace, harmony, reconciliation and the feminine, whereas the kingfisher is a masculine symbol. Birds of prey may point to the dreamer being under attack. Like a swooping magpie.

A dove may appear as a symbol of peace and serenity, perhaps the calmer nature of the dreamer. Or the dreamer may be seeking inner peace or tranquillity in their life.

CATS

Cats represent the archetypal feminine in our dream world. Feminine energy is intuitive, nurturing, and creative. Cats are a sign of independence, strength, and often fertility and are associated with sexuality and sensuality. This may be about the dreamer's own psyche or relationship with other women in their life. There may be a message about trusting one's intuition and instinct. Cats are vigilant and wary, checking out the environment for danger or threats. They are adaptable and agile.

In some cultures, cats are seen as protectors or symbols of warning. Cats embody the state of contentment and are able to take care of themselves. When cats are not out hunting, playing, or mating, their default position appears to be a state of calmness and peacefulness. Cats are mysterious and can represent the secretive or hidden side of the dreamer's nature. There is a duality about the cat's nature. They can be both aloof and playful, gentle and fierce. They are clever at finding the best hiding places. When it's hot, they quietly find the coolest place in which to lie, and when it's cold, there they are, toasty in the sun or by the fire.

Cats appear to be indifferent and ambiguous. They come for a pat or a cuddle when they want one, not when their owner wants. It is said they have nine lives. Cats can be a sign of jealousy or of being catty. They are territorial. They are destructive as they eat birds and wildlife. Black cats are thought to be bad luck. Alley cats are thought to be promiscuous.

Big cats, like lions or tigers, are symbols of strength and success. These are also animals to be feared as they are mostly looking for prey. They are fast, courageous, cunning, and have a strong survival instinct. They are often angry and powerful and evoke fear. They can be cruel.

SNAKES

Snakes are archetypal symbols that have both positive and negative associations. On one hand, they are the agents of healing and transformation, and on the other, they are thought of as evil predators. Snakes and lizards belong close to or beneath the ground. They dwell just below the level of consciousness. Snakes or serpents are a common image in our dreams. They appear as a fascinating and often frightening symbol when there is an instinctual integration of a new level of consciousness. The image of the snake or serpent shows us the ambivalent nature of the unconscious, as the bite of the serpent can be filling the dreamer with a destructive poison, or it can be medicine that heals and transforms. Snakes are often associated with hidden knowledge and may appear when one is searching for a deeper insight into their own inner world.

The ouroboros, the symbol of the snake biting his own tail, represents the circle or wheel of life, regeneration and eternity. It is a symbol of wholeness. Jung said, 'The idea of transformation and renewal by means of a serpent is a well-substantiated archetype.' There are many meanings for the presence of snakes in our dreams. Mostly these are frightening dreams. We certainly pay attention when the serpent appears! The snake may reflect the dreamer's fears or unresolved anxieties. Snakes are a phallic symbol, often associated with the male penis. Thus, they are a very potent and powerful masculine image. This means they also embody sexuality, desire, and creation.

I have had clients dream of being bitten by a snake, stared at by a snake, and spoken to by a snake. In the biblical story of the Garden of Eden, the snake is associated with the coming to consciousness of humanity. The snake tells Eve that eating the forbidden fruit of the tree of knowledge, of good and evil, will make one wise. This will transform as one holds both good and evil, attraction and fear, transforming an old way into a new way of being. But will this new way bite you, hypnotise you?

The *wagyl*, or the serpent of the Indigenous Dreaming, is the local Noongar version of the archetypal rainbow serpent. It has been central in the Indigenous psyche for thousands of years. The *waygl* lays down the path of life. He is the giver of life and the protector of life. To the Indigenous, the *waygl* is sacred, their hero. For the non-Indigenous, the *waygl* is to be respected and honoured. This serpent is the symbol of strength and creativity.

In mythology, Thoth, the Atlantean, who later returned as Hermes and was the father of alchemy, used the symbology of two snakes intertwining around a sword to represent healing. Thus, the serpent is associated with healing, as on the staff of Asclepius, the physicians' emblem. This healing is embodied by the serpent as a mediator between heaven and earth. In certain yogic practices in India, 'serpent power' is the goal of spiritual development for a oneness with the cosmos to be achieved.

The snake is charged with fear as it is laden with poisonous venom and can be dangerous. It is common to dream of a pit or pile of snakes on the floor around you. A snake can be deadly, but it can also be an image of transformation. It can shed its skin, survive, and renew. It can heal itself. The transmutation of the life-death-rebirth cycle is exemplified by the shedding of the snake's skin. The serpent is a traditional symbol of wisdom. Snakes also are representative of instinctual energy, especially when they appear in large numbers. Snakes are chthonic in nature, cold-blooded. They hold a mystery and a fascination.

Because the snake has many meanings, the dream image becomes personal and dependent on the client's own associations. I recall a client dreamed of being bitten by a rattlesnake. His association was the rage he felt from his toxic father who constantly drained him. He said this really rattled him. The snake dream opened him up to these important unexamined feelings.

The final dream of a client dying with ovarian cancer was of a python curled up asleep at the base of a church altar. There were two lit candles on the altar. The python looked her in the eyes, and she was not afraid. She said she felt comforted by its gaze. We talked of how the python was benevolent and soothed her, while her cancer had squeezed the life drive out of her with its power, again like the capability of the python. In the dream, it offered comfort by seeing her in her final days, as the altar was there to offer support. The candles offered divine light for her final journey.

If you dream of a snake, it is good to ask yourself:

- Is there anything or anyone in my waking life that I fear?
- Is someone around me venomous or loathsome?
- Or am I being venomous or loathsome? Cold-blooded even?
- Is it safe to shed, to let go and embrace the new?
- Am I feeling fearful of change?
- Am I in a rut?
- Am I feeling powerful, or perhaps powerless?
- Am I feeling rattled?
- Is there a snake in the grass? Someone or something unseen? Untrustworthy?
- Can I dance freely like the snake when the charmer calls? Will I dance to his tune?

FISH

Fish may represent the origins of humanity's physical and spiritual being. They are ancient and primitive symbols. They live in deep water, in oceans and rivers, symbols of the unconscious. The fish may symbolise the depth of the unconscious, which is fluid, oceanic, and a place we fish to find insights, hidden treasure. Dreaming of a fish may point to the emotional depth of the dreamer.

As the water is representative of our emotions, the fish may be laden with feelings, and this is the psyche's way of showing us these feelings. Fish also represent inspiration and creativity, or unconscious insights, as the unconscious is often represented as the sea. They may signify abundance or a period of prosperity in life. Fish undergo metamorphosis as they grow and thus may indicate the dreamer's own process of transformation or need for renewal and change. If the fish are in an aquarium, this may be pointing to how restricted one's freedom is, or perhaps self-expression or spirituality. Or the fish may feel happy to be contained and looked after, away from predators. If the fish are in a fishbowl, perhaps your life is too exposed, too visible. This may be a good time to check your personal boundaries. If the fish is visible just below the surface of the water, perhaps an insight or wisdom is to be brought to consciousness. The dreamer's associations are vital here.

Fish are hard to pin down and difficult to catch. They are illusive, adaptable, and flexible. They are smooth, fluid, slippery, streamlined, shimmering. Fish have been associated with fertility and creativity as they can spawn hundreds of eggs. They swim in schools and may symbolise learning or the beginning of becoming conscious. Christianity often uses a fish as a symbol. If eating fish in the dream, perhaps the dreamer is needing spiritual nourishment. Is the fish out of water? If so, perhaps this is how the dreamer is feeling. Is something fishy? Are they fishing for compliments?

The whale is a huge mammal and is a close relative of the dolphin. Some whale species are known to cause havoc to fishermen, capsizing their boats and stealing their haul. They have been hunted for centuries for their oil, whalebone, leather, and ivory. In the Bible, the story of Jonah and the whale is symbolic of renewal. The whale has a huge belly and may be a symbol of the mother.

SHARKS

Sharks are a common dream symbol. The shark is a dangerous predator and evokes fear in the dreamer. The shark is powerful, intelligent, and instinctual. It is a survivor. It lurks just under the surface of the water and may represent danger that is close at hand. Survival instincts and bodily responses of fight, flight, and freeze may surface. If the shark appears in your dream, explore your feelings of vulnerability or feelings of defenselessness. They have a killer instinct. Sharks may be symbolic of a defense, attempting to keep the dreamer physically or emotionally safe, or safe from awareness, or from making significant life changes. The shark may represent a shadow part of the self or unconscious desire. Does the dreamer have money issues? The shark may be a loan shark. Sharks can circle their prey. In some cultures, the shark's fins and teeth are very valuable.

SPIDERS

Spiders can be frightening in a dream, especially if the dreamer is caught in the sticky spider's web or if the spider is about to or does devour the dreamer. Or perhaps the dreamer is the spider. On the positive side, the spider symbolises the creativity of the feminine, as she industriously weaves fine, intricate, and beautiful designs of life. Like the spider, it takes a person much patience, planning, and execution to succeed when pursuing goals and ambitions.

Spiders are frightening and arouse fear in the dreamer, making the dreamer feel vulnerable. It is good to ask if you are feeling trapped by fear or other emotions. Is there a phobia present? The dreamer may be feeling like an outsider and may be spinning a way to keep their distance from others. Feelings are very important and need to be explored so the dreamer may escape the emotions that are entangling and may feel inescapable. Spiders can represent the shadow self or unconscious desires that are hidden from the dreamer. There may be a need to explore and bring to awareness and integrate these hidden parts of the self.

If we dream just of the web, it is important to study its precise pattern.

Then look for the weaver of this web. Is it a spider? Spiders exert control over their environment through spinning their webs, which they use to trap prey. They are resourceful, creative, and cunning. Perhaps the dreamer needs to look to their own resourcefulness and find creative solutions to any life issues being faced. There may be a need to untangle or navigate a way through a situation. The web can symbolise entanglement or being trapped in a sticky situation. The dreamer may be fearful or anxious.

Appendix: Starting a Dream Journal

Writing a dream journal is a beautiful and purposeful way to become familiar with unknown parts of yourself. It is a way to engage in an ongoing conversation and a connection with your inner life. If you have a desire to engage in this process, here are some practices I find useful.

- Sleep: It is good to be mindful about having a commitment to your routine around sleep. Daily physical exercise and spending time outdoors in daylight facilitates the circadian rhythm, and going to bed at the same time each night is helpful. It is recommended to disconnect from devices and restrict blue light from screens ninety minutes before bedtime. Having a warm bath with magnesium or Epsom salts in the bathwater helps muscles and the body relax; adding a few drops of lavender essential oil can also help. Be mindful of caffeine and alcohol intake. The practice of meditation, deep breathing, or playing gentle, harmonious music can be restful. A quiet, dark room and comfortable bed are helpful. If you suffer from insomnia, you may try the subtle use of 'white noise' and seek medical advice. Try to not become preoccupied about your sleep as this can lead to anxiety. Resist making a story in your mind about your sleep. Insomnia can become a habit.

- The longer and more soundly you sleep, the more intense your dreams will be. As you go off to sleep, ask gently for a dream. 'I would like to remember my dream.' I am sometimes playful and say, 'Hey, Siri ... I mean, psyche ... tonight I would like a dream about ...'
- If you have previously had a frightening dream or nightmare, gently say, 'I would like to remember a harmonious dream.' You are practising dream incubation. A dream will soon be given if you do this each night for about two weeks. This sets your intention.
- Keep a notepad or your dream journal and a pen or pencil by your bed, so when you wake from a dream, you can quickly jot it down. It is good practice to briefly list the occurrences of the day in your journal before sleep. Don't attach to them; they are just data. This may assist in recall. If preferable, record the dream on your electronic device. Try not to fully wake up. Then immerse yourself back into the dream. This is something I practise and have found works well.
- The next morning, rewrite the dream in your journal in the present tense. Note your feeling on waking. Note the mood and feelings in the dream.
- Give your dream story a title. Date your dream to assist in the review process. Then later, you can start to identify a theme or a pattern.
- Writing down your dream enforces a deeper connection to the dream. Read the dream aloud twice. Take notes and draw pictures of images and patterns. This puts you in a more precise relationship with the dream story. The more you can articulate what is happening or appearing in the dream, the more conscious

you will become and the more familiar with what you don't yet know. Be curious about this story. Notice any changes in feelings, tones, and images. Note the landscape, scenery, figures, characters, events, objects, colours, and action.

- It's best to not attempt to interpret or analyse the dream, though at some level, you may understand the general meaning. Be honest and try to remain objective and non-judgmental. Resist the ego's intervention.
- If there is some urgency in understanding the meaning of the dream, accept that there is much value purely in remembering and recording the dream. The dreamwork goes on percolating and processing when you are also awake.
- Take time to reflect on what is going on in your living world at present. Are you experiencing any emotional issues or issues of the heart or body around your family, home, or work? Note any of these issues in your journal below the dream.
- Now take time to ask what is going on in the dream. Write this down.
- Describe each character, each object, and each scene fully. As Jungian James Hillman once put it, 'make a friend' of these characters.
- Go into thoughts and feelings associated with these dream images. Ask how you feel in the dream. How are the dream characters feeling? Were they joyful, fearful, anxious? Start with simple emotions, like glad, mad, bad, sad, or afraid.
- Read the images sequentially and patterns or themes will slowly emerge. This is often exactly what the unconscious is emphasising. It is telling you to take note and pay attention.
- Describe each person in the dream fully. Note their gender, age, colouring, and clothing. Do you know these people? Are they familiar in any way? Do you like them? Do they speak, or want to speak? If so, what would they like to say?

- Can you see yourself in the dream? If so, how do you look? What age are you? What are you saying, feeling? If you are younger, try to recall what was going on in your life around this time.
- Describe the landscape and the environment. Is it familiar or foreign? Note the colour of the sky and earth, and also if there is a change in the surroundings.
- Write down any action words, for example, 'running'. Then note whether it is running to or from and why.
- Finally, ask: What does this dream have to do with me? What does this dream mean? The psyche has an imaginal intelligence, a knowing. Our path is to be curious about the dream's intent, its desire. The deeper we look inwards, the more we will see. It is like peering into a looking glass. The more you engage with and connect with your dreamscape, the more you will notice stronger and more insightful dreaming occurring. The aim of the psyche is to facilitate healing and balance and to bring the message into your conscious world. Each dream is a valuable contribution to your life.
- Ideally, discuss your dream with a psychotherapist or psychologist. In telling dream stories, we are re-experiencing them, making them more real, and insights may develop as we listen to the dream we are describing. If you have a dream image that seems important, take the time to get to really know it. This image comes from the unconscious. The dream language holds emotions and feelings as well as rational thought. The dream can promote balance and contribute towards emotional healing and psychological and physical health because the mind and the body are so linked. Working with these images can transform what feels not real into a possibility or even a reality. These images are a gift, data to your conscious self from an unknown part of the self, the unconscious. This helps to engage and acquaint you

with a part of yourself that you possibly have become disconnected from or have never been connected to.

- To work with the images—the process of creative visualisation—commence by taking some time away from distraction by finding a peaceful place that is conducive for contemplation. Be sure you are comfortable and warm and away from electronic devices. The aim is to be physically relaxed yet mindfully paying attention with focused awareness on the present moment. The aim is to create solitude and inner silence so you may gaze inwards.
- During this process, I follow a meditative practice like this. Gently close your eyes and follow your breath. Take the breath slowly to all parts of the body, bringing warmth, heaviness, and complete relaxation. As you breathe in, say, 'This is my in breath.' Breathe out and say, 'This is my out breath.' Take the breath down to your tummy. Feel it push out as your hand gently rests on your lap. Continue this, and gradually the mind chatter will settle. Allow yourself to enter the silence, and let your body sink heavily into a state of deep relaxation.
- Now recall and reimagine your dream. Replay it. Immerse yourself in the dream matrix, image by image. Check within and notice how your body is feeling. If you are holding tension in a certain part of your body, send warmth and light to this area. Gently massage it, contract, then release it. Let it go.
- Is there an image or a section of the dream that demands your attention? For example, this may be a long, silver snake with two heads. The aim is to become more familiar with this dream image.
- Fully explore this image, its size, shape, colour, texture, and smell. Make the image an object of your contemplation. Allow your breathing to adjust to the image; allow your heart to do the same. Befriend this image. Get closer to it. Be curious. What or who is this image? You are safe, so no need to feel afraid. You

have dreamt it. See the image in the dream story, in the dream landscape. Now try to relive the emotions associated with it. You are finding a way of relating to the unconscious image as it comes to you. We are setting in motion a flow of energy between the dream story from our unconscious and our conscious mind.

- Now explore the feeling you are holding in your body associated with this image. Is there tension? Where in your body is this feeling located? Go deeply into this area. Does the feeling have a colour, a temperature, a weight? Be creative with this. The dream inhabits your body as well as your mind. The two are connected.
- Explore the image as a lived experience. Walk around in the dream, explore it. Insights may arise. Meet them, no matter how confronting. There is a need for the insights to be revealed, to become conscious. Breathe into the insight without judgement, with energy and with love. Hold this insight, the image, and bring in the accompanying feeling. Cradle or hold these in your mind, in your body, and in your heart. Healing is happening.
- You may wish to allow this dream symbol to stay and travel with you in your daily life. A dream of a black sheep, for example, that has become estranged from the flock. Explore it, befriend it, dialogue with it, try to understand it, and keep it close. It is not trivial.
- We are discovering a way of relating to an unconscious image as it comes to you. You are using your imagination creatively.
- Go back to noticing your breath. Inhale—the gift that connects us to Eros, the life force—then exhale. Consider the dream image. Sit with it. Feel and think into it. Now you can have an engagement or relationship with it. It no longer only resides in the dream. Thank the psyche for the dream and yourself in your endeavour towards wholeness.
- It is valuable to now add this self-knowledge to your journal. Giving language to the experience grounds the dream in the

real, in another dimension. Perhaps draw or paint your dream; write a poem or a short story. Add what it is you have discovered to your dream journal. Enjoy this creative process. It has the potential to add joy to your world.
- Remember, record, re-feel, reflect, reimagine, and rework this gift that comes from within. The dream will then come alive.

Glossary

ANIMA (Latin, 'soul'). The unconscious, feminine side of a man's personality. She appears in dreams as images ranging from seductress to spiritual guide. She is the Eros principle, and a man's anima development is reflected in how he relates to women. Identification with the anima can appear as moodiness, effeminacy, and over-sensitivity.

ANIMUS (Latin, 'spirit'). The unconscious, masculine side of a woman's personality. He personifies the *logos* principle. Identification with the animus can cause a woman to become rigid, opinionated, and argumentative. More positively, he is the inner man who acts as a bridge between the woman's ego and her own creative resources in the unconscious.

ANOREXIA. An eating disorder characterised by an absence of appetite, intense fear of gaining weight, and a distorted body image, leading to restricted eating behaviours and significant weight loss. A range of physical and emotional symptoms include extreme thinness or emaciation, persistent fatigue and weakness, difficulty concentrating, insomnia, fainting, thin hair, dry skin, irregular or absent periods, social withdrawal or isolation, depression and anxiety, obsessive thoughts, and perfectionism.

In anorexia nervosa, the severe physical and psychological consequences if left untreated are enough to threaten health or life.

ARCHETYPES. Universal patterns or motifs that come from the collective unconscious and are the basic content of religions, legends, fantasies, and fairy tales. They appear in dreams and visions and carry a symbolic meaning.

ASSOCIATIONS. A spontaneous flow of interconnected thoughts and images around a specific idea determined by unconscious connections.

ATTACHMENT. The relationship or bond between humans that is formed and influenced by early childhood relationships with parent figures. There are three major functions of attachment relationships—to promote proximity seeking, provide a safe haven, and offer a secure base—all of which facilitate self-regulation and emotion regulation.

BIPOLAR DISORDER. A mental illness that causes unusual and extreme shifts in a person's mood, energy, activity levels, and concentration. These shifts can make it difficult to carry out day-to-day tasks. There are different types of bipolar disorder, including bipolar I and bipolar II.

BOUNDARY. A protective limit established between oneself and others with the goal of defining where one ends and another begins. Clear boundaries enable individuals to honour their own needs and support authentic relationships.

CIRCADIAN RHYTHM. This is the 24-hour internal clock in the brain that regulates cycles of alertness and sleepiness by responding to light changes in our environment. It is the internal regulator for sleep and wakefulness. Getting sufficient sunlight facilitates the rhythm.

CHTHONIC. Chthonic means dwelling beneath the earth. It may relate to the earth or to the Underworld. Snakes and amphibians are considered chthonic creatures in many cultures.

COGNATIVE BEHAVOUR THERAPY (CBT). A psychological treatment carried out by clinical psychologists for a range of mental health problems. It teaches coping skills for dealing with different problems. It focuses on how your thoughts, beliefs, and attitudes affect your feelings and actions.

CONSCIOUSNESS. The present state of awareness in which you are able to perceive your surroundings, thoughts, sensations, and emotions. It encompasses a wide range of mental processes, including perception, cognition, self-awareness, and subjective experience.

CORTISOL. A stress hormone involved in the fight-or-flight response that activates the body to engage with or remove itself from a perceived threat.

CRONE. This term has its roots in folklore and mythology. A crone is typically depicted as an old woman characterised by her wisdom, experience, and mystical or witch-like quality. She may be a healer, sage, or spiritual guide.

DEFENSE. A protective mechanism of protecting the ego.

DISSOCIATION. An adapted stress response in which a person is physically present and partially mentally detached, numb, or shutdown due to an overwhelming of the nervous system. A situation in which two or more mental processes co-exist without becoming connected or integrated. Known as dissociation or splitting.

DYSREGULATION. A state of physiological imbalance in the nervous system.

EGO. The part of the personality charged with harnessing the id's libidinal energy and is governed by the reality principle. It plays a crucial role in identity as it is the foundation for constructing the persona. The ego is the centre of consciousness, and the feet of the ego lie in the unconscious.

EMDR. Eye movement desensitisation and reprocessing facilitates the reprocessing of traumatic memories and other adverse life experiences and brings them to an adaptive resolution, with the use of eye movement during the processing of these memories. A therapy process for healing trauma.

EMOTIONAL REGULATION. The ability to respond to stress in a flexible, tolerant, and adaptive way, allowing our nervous system to return to baseline.

EMOTIONAL RESILIENCE. The ability to be flexible and rebound quickly while processing a wide variety of emotional states.

EMPATHY. The power of projecting one's personality into (and so fully comprehending) the object of contemplation. Being able to put oneself in the place of another.

EROS. The god of love and desire in Greek mythology. Used by Freud to personify the life force and sexual instinct.

Glossary

GRIEF. A normal response of intense emotional suffering caused by loss that often includes psychological distress and anxiety. The stages of grief include denial, anger, bargaining, depression, acceptance, and finding meaning in the loss. These stages are not necessarily felt sequentially, and some may be absent.

INDIVIDUATION. A Jungian term signifying the conscious realisation of one's unique psychological reality as a unique individual, separate from others, while developing one's own personality and identity. It is also seen as the path towards psychological wholeness and fulfilment.

INTEGRATION. The process by which parts are combined into a whole.

INTERDEPENDENCE. A mutual supportive connectedness within a relationship that allows boundaries, safety, autonomy, and full self-expression.

INTERPRETATION. The process of elucidating and expounding the meaning of something abstruse or obscure, as in dream interpretation. This is a meaning that is over and above that of the client.

INTUITION. An internal knowing and inner insight that, when listened to, guides us towards our authentic path.

HYPNOGOGIC STATE. The transitional state of consciousness between wakefulness and sleep.

METAPHOR. An expression that describes a person or object by referring to something unrelated that is considered to highlight similar characteristics between the two. Metaphors are a powerful tool as they can evoke vivid imagery, convey complex ideas, and provoke thought and emotion.

MYTH. A folklore or a set of stories, traditions, or beliefs. Myths are central to all cultures and civilisations throughout history.

OBSESSIVE-COMPULSIVE DISORDER (OCD). Features a pattern of unwanted thoughts and fears (obsessions) that lead one to do repetitive behaviours (compulsions) that cause significant distress and interfere with daily life.

PARADOX. A seemingly contradictory or absurd statement that, when investigated, may prove to be well-founded or reveal a deeper truth or insight.

POSTNATAL DEPRESSION (PND). A common form of depression also known as postpartum depression (PPD), affecting more than one in every ten women within a year of giving birth. It is not the 'baby blues', which usually lasts no more than two weeks after the birth of a baby. Signs of depression are persistent feelings of sadness or low mood, fatigue, difficulty looking after self and baby, withdrawing from contact with others, problems with concentration, and frightening thoughts about hurting the baby.

POST-TRAUMATIC STRESS DISORDER (PTSD). A mental health condition that can develop after experiencing or witnessing a traumatic event. Symptoms can vary widely from person to person but generally fall into four categories: intrusive memories, avoidance, negative changes in thinking and mood, and changes in physical and emotional reactions.

Glossary

PROJECTION. A defense mechanism unconsciously used in order to cope with difficult feelings or emotions by displacing one's own negative traits or emotions onto another person, animal, or object.

REPRESSION. A defense mechanism by which an unacceptable thought or idea is rendered unconscious.

SELF. A term created by Jung to define the archetype of wholeness and the regulating centre of the personality.

SHADOW. An unconscious part of the personality characterised by traits and attitudes, usually negative but sometimes positive, that the conscious ego tends to reject or ignore. It is personified in dreams by persons of both sexes. Conscious assimilation of one's shadow usually results in an increase of energy.

SYMBOL. A symbol is something that stands for or suggests another entity, action, belief, visual image, or idea. The symbol is the best possible expression of something essentially unknown. People produce symbols unconsciously and spontaneously in their dreams.

THANATOS. The Greek god of death used by Freud to personify the death instinct.

TRANSFERENCE and COUNTERTRANSFERENCE. Unconscious emotional bonds that arise between two persons in an analytic or therapeutic relationship. In transference, the client displaces onto the therapist feelings, ideas, etc., that derive from previous figures in their life.

TRAUMA. Any experience that causes the individual to lack the ability to emotionally regulate or process and then release the event, causing dysregulation to the body's nervous system. Trauma impacts each individual differently due to their own conditioning and modelled coping skills and cannot be quantified or measured.

Acknowledgments

Firstly, I extend my gratitude to my clients who entrusted me with their innermost thoughts and feelings within our therapeutic alliance. They have granted me the privilege of accompanying them through times of vulnerability and often distress.

I am grateful to Jungian analyst Dr. Sally Kester for her invaluable support and encouragement. She has been my teacher, analyst, mentor, colleague, and friend, enriching my journey with her generosity of heart and wisdom.

I wish to express my appreciation to Dr. Jan Resnick and The Churchill Clinic for my eclectic and enriching training, providing a strong foundation for my practice.

My thanks extend to my numerous teachers and supervisors over the years, especially Margaret Bercovic, Nancy McWilliams, Neville Simmington, Wendy-Lynne Cooke, Andre de Konning, Andrew Samuels, and Robbie Bosnac, as well as my supervision group Britt Garrett, Susan Thorman, and Elli Roeder. Thank you especially to Britt for encouraging me to continue writing this book.

Thanks to writer Donna Ward for getting me started.

Many thanks to friend and graphic artist Neil Turner at Turner Design for the book cover artwork.

Special appreciation goes to Professor Arlene Chan, my brilliant oncologist, whose expertise and care have been invaluable.

Gratitude to my beautiful support team of holistic women, especially while I was undergoing cancer treatment: Sarah Gamble, Maree Williams, Karen Anderson, Michelle Raye, and Jenny Jones.

I am grateful to Victoria Castiglioni for her contributions during the completion of the book.

Thank you to Robert Hinshaw for reading my manuscript.

Thank you to my editor Daina Lindeman, Ann Dettori at Independent Ink and typesetter, Julian Mole at Post Pre-press.

Lastly, but certainly not least, I extend my heartfelt gratitude to my family, especially my wonderful husband, Maurice, for his unwavering support and for being an integral part of this journey. My daughters, Remie, for always being available to discuss a sentence or an idea and bringing her wisdom, and Georgie, who sets an amazing example as a clinician, researcher, and frequent publisher. Thanks Will for your interest in my work, especially when a teenager.

How blessed I am.

ABOUT DEBBIE PAULIK FORD

Debbie's career began in nursing. She trained at Princess Margaret Hospital for Children, which equipped her with a holistic understanding, blending knowledge of both the body and the psyche. She has practised as a psychoanalytic psychotherapist in Western Australia since 1995, initially in Chelsea Village, Nedlands, and currently at the Centre for Jungian Psychology and Psychotherapy in Fremantle.

Her involvement in the field extends beyond clinical practice; she served as a committee member and former Vice President of the CG Jung Society of WA. Over the years, she also contributed as a lecturer and supervisor for trainee psychotherapists, facilitated meditation and dream groups and provided volunteer services at Canteen for more than fifteen years. Additionally, she dedicated five years to the board of Relationships Australia, WA.

www.ingramcontent.com/pod-product-compliance
Lightning Source LLC
Chambersburg PA
CBHW082201070526
44585CB00020B/2222